To Kiss the Chastening Rod

To Miss Jane Christiana Fox

To Kiss the Chastening Rod

*Domestic Fiction and
Sexual Ideology in the
American Renaissance*

G. M. Goshgarian

Cornell University Press

Ithaca and London

First published 1992 by Cornell University Press.

International Standard Book Number 0-8014-2559-X
Library of Congress Catalog Card Number 91-55560

Printed in the United States of America

*Librarians: Library of Congress cataloging information appears on
the last page of the book.*

⊗ The paper in this book meets the minimum requirements of the
American National Standard for Information Sciences—Permanence of
Paper for Printed Library Materials,
ANSI Z39.48-1984.

for the woman in Spitak
who was staying put
in spite of God and man

CONTENTS

Partez de l'idée du malentendu fondamental.
—Jacques Lacan, *The Psychoses*

Spare the rod and spoil the child.
—Solomon, Proverbs

Denn das Tier ist mit Gott eins, aber nur an sich.
—G. W. F. Hegel,
Lectures on the Philosophy of History

PREFACE

"Herman Melville Crazy," trumpeted the *New York Day Book*'s notice of *Pierre; or, The Ambiguities,* compressing the general tenor of critical reaction to the novel into one shrill note. Melville must have known he had it coming. He had taken the wraps off a subject, incest, that "universally-received rules of moral and social order" required one to keep "shrouded in a decorous darkness." And he had coupled this offense with a related one, compounded of "affectation," "remote analogies," "absurd forms of expression," "distorted fancies and conceits," and "genteel hifalutin, painful, though ingenious involutions of language." The upshot was "a kind of prose run mad" which dissolved solid truth in "unbounded . . . nothingness" and confounded "virtue and religion" with "their opposites." In a word, the "raving lunatic's" "diseased imagination" had boiled over in a "monstrous," "unhealthy," outrageously "improper work," compelling the guardians of moral and aesthetic rectitude to "freeze him into silence." And they did, with a vengeance.

The present book began life as an attempt to get back into the spirit of their hysteria. If Melville merited muzzling for "sous[ing]" readers in a "torrent rhapsody" that treated "the holy relations of the family with supersensuousness," how, I wanted to know, did the primitive pre-Freudians of the age of *Pierre* treat the same sacred subject? (Melville's novel, it will be remembered, was conceived four years before Freud was.) What decorous domestic vision had Melville's distorted fancy distorted? I began fishing for an answer in the vast sea of domestic novels, but also marriage manuals, medical guides, and multipurpose vade mecums, which had flooded the American book market while a cubic meter or so of *Ambiguities* stagnated in Harper's warehouse. What I hauled up was a sunken treasure of some of the most genteel hifalutin, distorted, affectedly absurd and involuted prose it has ever been anyone's good fortune to discover by accident. With it came the usual surprise: the sane had understood their raving lunatic well enough not to want to understand him any better. The distortions and involutions of *their* books on the holy family testified to their resolve to keep the subject of Melville's wholly unmentionable. Freezing him into silence, shrouding him in darkness, they sealed off a region of horrors whose exclusion largely determined the shape of things in their own.

That, at any rate, was my initial impression. But the longer I peered into the darkness Melville's contemporaries put between him and them, the less plausible seemed the idea that theirs was exclusively, or even primarily, a strategy of exclusion. For the fictioneers and advice-mongers who specialized in distinguishing "virtue and religion" from their repulsive opposites also did quite the opposite: the things they distinguished had a habit of turning into the things they distinguished them from. Melville's book-length "*double entendre*," as one righteously indignant reviewer rightly called *Pierre*, redoubled what was already double. Bestsellerdom's paragon of "virtue and religion," the Victorians' famously passionless "True Woman," furnished the clearest proof: she moonlighted as a vicious and sacrilegiously incestuous Female Animal. And she did so in the very bestsellers that celebrated her passionlessness; the genteel readers who gagged on Melville's incest novel slurped down countless others with their afternoon tea. If the author of *Pierre* "struck with an impious . . . hand at the very foundations of society," so did the pious people who were paid to keep the foundations firm.[1]

But then why were they spared the pillorying that was Melville's portion? Plainly, something distinguished his double entendres from theirs. Moreover, something plainly still does. For the last decade and more, literary critics and social historians have been exploring the jungle of mass-market novels and advice books that overran the literary marketplace in the 1840s and 1850s. Yet none of these scholars (with rare, partial exceptions) reports having sighted anything resembling an incestuous female animal. On the contrary: like the critical establishment of Melville's day, the historians and critics of our own suggest that a *respectable* mid-century writer shrouded even ordinary sex in decorous darkness—to say nothing of incest.[2] It would be overweening to dismiss all these scholars as blind; it is impossible to overlook Victorian America's fascination with female incestuousness. The only reasonable conclusion seems to be that best-selling antebellum writing was as subversively incestuous as *Pierre*, and that it simultaneously wasn't incestuous at all. No less than Melville, the champions of the "moral and social order" "struck at its foundations"; they did so, however, not with an impious, but with an (im)pious hand.

This book examines their (im)piety. As befits its subject, it takes the form of a series of detours. The book as a whole addresses the question of Melville's mental health. But it does so by appraising the standards of sanity the deviant is supposed to have deviated from, with the result that the author of *Pierre* is scarcely ever mentioned (though he, and especially his novel, are silently evoked at every turn). Melville aside, my subject proper is the best-selling American domestic (or "woman's") fiction of the 1850s, discussed in Chapters 3, 4, and 5. Here too, however, I stray from the topic from the first, since my main interest lies in the incestuous sexuality that is, precisely, *not proper* to these sexless texts; I read them as so many massive double entendres, which their paradigmatically proper authors would no more have recognized as being theirs than, say, the French recognize the expression "double entendre" as being *theirs*. To justify this admittedly improper sort of criticism, I begin the book by making a detour from its subject proper: How, I ask in Chapter 1, can a text deviate from itself to the point of becoming its own exact opposite—while remaining exactly what it is? What "involution of language" could have permitted Melville's genteel contemporaries to be Melvillean and anti-Melvillean at once? The answer I give is, briefly, that such textual duplicity emerges out of the contradictions fiction reveals in other ideological discourses, to the extent that these discourses forge their unity in fiction. This necessitates one further detour, implying as it does that the road to the duplicitous text runs through those other discourses that divide the text against itself. In the case of the best-selling fiction of the 1850s, textual duplicity has its deepest roots in mid-Victorian sexual duplicity. I try to show this in Chapter 2, which analyzes antebellum America's self-contradictory conceptions of sex and the family as they are reflected in the writings of moral reformers, medical men, phrenologists, marriage counselors, and other self-appointed servants of the common weal.

The moral of the whole might as well be stated here: Melville's critics were right. Incest leads to insanity.

Fortunately for me, many people recklessly ignored that home truth to help me write the present book; many more helped me while I was writing it. I mention only a few, and apologize to all the rest. My parents, George Goshgarian and Isabel Calusdian Goshgarian, made things vastly easier by serving as long-distance secretaries, couriers, and all-round factotums. Avedis Sanjian provided much appreciated encouragement as I was getting started. Constance Coiner proved to be a friend in need time and again; George B. Goshgarian directed a steady stream of pertinent clippings my way; Levon Chorbajian chased down the odd sociological reference; Khachig Tölölyan supplied project-sustaining assistance at two critical moments. As for the long critical moment that stretched from a planned three months to three *years* and three months, I could not have weathered it in better company: from my boss, Ulrich Halfmann, to my students, the English and American studies people at the University of Mannheim provided an environment as stimulating as it was relaxed, leaving even a dedicated procrastinator no choice but to accomplish something. And they extended the best kind of hospitality there is—the kind that makes a guest forget s/he is one.

Although this book was substantially completed before I began working at the University of Reims, I would like to thank all those there who facilitated the task of revision by helping me adjust to the many unique features of the French university: in particular, Guy Frossard, Jean Pauchard, Adrian Park, and Fernand Vaillant. And a special thanks to Nathalie Ghionis for her friendship and support.

As to those who gave me a hand in the narrower sense, my first debt is to Robert Maniquis, whose comments on various sections of the manuscript eliminated many an error of strategy and style. Jochen Barkhausen, Valérie Burling, Constance Coiner, Nicole Dubois, Jon Klancher, Raymund Paredes, Bleuette Pion, and Ross Shideler also made useful criticisms of parts of the manuscript, as did the two attentive readers for Cornell University Press. I benefited immensely from long arguments about politics and philosophy with Warren Montag, and from discussions over the years with Michèle Delisle, Jens Kruse, Marilyn Manners, and Linda Paulson, among many others. Bernhard Kendler, of Cornell University Press, was a model of kindness, courtesy, and wit; Patty Peltekos edited the manuscript with scrupulous care.

Finally, I thank Philip Bardsley, Ewald Dietrich, and Patrick Ravaux for leading me through the thickets of international computerdom, and Marie-Hélène Wieczorek for finagling me access to the *salle d'informatique* when it counted.

G. M. GOSHGARIAN

Reims, France

To Kiss the Chastening Rod

1

THE FICTIONAL SUBJECT

Was he sincere, when with apparent enthusiasm he had applied to me the epithet, *beautiful?* . . .

For the first time I looked upon myself with reference to the eyes of others, and I tried to imagine the youthful figure on which I gazed as belonging to another, and not myself . . . and as the image smiled back upon the original, there was such a light, such a glow, such a living soul passed before me, that for one moment a triumphant consciousness swelled my bosom, a new revelation beamed on my understanding—the consciousness of woman's hitherto unknown power—the revelation of woman's destiny.

—Mrs. Caroline Lee Hentz

Shortly before the Christmas of 1850, George Putnam's New York publishing firm launched, without fanfare, *The Wide, Wide World*, a sprawling first novel by the unknown American writer Susan Warner. A number of other publishers had rejected the manuscript. This was arguably evidence of their superior literary standards, but it reflected very poorly on their commercial sense. *The Wide, Wide World*'s sales mounted steadily, if unspectacularly, throughout 1851, then took off on a trajectory without an arc. By the middle of 1852, the book had sold in the neighborhood of fifteen thousand copies. Before 1853 was out, it is supposed to have exhausted sixteen American editions and had been pirated by a dozen English publishers, just one of whom eventually marketed eighty thousand copies.[1] Though soon outstripped by the phenomenal *Uncle Tom's Cabin*, *The Wide, Wide World* continued to draw paying customers on both sides of the Atlantic to the end of the nineteenth century and beyond; it saw some eighty reprintings between 1851 and 1905.[2] According to Putnam's son, it was still in demand on the eve of World War I. An estimate made just after World War II put its cumulative sales in the United States alone at around half a million.[3]

The Wide, Wide World's stupefying success was unprecedented;

never before had an American hardcover novel sold tens of thousands of copies within a year or two of publication.[4] But in the early 1850s several did, and the publishing industry began to take astonished and delighted notice of the fact that the market for belles lettres could now absorb individual titles by the wagonload. In 1855, a trade journal was crowing that "to dispose of *fifty thousand* copies, of any moderately good book, is among the ordinary events which every American publisher deems himself entitled to anticipate."[5] This was an exaggeration, but—by publishers' standards—not much of one. While accurate figures are hard to come by, certain is that at least three American novels released in the 1850s sold 100,000 copies or more in book form before the Civil War. Perhaps another dozen sold over 25,000 copies, and many more passed the 10,000 mark. The age of the best-seller had arrived.[6]

Its arrival involved more than mere numbers. The *quality* of the writing America bought plummeted in proportion as the quantity soared. The fiction business of the 1830s and 1840s had been dominated by craftsmen as skillful as Cooper, Dickens, Longfellow, and Bulwer-Lytton; the mass marketplace of the 1850s was overrun—in Hawthorne's memorable phrase—by a "d——d mob of scribbling women," together with a few equally execrable scribblers of the opposite sex. Almost overnight, literary craftsmanship was eclipsed by scribbling, and prose that everyone (its perpetrators not excepted) considered subliterary began to outshine its inestimably more brilliant competition. Worse, the lackluster "trash" (Hawthorne again) tirelessly generated by the scribblers *continued* to outshine the competition for decades to come.[7] Indeed, many of the very *titles* that burst upon the mid-century mass-literary firmament were still delighting the benighted millions forty and fifty years later; Joyce's Gerty MacDowell was only one of an obscure throng of moonstruck adolescents steeped in their grandparents' favorite fiction.[8] Not until World War I did these novas whose flame no Melville could dim cease to bedazzle the public imagination, and even in this twilight of the scribbling horde the most durable favorites continued to glow steadily on the subliterary horizon.[9] Viewed in retrospect, then, *The Wide, Wide World* takes a central place in a major cultural constellation; the fictioneers who surged to stardom in the publishing revolution of the fifties were to preside over the long night of American letters for something like half a century.

Not that the night is over. If the peculiar charms of the scribblers'

Sunday-school epics have flickered and faded, those of their pre-ferred narrative *mode* have not.[10] The U.S. fiction industry continues to thrive on aesthetically unassuming but monumentally earnest prose sagas that, like Warner's, stick prudently to home truths and the aesthetic lowlands, and yet loom up before the peoples as distinc-tive, irreplaceable, cherished cultural landmarks. Warner did not, to be sure, invent that kind of fiction; but she came along at just the right moment to help it ring in a new era in American mass-literary history. Before her, the country's subaltern "cultural work" had been performed by a multitude of pious parables and blood-and-bullion romances whose individual avatars even aficionados must have had trouble sorting out; from about the time she zoomed to prominence, the blockbuster sui generis began to set the cultural pace. Unlike their ancestors, like their descendants, mid-century Americans hon-ored their best-sellers as *unique* works of (subliterary) art. They were advertised and even reviewed on an individual basis; quoted, an-thologized, dramatized, and parodied; issued, as a rule, in formats destined for the parlor rather than the pantry; and not uncommonly enshrined in marbled duodecimo collected editions whose solidity bespoke a prophetic awareness of posterity's claims.[11] In short, Victo-rian readers regarded *The Wide, Wide World* and its unsufferable ilk the way modern readers do *Love Story* and its: not as interchangeable "'copies' which have no original,"[12] but as rare originals many an avid admirer would have given his eyeteeth to be able to copy. In an unbroken line with today's drugstore classic, the first American best-sellers thus pose the question of what continues to be (after cook-books, and not counting the comics) our favorite brand of writing: the one-of-a-kind mass fiction.

That is one reason we should still pay some attention to them. Another is that they speak to current preoccupations with female sexuality. They do not, of course, stoop to mentioning sex; fa-mously, they stand as mute monuments to the prudery of their age. Yet encrypted in these massively moral *contes*, in an idiolect as for-eign to them as it is intimately theirs, lies a story of sexual aber-ration a Byron would have blushed at. Its subject is incest; its pro-tagonist, innately incestuous woman; its theme, that only the morti-fication of the female flesh can close off another and infinitely more mortifying prospect: that of having to recognize in the true Ameri-can woman's proverbial purity a colossal blind for her con-genital corruption. The curious mode this tale is told in is accordingly such as to prevent it from being told. In both senses of the word, the best-sellers *contain* their immoral moral: it consists in an insight they block out of their field of vision, it persists in an inside whose suppression entails their internal scission. It exists, in other words, as their *not-saying* anything about it, in other words that are the same words they contain it with. The scribblers proclaim at every turn that their pure fiction is pure fiction; that (dis)avowal of their (im)purity is where their real truth lies.

A double reason, then, for disinterring this body of work: to take the measure of its treatment of gender; to find out what it reveals about its still vital "genre." But, as the words indicate, these two lines of inquiry tend to merge. What, we will therefore also be asking, do the scribblers murmur about the kinship between gender and their "genre"? And what does incest have to do with it?

Gender, genre, degeneracy: it is to explore that relatively narrow range of issues that we mean to plod through the wide, wide world of scribblerdom. As it is by no means virgin territory, let us begin by consulting the existing maps.

Mirrors and Dark Undersides: Theory

"What," Hawthorne sourly wondered, in the same breath in which he cursed his competition, "is the mystery of these innumerable editions of the 'Lamplighter,' and other books neither better nor worse?—Worse they could not be, and better they need not be, when they sell by the 100,000."[13] Such theorizing as scribbler scholarship makes room for generally mimics the ritual gesture first rehearsed here. In one way or another, it puts the scribblers back in their subaltern place for doing in their prose what their sisters were supposed to be doing at home: not producing, but *re*producing.

Take, for instance, Donald Koch. "The remarkable success of *The Lamplighter* 'and other books neither better nor worse,'" this latter-day Hawthornean flatly declares, "was never a 'mystery'" at all. Koch goes on to prove by example how quickly Hawthorne's fretful obiter dictum can be erected into a full-blooded theory of the scribbler novel:

If occasional genius fretted over these best-sellers, the popular mind was in complete rapport with them. At a time when national life was in great turmoil, the American domestic sentimentalists produced a folk fiction with all of the appealing characteristics that distinguish a *genre*. A great part of the popularity of their novels arose from the sense of security and satisfaction they imparted. . . . In the absence of answers to larger social dilemmas, these books with their stereotyped formula and optimistic philosophy were at hand to offer a comfort.[14]

Great literature as unsettling creation, popular writing as soothing repetition: an odd echo haunts this Hawthornean homily. For not only does the passage insist on the reproductive function of mid-century mass fiction; it *performs* the main offices assigned its object. At a time when national life is in great turmoil (1968), domestic criticism (re)produces a stereotypical formula with (almost) all the appealing characteristics that distinguish one's mother. Just as she might have, Koch offers himself the comforting reassurance that genius's other, the "popular mind," mindlessly imitates something else. From Plato to Pattee, critics have been reproducing just this solution to their favorite mystery—and with it, presumably, the sense of security and satisfaction it imparts. But let us not repeat Koch's mistake of equating repetitiveness with insignificance. In its contemporary context, his classic recitation is an answer to a literary-critical *and* a larger social dilemma. Activating a logic by no means outdated, it equates a "*genre*" (the "domestic") with the reproductive, and the reproductive with the non-productive; it then denies the works in the genre that does no work the status, precisely, of the literary *work*.[15] Archetypal and historical at once, generic and scribbler-specific, Koch's formula writes scribbling off as a consummate sort of inferior mimesis.

What does scribblerdom imitate? It imitates itself. There is a "complete rapport" between the "best-sellers" and the "popular mind." A *complete* rapport: the "stereotyped formula[s]" of the "domestic sentimentalists" are indifferently the substance of the novels and the stereotypical mind that reproduces itself in them. And yet a complete *rapport*: reading the scribblers, the popular mind relates to something that is the same as itself but also other, narcissistically confronts itself-as-other. The (non)work performed by Koch's "folk fiction" is the (re)production of sameness as difference. For the untold thousands who stubbornly preferred hackwork to Hawthorne, the road to the bookshop led straight back home. The mass reading audience was fixated in a kind of collective mirror phase, enthralled by an image/imitation of itself.[16]

That way of looking at bestsellerdom remains both popular and productive. But it also exhibits certain anomalies. The strategy of dismissing mass art as strictly derivative, while explaining its massive popularity on the self-same grounds, works smoothly enough when applied to the individual "folk fiction"; without much strain, it can be made to accommodate entire genres as well. Applied to folk fiction as a whole, however, the logic of the "complete rapport" inconveniently reverses itself: derivative only of itself-as-other, mass culture is, at the limit, not derivative at all. If the particular mass work borrows its identity from the formulas it merely mirrors, the *universe* of "stereotyped formula[s]" forms a closed system of representations which refers to nothing other than itself, can refer only to itself even when seeming to refer beyond itself.[17] Mass culture reduplicates the popular mind which reduplicates mass culture: in the aggregate, all the stereotypes make up an *original* work of "folk fiction." By its very unoriginality, scribbling returns us endlessly to a world of its own devising.

That, however, is what "occasional genius" is supposed to do. Hawthorne put his finger on a mystery after all: from a certain point of view, the reproductive is as creative as the creative. Hackwork (generally) and the great work (individually) can be treated as unique and self-validating modes, instances of self-rapport separated by an absolute nonrapport. Hawthorne's genre and that of the scribblers are, the conclusion seems to be, incommensurable.

Criticism does not find the idea uniformly unattractive. Indeed, ever since the scribbling horde loomed up on the literary horizon, the notion of the scribblers' incommensurable difference has helped maintain an essential line of demarcation between genius and the mob. But, lest incommensurability degenerate into mere absence of measure, the same line has also always had to be crossed; otherwise, greatness and its guardians could only invoke the unstable criterion of *taste* to defend the hallowed distinction separating the literary from the subliterary sphere. The reinforcements called up to beat back such relativism have been, invariably, truth and the real.

Henry Nash Smith's excursus on scribblerdom is therefore the classical supplement to Koch's:

[The English scribbler] Margaret Oliphant . . . accuses Hawthorne of straining the minds of his readers by compelling them to struggle with baffling problems. Mrs. Oliphant's attack is directed precisely at . . . his establishment of a realm of imaginative truth in fiction, a truth of ro-

mance distinct from the mere imitation of outer reality. . . . When the
fantasy life of the American Common Man and especially the Common
Woman became available for inspection in the fiction preferred by the
suddenly expanded reading public, it revealed that both Hawthorne and
Melville, in setting out to explore the dark underside of the psyche, had
been moving in a direction directly counter to that of the popular culture. . . . Fiction conceived as a penetration of the unconscious seemed
threatening to the newly articulate middle class, which craved not challenge but reassurance.[18]

The reassurance that an Oliphant stands lower in the scale of being than a Hawthorne comes at the price of a reversal complement-
ing the one traced a moment ago. As mass culture, though derivative, is on Koch's evidence also creative, so the creative work, as
Smith testifies, is for its part also derivative. In its mimetic freedom,
true art subserves the truth. Imaging a world of its own, the original
work yet mirrors reality as it really is. The proof is that it encom-
passes what passes to the backside, as it were, of the "middle class's"
looking glass. The genius of genius is to bare even the "dark underside" of things.

How does one know when one is looking at that obscure object?
What distinguishes the "truth of romance" from mere moonshine?
The truth of romance does. The touchstone that permits one to
identify the truth in fiction is produced in the realm of the "truth in
fiction": "imaginative truth" provides the measure both of itself and
untruth, assigning "the popular culture" its proper place on the
other side of the underside. The basic truth of romance thus concerns the status of the "truth of romance"; it says that the inner life
of the "Common Man and especially the Common Woman" is a fat-
uous "fantasy" on the far side of the truly real.

But then what is agitating Mrs. Oliphant?

It is too early to tell. One can, however, already note Smith's satisfaction over her agitation. As a guardian of the imaginative truth, he
has every reason to be satisfied: our apprehension of the truth in
fiction depends on a Mrs. Oliphant's apprehensions. If the popular
culture did not feel threatened by true fiction's penetration of the
unconscious, it would not throw up the bright screen against which
alone the dark underside becomes visible. Genius can, perhaps, produce the truth of romance independently of scribblerdom (that, at
any rate, is Smith's assumption); but we can *see* it only because the
scribblers reproduce the cheery blankness that is its absence. Truth

emerges only as the generic difference between the all-inclusive wholeness of high art's vision and the *ex*clusive wholeness of "the popular culture's."

Yet this latter wholeness is not, despite appearances, Koch's "complete [self-]rapport." For Smith's "fantasy life" is not unfettered; his scribblers are not at liberty to scribble just anything, to run in whichever direction they please. They are constrained to run *away*, in a direction directly counter to the one taken by genius. By that flight they reveal that the truth governs them too. But it governs them from the outside, without their knowing anything about it; from the point of view of the imaginative truth, the positive content of their fantasy counts only as an index of its vacuity. Of its vacuity, not its insignificance: scribbling is of no account, it does not so much as encounter, let alone negate the truth, but it is not therefore *nothing*. It is *truth degree zero*. The limited and delimiting task of the Commoner as writer ("especially the Common Woman") is to stand in for the hole that only the wholeness of truth can fill. The meeting folk fantasy forever misses by running directly counter to the Hawthorno-Melvillean darkness *is* the essential mode of encounter between genius and the mob.

This equation of popular fantasy with the null set which founds the only truth that counts has, mathematically speaking, an undeniable allure. But, critically speaking, it has a suspicious ring. To say the least, it is odd that Mrs. Oliphant should know enough to fly in exactly the right direction from a truth which escapes her; that the Commoners should tremble before the threat of a penetration whose possibility their optimistic philosophy denies; and that the scribblers should so obsessively retell the story that so optimistically denies it. Simply taken at face value, Smith's evidence would seem to point less to Smith's conclusion than to one he puts by: that the scribblers' text might be woven around the very hole its fantasy of wholeness makes disappear, and so might betray in its warp and woof precisely what it is supposed to conceal. But that idea is inadmissible, for essential reasons. It implies that the difference a Smith situates *between* the genres of genius and the mob should be conceived as a sort of generalized heterogeneity traversing both; that the black-and-white distinction between the dark underside and the other side is a reassuring fantasy about a reassuring fantasy; and therefore that the *scribblers'* ostensible self-rapport sustains the *Hawthorno-Melvilleans'*. More is at stake in traditional scribbler theory than scribblerdom.

One can, of course, decide that the theory is rooted in fantasy without concluding that the complete rapport so dear to it is sheer illusion. Folk fiction's eternal Same may be, precisely, *fiction*, reproductive *work* and not non-work, the very real product of the very real fiction factory in the very profitable business of fabricating it. To refuse the classical dichotomies does not, then, oblige us to dismiss Hawthorne's mystery. It is perhaps enough simply to turn it around, rewriting his question about the representation of *sameness as difference* as one about the representation of *difference as sameness*. The mystery is not necessarily diminished thereby.

From a certain point of view, it is even enhanced. For the new question not only suggests that the scribblers have an underside as dark as their more exalted competitors'. It further reminds us that they *seem not to*: the most mysterious thing about bestsellerdom's underside is that it also isn't one. The classical theory of domestic fiction is not so much wrong, then, as it is one-sided. It goes to show that the scribblers manage to conceal their shadowy side in the blinding light of the sunny side, that they make it disappear by putting it on view.[19] Bestsellerdom hides its dark secret the way the Minister hid his letter.[20]

This remains one of the best ways to hide things. The easiest way to prove it is to turn to practical scribbler criticism, which, with rare exceptions, aids and abets its authors in forging their fictional self-rapport.[21]

Mirrors and Dark Undersides: Practice

A good deal has been written about the "domestic," "sentimental," or "women's" novels of the mid-century, much of it recently. There is a consensus on the basics: that the scribblers focus on middle-class home life; appeal massively to their readers' tenderest emotions; deal in types rather than psychologically individuated characters; write with evangelical ends in mind; and compulsively chronicle the improbable career of a pious, nubile, aboriginally middle-class but temporarily déclassée white American girl whose exemplary fortitude under a storm of adversities is rewarded with a spouse, solvency, and salvation. Beyond that, the critics only agree about what they should disagree about: chiefly, their authors' perception of the Victorian "woman question."

The disagreement, it seems, could hardly be greater than it is. One group of critics makes the scribblers hidebound antifeminists; a second pronounces them foremothers of the women's movement; a third argues they were neither, or else both. The first view is the traditional one. It was succinctly articulated in the 1940s by Alexander Cowie, for whom the domestic novel "may be roughly defined" as "an extended prose tale composed chiefly of commonplace household incidents and episodes loosely worked into a trite plot involving the fortunes of characters who exist less as individuals than as carriers of pious moral or religious sentiment. The thesis of such a book is that true happiness comes from submission to suffering."[22] Such "sex-warfare" as breaks out in this fiction (still following Cowie) "generally ends in an ignoble truce whereby the woman barters all her advantages for a scrap of paper—a marriage certificate." This jibes with the "distinctly conservative" character of the domestic novel, which "functioned as a sort of benign moral police whose regulations were principally comprised under the heads of religion and morality." The best-sellers' popularity, one infers, reflected their customers' allegiance to the Victorian social order—first and foremost, to the patriarchy.[23]

Cowie's remains the majority opinion, at least if one counts all those who pause over the scribblers just long enough to type them as professional apologists for prevailing social arrangements.[24] Since the 1950s, however, traditionalists have had to contend with counterclaims that insist on the protofeminist character of domestic prose. Helen Papashvily was the first to recast the scribblers as closet subversives. Under a placid surface, according to her, their anodyne moral *contes* "were handbooks of . . . feminine revolt. . . . These pretty tales reflected and encouraged a pattern of feminine behavior so quietly ruthless, so subtly vicious that by comparison the ladies at Seneca appear angels of innocence. . . . These books were . . . a witches' broth, a lethal draught brewed by women and used by women to destroy their common enemy, man."[25]

When this was written, Papashvily qualified as an eccentric. When the post–1968 generation of feminist critics exhumed the scribblers some twenty years later, she was retrospectively transformed into a pioneer. Eager to reclaim earlier women's writing for a newly (re)constructed feminist tradition, the revisionists of the 1970s resurrected Papashvily's thesis—though they formulated it less exuberantly than she did—that the domestic novel decried the oppression of women while paying lip service to prevailing moral norms. The idea has by no means seen its day. It is codified in Nina Baym's by now classic survey of scribblerdom, called, straightforwardly, *Woman's Fiction*.[26]

Woman's Fiction celebrates the domestic novel as a "progressive," "pragmatic feminist" account of the "'trials and triumph' . . . of a heroine who, beset with hardships, finds within herself the qualities of intelligence, will, resourcefulness and courage sufficient to overcome them." Baym builds her case on two kinds of evidence. First, she combs the novels for illustrations of masculine self-indulgence, cruelty, lechery, misogyny, and double-dealing in order to establish that, in scribblerdom as elsewhere, villainy customarily wore pants. Second, she puts a pragmatically feminist face on the very exhibits Cowiesque critics produce to document the scribblers' conformism; Baym's argument is that what may look like craven compliance is actually stealthy self-assertion, the only practicable strategy for coping with the "oppressions and cruelties, covert and blatant, of men." Thus if, in traditional perspective, the heroine's submission to the inscrutable decrees of Providence attests the best-sellers' traditionalism, for Baym it becomes "a pragmatic strategy for dealing from a weak position with the threats and aggressions of the powerful": "kiss[ing] the rod. . . . lifts [the heroine] up in her trials and enables her to survive, to carry out her responsibilities, and to bear with deprivation and loss." Again, where Cowie's domestic maiden scrambles ignominiously to net a mate, Baym's bachelorette conducts a systematic search for "a network of surrogate kin" to compensate the deficiencies (usually father's) of her biological family. It follows that the typical domestic fiction is "not only [the story] of a self-made woman but that of a self-made or surrogate family." Logically, then, "most of these novels conclude with a marriage that represents the institutionalizing of such families."[27] One could go on; but this perhaps suffices to show how shifting the critical light makes parables of submission over into indictments of oppression, profiling the scribblers as prophets, not of conformity, but of realistic reform. Their audience is of course transformed along with them: mid-century woman must have bought the best-sellers because she relished their portrayal of "*Homo tyrannicus, Homo timidus,* and *Homo tenuis*" as—in Frances Cogan's arresting metaphor—"spiritual barbells the domestic heroine lifts . . . to strengthen her own intellectual and ethical muscles."[28]

Alternatively, she bought them for mirroring her ambivalence about her prescribed social role. This is the thesis of the dialectical school of scribbler criticism. Its major spokeswoman, Mary Kelley, detects in the tales of the "literary domestics" a "positive, forceful message [about women's domestic role]" that "rode and was partly generated by an undercurrent of dissatisfaction and despair."[29] Both the forceful message and the despair grew out of protofeminist impulses. But the impulses clashed: the literary domestics' "eagerness to glorify woman in the name of her mandated ethic of life, selfless service to others, warred with their apprehension that woman's condition was actually demoralizing and debilitating." The apprehension did not erupt in fiery protest only because an overriding allegiance to prevailing ideals of femininity precluded a combative feminism: "society's and their own sense of female vocation and female place" modulated the scribblers' dissatisfaction into uneasy advocacy of the ethic of self-denial.[30]

The dialectical thesis has a palpable advantage over the other two: it accounts for them, neatly demonstrating how domestic fiction has managed to elicit readings as divergent as Cowie's and Baym's. For Cowie is certainly right: the best-sellers convey Cowiesque messages with a vengeance, tirelessly intoning that, for the weaker sex, true happiness lies in sweet surrender to God and man. But Baym is also right: such messages are consistently qualified by their Baymian context. The novels abound in wonderful women who must defeat the dastardly designs of *Homo tyrannicus*, or make good the dire deficiencies of *Homos timidus* and *tenuis*. One therefore cannot help but agree with Kelley: from *The Scarlet Letter* to *The Hidden Hand*, the best-sellers of the 1850s methodically establish a double perspective on the gender hierarchy, quietly denouncing woman's oppression even as they apologize for the social order that oppresses her.

The problem with this kind of commentary is not that it paints a false picture. The problem is that the picture it paints resembles the original too closely to reveal much about it. To be sure, the hints of woman's dilemma usually lurk in bestsellerdom's darker reaches; this gives criticism a pretext for hauling them into its light. But certain of the novels spare one even that little trouble. Augusta Jane Evans's heroine Beulah, for instance, frontally challenges the oppressive order of things: she jeopardizes her marital prospects for the sake of her literary career, shelves her Bible for an agonizing study of morals and metaphysics, and even dares draft an article "designed to prove that woman's happiness [is] not necessarily dependent upon marriage." Only after her iconoclasm has brought her teetering to the brink of atheism and spinsterhood does this Margaret Fuller manquée concede the error of her ways, and even then it is with more than a twinge of regret that she forswears freethinking, philosophy, and feminism for the God of her fathers and a forbidding father figure of a husband.[31] Plainly, if criticism's mission is to show that antithetical feminine impulses collide in domestic fiction, then *Beulah* is above criticism; it says as much about itself (and, by extension, its sister novels) as the critics can say about it. One is therefore not surprised to find a recent essay celebrating it as a limit text, the ne plus ultra (with Evans's *St. Elmo*) in the sentimental line.[32]

The present study might be described as an attempt to move criticism beyond *Beulah*. Its objective remains Kelleyesque: to pinpoint "the contradiction of an unavoidable domestic destiny," the "principle of crisis" on which domestic fiction is premised.[33] But the best-sellers as read by the dialectical school—essentially, the best-sellers as read by *Beulah*—offer us only a faint echo of these disruptive things. They offer us, in a word, not contradiction, but cognitive dissonance: a "split between an inner vision and a desire to conform," a rebel ethic the heart of scribblerdom "both claimed and rejected."[34] Contradiction lies elsewhere: in the split between this split and a desire the scribblers neither claimed nor rejected, but simply disallowed—so that it might (re)appear as the "inner vision" that *was not it*. If we are to report on *this* theater of the "warfare within" *Beulah* (appropriately incongruous notion), we need to settle accounts with the principle of crisis on which the dialectical approach itself is premised.[35] It too involves something of a split: between a desire to shake off the shackles of patriarchal scribbler criticism and an inner vision that conforms to the desire of the critical fathers.

For example, Smith or Koch. Kelley's reflective "literary domestics" bear a strong family resemblance to tradition's mindless mimics: they too faithfully mirror their own minds. "These writers," in Kelley's words, "reported on their own phenomenon." Logically, this makes criticism (or history) a report on their self-report; phenomeno-logically, it makes it an authentification of their self-rapport. Not that it is enough simply to transcribe the literary domestics' report; obviously, it must first be verified, or, at a minimum, "sift[ed], arrange[d], and organize[d]." What does one sift out? Plainly, the most authentic reporting, that which most truly reflects the domestic phenomenon. Where is the standard that permits one to identify it? Necessarily, in the self-report itself, in that essential part of it which can serve as a measure of the truth of the whole. This is where *Beulah* (or whichever text one likes) comes in: it embodies bestsellerdom's equivalent of the "truth of romance," the highest realization of scribbler self-rapport. Tradition, in the persons of Koch and Smith, moves between the bounds of a nugatory folk "fantasy" and Hawthorno-Melvillean epiphany; the Kelleyans challenge that critical vision by tracing *within* scribblerdom the progressive unfolding of the scribblers' own, Beulan truth. The challenge accordingly reproduces the structure of the system it challenges. The only difference is that we now find *inside* popular culture the truth as well as its null set, the latter in the guise of "domestic dream[s] of celebration" or occasional "idealized fantasies"—both given the lie by Beulah's more authentic ambivalence. Affirming the logic of the "dark underside," the dialectical approach diverges from its patriarchal predecessors only in claiming a slice of that fundamental region for scribblerdom.

Analysis of particular works follows the same pattern; it too traces a progression, within the individual text, from dark side to sunny side, fantasy to truth. Practically, this gives rise to a kind of consciousness-raising after the fact. Aware that she is working in a sphere in which "self-discovery was not total," the analyst inevitably finds herself assuming the role of critical *therapist*. Her task becomes that of bringing out the varying *potential* for full self-consciousness whose horizon is in one sense *Beulah*, and in another the critic herself (since it is the critic who recognizes this horizon in/as *Beulah*). Thus Kelley gently coaxes her textual interlocutors into confessing that their celebratory dreams are in fact "defensive, ambiguous, [and] conflicted," troubled by "stirrings of discontent," shot through with "notes of distress," riven by "inner turmoil," and so on. In a word, she teaches them to teach us that they *knew better*.[36]

At a practical level, such an approach produces vastly more interesting results than the blanket dismissal tradition has treated the scribblers to. But what interests us here is less the difference than the common denominator: the *fictional subject*, that (un)knowing textual mind which forges the self-rapport of the domestic novel as read by all its critics to date. Especially its dialectical critics, who demonstrate better than all the rest the fictional subject's unifying function. No matter that they dwell lovingly on Beulah's (and her sisters') split, their proof positive that bestsellerdom engaged the baffling problems the jaundiced meanly accuse it of ducking. That self-rapport should crystallize as the posing of a baffling problem is not at all a baffling problem: the solution is already there in the poser, the overarching textual mind supposed to be of two minds about things. Simply, because the scribbler text that is not one (half) *knows* it, its "primary and self-defined nature" emerges as that of a (self-questioning) self.[37] The text is one after all; its confession of confusion proves it; indeed, the more baffled the self-report, the greater the self-rapport. No textual split that does not bring the fictional subject closer to the wholeness of an integral vision of its divided self—to that realm of imaginative truth in fiction where self-discovery would surely be total.

The result is a circle. For, by a tautology worth pausing over, to posit the fictional subject as sole poser of all possible scribbler posers is to pose oneself only such posers as this supposed "self-consciousness" can consciously pose. One can avoid that critical echo chamber only by approaching it from a critical position calculated to decompose it: one must shatter the text's self-composure by exposing its subjective pose *as* a pose, as the imposition on its composite elements of an only apparent self-rapport. To expose its pose means to pose it as a textual *effect*; we propose to call it the fictional subject-effect. That this effect is quite as real as it is fictional will by now be evident: we have just seen it repeatedly *realized* in scribbler scholarship. But it also involves a certain imposture. Posturing as the whole text, when it is in fact only a textual effect, the fictional subject banishes to its dark underside everything in the text counterposed to its subjective unity; it renders invisible all those posers it cannot possibly pose without problematizing its "primary and self-defined nature." That domestic fiction harbors such unposable problems must of course be demonstrated, not presupposed. This, however, is precisely what it is impossible to demonstrate as long as one attends only to the fictional subject's self-report, in the charitable intention of helping it realize its total self-rapport.

Making the fictional subject effect an *object* rather than the *basis* of analysis means raising the possibility, anathema for therapeutic criticism, that one's text stands in an incurably contradictory relation to itself. The kinds of contradiction which emerge in that perspective might be described as the difference between the text considered as subject and as a defective mechanism for obliterating everything in itself which resists subjection. Or, if one prefers, as the difference between the posers the fictional subject poses, and those it cannot possibly pose—because *they* pose *it*. But before examining scribblerdom for evidence of that kind of split, it may be useful to say something more, and more abstractly, about the non-fictional subject.[38]

There Is More to Ideology than Meets the I

The unity claimed by works of fiction might be likened to that of ideology, which can be loosely defined, following Louis Althusser, as the set of representations and practices which engender social subjects by endowing individuals with imaginary visions of their real relations to the world.[39] The supposed unity of ideology, in turn, resembles that of those "normal" subjects who "live out" the imaginary identities ideology engenders. Very schematically, the mechanism that produces the imaginary self-rapport of both ideology and the ideological subject may be conceived (still following Althusser) as a "mirror structure" involving identificatory relationships between individuals and imaginary Representations of themselves (for example, women and Woman: see the latter part of the epigraph to this chapter), and, secondarily, between individuals and similar individuals. Each position within this "duplicate mirror structure" reflects and validates the other; subjectivity *is*, in some sense, the resulting process of reciprocal self-reflection.

But the relations the dual mirror structure mobilizes are not merely imaginary. As Althusser indicates by way of a few laconic allusions to psychoanalysis (elaborated a bit here), ideology's "mirrors" depend on language. The cognition that "I am made in God's image," for example, not only binds the "I" of the statement to his divine Representative; it presupposes the speaker's identification with the "I" that represents him *in* his statement. The obviousness of the latter identification (I am obviously the person I refer to when I say "I") masks a circumstance that, exposed, imperils the very notion of identification: the price of access to the signifier "I" is submission to the basic condition of any signifying activity, namely, that a signified be absent from its signifier in order to be re-presented there. Yet this presence rooted in absence is the only possible form of self-presence: only by disappearing behind the signifier can an individual signify that he is a "self," and so *become one*. If one adds that no signifier designates what it signifies except in relation to another signifier, and so on to infinity, one begins to see that an "I" emerges as the effect of a double division: that of its definition in terms of a

signifying system not only exterior, antecedent, and indeed indifferent to any particular "self," but also incapable of producing the
kind of fixed significations that could ground a self's supposed self-
sameness. Fundamentally split by his accession to language, frag-
mented by its operations once he has acceded to it, a subject can *have*
an identity only insofar as he perpetually pursues one, along a chain
of identificatory metaphors promising him an impossible wholeness
while endlessly effecting his division, and thus his symbolic death.

This state of affairs both motivates and subverts ideological identification. Motivates it, because ideology retrieves for each "I" a discursive "image" of the wholeness her accession to language puts out
of reach: the dual mirror structure is perhaps best imagined as a
kind of discursive machine that repeatedly arrests the restless movement of the signifier within which the subject's inaugural self-divi-
sion is repeatedly re-enacted. Arrests it in order to put in its place
the "mirror" of an automatism, a recurring configuration of meanings whose fixity tends to collapse meaning back into meaningless-
ness: no better example than the self-rapport that recurs with such
deadening reassurance in (the scholarship on) mass culture. But,
precisely because the dual mirror structure is this *linguistic* auto-
maton—because one's ideological mirror image is reflected in mirrors made of *discourse*—the reassuring self-rapport ideology produces is never more than a fiction. Notoriously, the stuff of
discourse slips, slides, perishes, will not stay still: caught up in the
social struggles that divide and redivide it against itself, language
spoils the dream of ideological stability it engenders and serves. Having torn a hole in the subject only to fill it with ideology's imaginary
vision of wholeness, it tears a hole in the fabric of the ideological
vision it weaves. The dual mirror structure thus fabricates an identity whose fundamental condition is its impossibility. This strange
compound deserves a name no less strange: let us call it (w)holeness.

(W)holeness is what poses as it opposes the (fictional) subject effect.

How is this hybrid produced? How does ideology impose the identity the subject unquestionably supposes to be her own? Briefly: by
putting before her not only an imaginary Representation of herself,
but also an Absolute Subject *through* whom she identifies with herself. This Subject is the One who is always, as it were, looking over
the subject's shoulder as she confronts her reflection in ideology's
mirror. Consequently, what she sees there is never simply herself; it

is herself insofar as He too sees her, and *as* He sees her. How, indeed, would she know that she had properly seen herself at all, if He—represented by His Word—were not there to assure her she had? (Here again, one could do worse than to consult that proto-Althusserian, Mrs. Caroline Lee Hentz; see the first part of the epigraph.) Thus the dual mirror structure joins two assymetrical "halves" whose mutual recognition coincides with the subjection of the one to the Other; at the same time, it produces the symmetry of the subject's relation to her "mirror image," as well as to other subjects "equal" to herself. In Althusser's formulation: the subject "is . . . a subject through the Subject and subjected to the Subject," while the Subject, for his part, recognizes "the terrible inversion of His image" in his subjects. (The classic example is God and man. Another is Man and woman. This book is largely about the mirror relation between those two examples.) Recognizing that she has been recognized, the subject simultaneously acquires both her independent sense of self and the sense that independent selfhood is a function of one's dependence on the Representative of an overarching order.

Out of this account of ideology as a duplicate yet assymetrical mirror structure comes the key notion of "interpellation"; here is Althusser's description of the *process* by which the non-self-identity of the speaking subject is obscured by the "primary 'obviousness' . . . that you and I are subjects" exactly identical to ourselves. Althusser likens this process to the everyday experience of being hailed on the street.[40] The conviction that I am indeed who I am supposed to be resembles the conviction that I and nobody else am the addressee of the "Hey you!" (or "Hey beautiful!": compare Mrs. Hentz) which rings out behind me as I am walking along; the act of turning around when hailed acknowledges that somebody else has acknowledged me, and so evokes the discourses and actions through which I live out my ideological identity. In this "little theoretical theatre," the one who calls out stands, obviously, for the Subject; the other is the subject, or rather *becomes one* from the moment she turns around. The scene as a whole, Althusser says, might simply be entitled "ideology"; "the existence of ideology and the hailing or interpellation of individuals as subjects are one and the same thing."

Should we take this to mean that there "really is" a Subject who recruits individuals for ideology? If not, what is the status of this mysterious Being? Althusser provides the elements of an answer when he notes that his theoretical theatre rests on a fiction: in reality, there are no individuals who are not subjects, which is to say that everyone is in ideology from before the beginning (even before being born, one has a gender, a nationality, a class affiliation, etc.—in other words, the foundations of an imaginary identity). Similarly, everybody has a place "reserved" for him in language. Before one speaks, one is spoken of; when one speaks, it is to assume an already established linguistic position, to set an "I" in the place of a "s/he." Individuals are interpellated, then, by a social and signifying order which, like the language that is its main vehicle, already includes the subjects the individuals will become. The Subject represents that order; but He represents it as overdetermined by its principal effect, the subject-effect. Interpellation casts the "normal" individual's imaginary relation to the reality that determines him in the only terms available to him once he has been interpellated; namely, in terms that disavow anything in the subject outside the closed circuits of subjectivity.

But those closed circuits are also open, for reasons we have touched on: the subject dwells not in wholeness, but in (w)holeness. The consequence is that the Subject, as the subject sees Him, bears the marks of her imperfection: He too—He above all—*leaves something to be desired.* It is well that He does. If the subject assents to her penetration by the Subject, freely "choosing" to be interpellated, it is in the secret hope of supplying the lack that makes even the Supreme Representative of Wholeness less than whole—and, by supplying it, of becoming whole herself, of *becoming one with Him.* But we are getting ahead of ourselves. *That* lesson is to be read not in Althusser, but in the scribblers. For the immediate pupose of suggesting a new angle of approach to their work, enough, perhaps, has been said about the Subject.

Proper (hi)Story

What does Althusser's conception of ideology have to do with the scribblers, or their critics?

Let us put the question differently. Which Subject interpellates domestic fiction's fictional subject?

On that question, the scribblers and their twentieth-century critics do not see eye to eye. As the scribblers understand it, their works are called forth by God, whose self-sameness they transcribe in a humbler register. We will examine this hypothesis in due course (Chapter 3). At the moment, however, it is the critics' ostensibly more secular hypothesis that interests us. For them, the Subject who interpellates bestsellerdom's surrogate subject (female eunuch, closet feminist, or cognitive dissident) is named History. Inconveniently, this primary obviousness is so obvious that it is nowhere spelled out in scribbler scholarship per se.[41] We turn, therefore, to a classic American statement of the principles involved, R. W. B. Lewis's *The American Adam.* Here is the kernel of Lewis's conception of (in our terms) the relations between History and the historical subject, whose kinship with his fictional cousin will not be slow to appear:

> Intellectual history, properly conducted, exposes not only the dominant ideas of a period, or of a nation, but more important, the dominant clashes over ideas. . . . The historian looks not only for the major terms of discourse, but also for the major pairs of opposed terms which, by their very opposition, carry discourse forward. . . . As he does so . . . the historian is likely to discover that the development of the culture in question resembles a protracted and broadly ranging conversation: at best a dialogue—a dialogue which at times moves very close to drama.[42]

The history of culture is the history of people talking to each other; nothing, it seems, could be more obvious than that. Accordingly, the intellectual historian's task is to listen in on the cultural conversation in order to discover what people were talking *about.* The procedure recommended is, in principle, simple: one listens for the major pairs of opposed terms that carry discourse forward. They are identified easily enough: they are the terms and ideas that turned up most frequently in the debate. In essence, then, intellectual history is an exercise in intelligent *transcription*: the historian is a kind of stenographer after the fact, who takes down the most insistent of the statements still echoing in the archive with a view to resurrecting the spirit of the conversation that generated them.[43]

Lewis's historian comes after the fact in another sense as well. The transcription he makes has already been made; before he picks up his pen, History has been written as *story* by those Ur-historians, "the best-attuned artists of the time." Like History, narrative art, at least if it is well-attuned, rehearses the debate that defines "the culture in question." Narrative provides the contemporaneous equivalent of the cultural conversation the historian later converts into the history

of culture. To be sure, it is an "imaginative and usually more compelling equivalent," one that crowds into a small space the comprehensive view of life everyday cultural conversation must laboriously
articulate in the orderly language of rational thought. But though
the accent here is on the more compelling, the basic *equivalence* of
fiction with ordinary cultural discourse comprises the burden of the
argument.[44] This becomes most evident precisely when fiction comes
in for the highest praise: "Narrative deals with experiences, not with
propositions. The narrative art, moreover, dramatizes as human
conflict what is elsewhere a thoughtful exchange of ideas; and art
projects—in a single packed image—conflicting principles which the
discursive mind must contemplate separately and consecutively."[45]

The well-attuned artist, then, dramatizes a cultural dialogue that
his heir the historian subsequently discovers to be very close to
drama. History repeats itself, in the most literal sense: historian and
storyteller alike only say what History's players have already said before them. Here is a remake of Hegel's philosophy of history that
drastically foreshortens the time-scheme while preserving the essentials intact. In the condensed American version, the owl of Minerva
is airborne well before dusk; but, as in the original, her flight path
retraces contours already laid down by History's dialectic. To intro-
duce a pair of terms we will often come back to, Lewis follows Hegel
in equating history-as-event (*Geschichte*—in this case, intellectual *Geschichte*) with the knowledge of history (*Historie*). For Lewis and his
tradition, in consequence, History reports on its own phenomenon
by speaking its own meanings. "Intellectual history *properly* conducted"—and this is perhaps more than a convenient verbal coincidence—records that which is *proper to* the "cultural conversation" au-
thorizing it. Observing the historiographical proprieties means
respecting the boundaries of History's own history of itself, means
properly reappropriating History's ongoing self-appropriation. *Geschichte* = story = *Historie*: through the proper historian, history
continues to speak in propria persona.

This implies that history *has* a propria persona. And therein lies
the relevance of the Althusserian Subject to Lewisian History. For
Lewis, History *is* a Subject, constituted by a dual mirror structure
that immediately reflects *Geschichte* in story and in *Historie*. More precisely: History is a Subject and its subjects and their imaginary con-
junction. Earlier, paraphrasing Althusser, we said that the specular
relation of Subject to subject ensures that, for ideology, nothing can

escape the closed circuits of subjectivity. Analogously, there is in Lewis's conception of history nothing outside the circuits of the properly historical. Repeating itself in (hi)stories, History achieves the ideological closure the Subject achieves by "repeating Himself" in individual subjects. Thus History ("a dialogue written in collaboration by many persons")[46] coincides with the totality of its voices the way the Subject coincides with His subjects, the way subjects coincide with "their own" discourse, the way any subject's discourse coincides with itself, or—beginning and end of the chain—the way a signifier coincides with its signified. History is authoritative metaphor and the Author of all possible metaphor. Rendering difference as a subordinate moment of the selfsame, History interpellates itself as (surrogate) subject.[47]

It does so in the only place it can: in narrative. Which is to say, in the best place it could. The best place, because narrative has already encoded in its *forms* the closure it "discovers" and narrates in its object. The model for such closure, Lewis reminds us, is the mode that is history's opposite and twin: fiction.

Conscious and Coherent Narrative

Not only is fiction history's model; there exists a model model, the "*conscious and coherent* narrative" (emphasis added) produced by a culture's "best-attuned artists."[48] The clear implication is that fictions are to be ranked according to the consciousness and coherence with which they reflect History—a point we will return to. But that point presupposes as it obscures another: the model for conscious and coherent reflection (of History, truth, the real) is given by the work of fiction *as such*. The proper historian works *toward* the adequation of event and story, narrative and the to-be-narrated; in fiction—Faulkner's no less than Fielding's—they are by definition one.[49] A history deviates from its object insofar as it is not accurate history, but *The History of Tom Jones* can no more deviate from the history of Tom Jones than a proper noun can designate something other than what it designates. Formally, in other words, fiction is perfectly coherent.

By the same token, it is perfectly conscious. Nothing in the world of the novel can escape the novel's notice, while everything included there is included because it has entered the field of vision the novel *is*. The novel's report on its own phenomenon *is* its own phenomenon; its knowledge of reality is co-extensive with its reality, its awareness is by definition complete self-awareness.

Does this total self-discovery and perfect self-coincidence account, then, for the fictional subject-effect?

Not quite; or, perhaps, not at all. For the consciousness and coherence that make fiction's surrogate subject the subject par excellence also threaten to render subjectivity superfluous. One can evoke the perfect congruence between fictional *Geschichte* and *Historie* to erase the distinction between them; the self-identity of a story can be taken to imply that the teller is only a shadow cast by the reality of his tale. What Benveniste remarks about a passage in Balzac—that in it "events seem to tell themselves"[50]—would appear, in this perspective, to hold for any story. The fictional subject, the proper conclusion seems to be, is quite literally a fiction.

The scribblers themselves, as will appear, are inclined to conclude just that. But they are unusual. Outside scribblerdom, it is the notion of events telling themselves that has a blasphemous ring. Far from undermining the subject-effect, fiction—witness our critics—ranks as one of its privileged domains. The question, then, is how the subject-form manages to "prop itself up" on a discourse whose formal properties might be deemed to cancel it out. What makes the text's coherence the coherence of a *consciousness*?

A certain fold in the text does. It is introduced into the seamless web of narrative and narrated by a third moment, that of the narration. Narration might be briefly defined as narrative's (un)folding, the process repeated, only to be annulled, each time a novel is read through to the end. Narration can then be distinguished from narrated as, in linguistics, "enunciation" is distinguished from "enounced," the stating of a statement from the statement stated. The well-known paradox "I am lying" helps situate the distinctions in question. Here "narration" and "narrated" plainly diverge: the subject of one is honest, the other is a liar. Yet this mini-narrative does not ordinarily present any obstacle to understanding, for reasons connected with the very distinction it illustrates. The formal paradox is neutralized by the space of the narration itself: thanks to it, one quite unproblematically distinguishes the narrating "I" from the one narrated, permitting the former to take the latter as its object.

Now this illustration is, here, more than an illustration, inasmuch as fiction may be taken to illustrate *it*. Fictional narrative redoubles itself as narration precisely through a constant disavowal of its integrity. Everyone knows that "anything can happen" in a story; it can always veer in an unanticipated direction, even rescind what it has previously given out as the truth. More fundamentally, even the most forthright of narratives holds the whole truth in reserve, constantly deviating from that other, always absent version of itself which is the narrated as a synchronic whole. In that sense, the nature of narrative is to be deceptive to the end—to lie, if only by omission. The "I am lying" any story affirms at every moment of its unfolding is therefore, from start to finish, indubitably true. As narration, fiction honestly confesses its own duplicity.

But it does so in a context guaranteed to give its own confession the lie. For, if anything can happen in a story, only one thing—and always the same thing—ever does. When the narrative has arrived at its destination—when the design of the story is at last fulfilled—what appeared to be the perfect freedom of the narration vanishes in the perfect rapport of narrative and narrated. Vanishes as we always knew it would: if a narration is buttoned down to its narrated only when the story ends, we were sure, when we began reading, that it eventually *would be*; hence we are sure, even while reading, that it always already *has been*. Thus the subject of the narration—of fiction's duplicitous "I am lying"—turns out to be dissimulating her role as stand-in for the integral textual "I" who can only ever tell the fictional truth. At every instant, the text-as-unpredictable-narration claims its freedom, and the text-as-predetermined-narrative cancels the claim. In accordance with the pattern played out by genius and the mob, narration's creative freedom—its freedom to lie—lies in a dimension of truth from which every escape is a return.

In Lewis as in scribbler criticism, the fictional text is readily imagined as a subject because that alternation is readily imagined as a dialectical unity. At liberty to wander wherever (folk) fantasy leads, narration simulates the subject's freedom to forge whichever identity she chooses. Yet whichever fantasy narration narrates, it necessarily chooses a textual identity. The fictional subject announces herself in the text's power to lie, but its lie is only a provisional deviation from an underlying selfsameness. The subject of the narration reduces to a moment within the dialectical whole which is the totalizing fictional "I." At the same time, that imperious "I" claims for itself the freedom of the "I" whose freedom it contains. The consciousness of the text's (im)possible non-coherence ("I am lying") is thus enfolded within the coherence that founds the textual "consciousness" in the first place. Hence the consciousness of the text is the consciousness of its coherence. The proposition is conveniently reversible: the coherence of the text is the coherence of its consciousness. The unity of narrative and narrated cannot but express itself through the narration which is its vehicle, and which cannot but convey a story's self-rapport while seeming endlessly to challenge it.

Story, as noted earlier, finds its general analog in Lewisian History. The *telling* of a story, one may now add, has its equivalent in the freely unfolding "cultural conversation" that, as it were, tells History. Thus History not only coincides with itself, but also *differs* from itself the same way fiction does. It is narrated by a subject—a collective one—which advertises its non-self-identity by forever contradicting itself, and which is yet trapped within the horizon of the Historical narrated as inescapably as the general fictional narrator is bound by the narrative she will have narrated by the time her story ends. History is as (deceptively) duplicitous as fiction is.

These two instances of self-coincidence coincide on the common ground of the subject-form. By the ideo-logic of the dual mirror structure, fiction becomes a self-identical subject by reflecting its own reflection *in* and *as* the Historical Subject. "The narrative art," Lewis says, "inevitably and by nature invests its inherited intellectual content with quickening duplicity; it stains ideas with restless ambiguity."[51] It has to: what it stains, as Lewis also tells us, is already stained. The duplicity inherent in fiction and bequeathed to History is also inherited from the History fiction reflects. What we have analyzed as a formal relation consequently doubles as a substantial one: the duplicitous coherence History inherits from its fictional heir is, precisely, historical, and so *real*. To prove worthy of its historical heritage, therefore, the narrative art must achieve at the level of content what it necessarily does at the level of form; it must put its duplicity at the service of a higher historical truth. It must, that is, appropriate *History's* coherent duplicity, which inevitably and by nature displays fiction's duplicitous coherence. Coherent duplicitousness: that, in a phrase, is the stake of History's interpellation of Himself as the subject of His stories.

Hence the kind of criticism we began by sampling. Its point of departure is the notion of proper History, of a Historical Subject that finds its model in the fictional Trinity of narrative, narrated, and narration. Its method consists essentially in making History the measure of a text's propriety at the level of content. Its question of questions is therefore that of the literary-historical hierarchy. Conceived as a report on the dual mirror structure linking History and culture, criticism comes down to asking—directly or obliquely—how *proper* a text is, how much History it appropriates. The ultimate fictional stakes remain, as always, truth and the real.

Mass fiction plays a vital if inglorious role in this critical scheme: it is that species of insufficiently duplicitous writing whose consciousness is not total, a subject whose cognitive disabilities prevent it from fully comprehending the cultural conversation of which it makes so substantial a part. It refers us, then, to the comprehensive Consciousness of History that englobes the popular mind—as the collective fantasy of Koch's scribblers refers us unawares to the all-embracing Hawthorno-Melvillean real, as fiction's duplicity automatically refers us to fiction's integrity. Or else mass fiction is revalued as Kelley revalues it; in that case, it approaches *being* the historical Subject that comprehends, among other things, the narrow limits of (inferior) mass fiction. Proper criticism must choose between, or move between, those two alternatives.

This grounds popular fiction's other, perhaps humbler function: to maintain the dominion of the proper in the realm one might have supposed to be reserved for the *im*proper. Well-attuned or ill-attuned, every text has its part in the grand Historical partita; echoing *Geschichte* simply by virtue of its participation in History's chorus for several voices, even the least prepossessing of narratives is prepossessed by the Historical Master Narrative that includes all cultural conversation, no matter how trivial. The consequence is that the "proper" has no proper opposite. For Lewisian critics, there can be no improper (hi)stories, only more or less proper ones—just as, for Hegel, there are no lies but only incubating truths, just as, for ideology in general, there are "bad subjects," but nothing and nobody outside the closed circuits of subjectivity.[52] The historico-fictional dual mirror structure ensures that, in fiction as in life, interpellation leaves no one and nothing out. Like the fictional "I" who ultimately cannot *not* tell the truth, the "popular mind" cannot not be conscious of History—even if it resolutely excludes History from its ken.

One can imagine no better illustration of the straits into which this scheme drives students of mass fiction than that provided by the latest scribbler scholarship, which is manfully struggling to decide whether the scribblers' vision of "herstory" should have its proper

place on the alternate syllabus. The critics are trembling before the
alternatives of dismissing domestic fiction on the grounds that it
blindly assents to the oppressive pieties of the age;[53] assigning it a
subaltern but still honorable place in the pantheon because, despite
its myopia, it sees more of the feminine dilemma than is commonly
supposed;[54] or defiantly elevating it to the visionary heights scaled by
the other "stunning" texts of the "other American Renaissance."[55] If
all the choices are somehow unsatisfactory, it is perhaps because
there is something lacking in the system that makes these one's
choices.

Sense and Non-sense

Criticism rooted in the belief that the grand Historical
Subject interpellates its conscious and coherent fictional subjects is,
to give it its proper name, "proper criticism." What might improper
criticism look like?

Not like its texts. The improper critic can put herself neither in
the place of the Historical mirror in which her texts find their (perhaps "contradictory") image, nor in the place of the fictional mirror
in which History finds its. Her place is the gap *in* the text *between* the
text and its image;[56] her object is not the (perhaps "baffled") wholeness which is the imaginary product of interpellation, but the
(w)holeness in which interpellation encounters, all at once, its condition, product, and limit. Improper criticism thus necessarily involves
violating a text's self-image; it is by nature unwholesome.

Yet the textual perversion the improper critic practices is, precisely, textual: it is a property of the text which the critic educes
(and, in that specific sense, *pro*duces), not a deviation she willfully—
some might say, perversely—induces. As will appear in a moment,
this internal deviation is also and immediately external, since it results from a (mis)appropriation of the text by the history that interpellates it. It is therefore all the more important to stress that the
deviation cannot issue from improper criticism's own, improper interpellation, witness the contradiction in terms: the critic who appropriates his text, even to unwholesome ends, is, by definition, engaged in proper criticism. The improper critic's proper object can
only be the hole torn in the text by one or another interpellation of
it as conscious and coherent whole.

There can be no question, here, of producing an anatomy of improper criticism. Indeed, one might cogently argue the impossibility
of anatomizing a critical approach whose object is less the body of
the text than the fractures produced in it by particular appropria-
tions of it. In any case, we will restrict ourselves to laying out the
bare bones of an improper methodology, deferring our plea for its
utility to the chapters that present its practical results. Thus the following skeletal outline offers itself only as a set of provisional answers to what we may provisionally call improper criticism's main
question: how does the gap left by the interpellation of the fictional
subject manage to manifest itself despite the imaginary coherence
that works to efface its traces?

In the typical domestic fiction, to stick to the example at hand, it
manifests itself in the paradoxical form of an *excess*; specifically, in
the excess of the *fiction's* meanings over the fictional *subject's*. We will
call the former the text's meaning-effects, in order to distinguish
them from what the fictional subject means, that is, what she means
to mean (in the sense of the French *vouloir dire* or the German
meinen). If the meaning-effects are in excess, the reason is simply
that the fictional subject cannot mean to mean some of them if it
means to mean others, except at the cost of shattering the identity
that forms the basis of its surrogate selfhood. To anticipate the example pursued at length below, no fictional subject can mean that
woman is naturally pure insofar as she is naturally corrupt and simultaneously claim that "is" as the basis of a textual identity; yet the
mid-century domestic fictions we will be examining effectively mean
that woman is, impossibly, just such an equation of purity with corruption. There is a baffling problem from which no self-consciousness, however total, can ever derive a sense of self, a split that, in
contrast to Beulah's episodic schizophrenia, cannot be healed. However sympathetic their critical therapists, novels thus sundered from
themselves are inaccessible to treatment. Indeed, for as long as one
investigates them on the basis of their self-report, their problem cannot even be diagnosed: approached as subjects, the best-sellers cannot *communicate* what, improperly speaking, ails them. The scribblers' fictional subject is constitutionally incapable of saying the
better part of what the scribbler text signifies.

Since to admit this would be to surrender the claim to integrity the
fictional subject embodies, the text-as-subject must exclude as
non-sense the meaning-effects unassimilable to its meaning properly

so called. In improper perspective, then, the fictional subject-effect appears as a product of the ongoing suppression of its "opposite," which we will call, for lack of a more respectable term, the "non-sense effect." Here is the fictional analog of that linguistic disjunction which opens a gap between the subject of ideology and herself, between the sovereign "I" and all that *in* it which is nevertheless not *proper* to it. Here, too, is what drives the fictional subject's quest for wholeness, the element whose simultaneous inclusion and suppression makes the text which-is-not-one want to be one. Here, finally, is the privileged object of improper criticism.

How does a text suppress those of its elements which are, from the fictional subject's point of view, non-sense? Essentially, by not narrating them. A set of significations in the text and yet not in the story, the non-sensical consists in a scattered set, so to speak, of unplotted points; it is by failing to integrate them into the continuum of the narrative that the text-as-subject denies that they make sense. In this way a story signifies its non-recognition of that "unbound"[57] dynamic which jeopardizes its self-rapport from a "within" it must, in self-defense, banish to an "outside." What is aptly called "narrative closure" *closes out* the meaning-effects the fictional subject cannot narrate as part of a cohesive whole. Yet this non-sense is signified by the same signifiers the text plots as a continuous narrative curve. The improper emerges, as a result, in the act of being suppressed; its suppression *is* the form its emergence takes. That is why the division involved differs from the coherent duplicity of Lewis's great debate, or the curable melancholia of Kelley's unhappy textual consciousness; rather than a contrapuntal distribution of thesis and antithesis, bright side and dark, we have to do with an "either/or," a contradiction one of whose terms must exclude the other as unthinkable. But because both are stated in the same place, we also have to do with an "and," with the impossible encounter of a meaning and the non-sense whose unassimilability motivates the meaning that excludes it. The perfect congruence of narration and narrated is thus accompanied by the radical disjunction of story and text. In improper perspective, *The History of Tom Jones* deviates at every turn from whatever one chooses to regard as the conscious and coherent history of Tom Jones. The closure brought about by the "binding" of narration to narrated is also permanently and radically breached, and so exposed as the imaginary appropriation of irreconcilable meaning-effects by a fictive self. In other words, as (w)holeness.

This kind of open closure is possible because texts mirror ideologies: it is history-as-ideology which interpellates fictional subjects. It follows that every text replicates the closure of another: for the ideology that assumes the role of textual Subject may itself be regarded as a text, a master narrative closed by virtue of having suppressed the contradictions that inhabit it. Ideology's fictional mirror image will accordingly reflect ideological contradictions "only in a form which at once provides their imaginary solution, or, better still, which displaces them by substituting imaginary contradictions soluble within the ideological practice of religion, politics, morality, aesthetics and psychology."[58] But fiction's supplementary displacement of contradictions already displaced by ideology not only further obscures them. Replacing (unacknowledged) ideological antinomies with their resolvable fictional equivalents, it also drags the antinomies into the light. The gap between the fictional subject and the text is, ultimately, fiction's rendition of another—the non-self-rapport that traverses ideology's imaginary coherence.

Why should the passage from ideological master narrative to fiction not only "solve," but also expose ideology's contradictions? Schematically: because the language of fiction, the means of its production (plots, types, styles, etc.) has a history of its own, one which crisscrosses but does not coincide with the history of a given ideology. Invested with the accumulated energy of other literary works and conflicting ideological projects, the indispensable instruments of any fictional production of ideology enjoy an autonomy that makes them more than mere instruments.[59] Unbidden, they engender an excess of signifying possibilities over whatever significance they are called on to convey; like the sorcerer's apprentice's broom, they defy the authority of the hand that sets them to work. Any particular narrative trajectory is thus automatically deflected by the very instruments that assure it. The internal division that characterizes the text may therefore be conceived as the result of a narrative's unceasing effort to maintain itself against the "narrative drift" marking it from its inception. Fiction cannot help lying even as it transmits the truth, and lying in a way no negation of the negation can transmute into another version of truth telling.

As narrative drift resists fiction's closure, so too does it resist History's: if the subject does not coincide with herself, the Subject she re-presents must not either. Truth must carry its untruth within itself, but as an irreducibly alien presence; History must be chronically

afflicted by a non-self-rapport it can only imaginarily recuperate as
the coherence of cultural conversation/story/*Historie*. It is this sort of
difference which preserves history from the stasis of an imaginary
self-coincidence—"history" with a small "h," to mark the contrast
with the totalizing History that presides over Lewisian criticism and,
with it, the whole gamut of scribbler scholarship. Lower-case history
is not, then, a closed set of meanings that preexist their well-attuned
narrativization, but rather an energy that resists any attempt at har-
monious signification; it is the history of that resistance, the history
of history's difference from itself. That is why criticism that takes its
stand outside fictional History is, (im)properly conducted, anything
but unhistorical—as we will go on to argue.

Reading Formations and Narrative Disorders

That each item in the literary inventory bears the accumulated traces of its historical trajectory is the condition of the fictional
non-sense effect. But what actually interferes with the proper trans-
mission of ideology "through" a given fiction is not the sum of all the
signifying possibilities that have accrued to a text's narrative signifiers, "less" whichever combination of meaning-effects one chooses
to regard as yielding the proper sense(s) of the text. Thus to confuse
the *condition* of the non-sense effect with its concrete realizations
would be to operate a historically rationalized dehistoricization of
the concept of the improper.

In fact, fictions and the ideologies that interpellate them collabo-
rate to assign a historically delimited, if constantly evolving content
to the categories of the proper and the improper, sense and non-
sense. That this holds at the level of the proper will no doubt be
readily granted in all but the most truculently fundamentalist circles.
It seems safe to say, for example, that the English peasants en-
amored of *The Wide, Wide World* in 1890[60] were not reading the same
book as either its writer and first reader, the schoolgirls who confes-
sed in the mid-1880s that they ranked the novel second only to *West-
ward Ho!*,[61] or, again, the feminist critics who, a century later, range
it alongside *Moby Dick*. If so, we must add a dimension to this thumb-
nail sketch of improper criticism: a text's proper meaning is a property of the text only insofar as it is also a property of the text's audience.

The idea may be put more precisely with the help of Tony Bennett's conception of the "reading formation," defined as "a set of intersecting discourses that productively activate a given body of texts and the relations between them in a specific way."[62] As Althusser conceives the subject as an effect of an ensemble of ideological practices, rather than its center and point of origin, so Bennett reminds us that a reader is not the self-sustaining source of an individual interpretation of a text, but rather an effect of those (contradictory) practices and discourses that regulate the uses of literature by a given group of people at a given time. Correspondingly, the text is conceived not as a repository of meanings established in advance of their reception, but rather as a discourse whose meaning evolves out of its relations to other discourses. Text and reader emerge as nodes within a network of historically evolving signifying relations. Reading, then, takes on the aspect of an interaction between various discursive practices, an interaction one can think of as *grounding* ideology's dual mirror structure, without being forced to the conclusion that it is *contained* by it.

Insofar as it serves one or another ideological project, this interaction—which we have assimilated to Althusser's notion of interpellation—might be approached as a *selection* by a reading formation from among the signifying possibilities a text sets up. Establishing the text's narratability and, with it, the fictional subject-effect, such a selection could only appropriate the fictional subject's claim of self-identity for the reading formation itself. A reading formation thus makes texts over into its own image, into progressive relations of the imaginary coherence it claims to possess as a synchronic whole. The texts a given reading formation prefers, then, will be those best suited to acting as mirrors of its coherence. So regarded, reading can be treated as the enactment of a duplicate mirror structure encompassing text and reading formation.

We have, it seems, come back to the notion of a (mass) audience in complete rapport with its favorite texts. But we have come back to it by the detour of the improper, which makes a difference. Like the "popular mind," the mass-reading formation does indeed find itself in "complete rapport" with mass culture; but, by the logic of (w)holeness, this rapport is a function of the *non*-rapport of the reading formation with itself, a fictional identity englobed by the non-identity that haunts the ideological. One may say, with Aristotle, Hawthorne, Koch, et al., that readerships verify their identity in fiction out of a "delight in [self-]imitation"; but one must add—upsetting the scheme—that such self-imitation entails self-limitation, generates self-identity and the opposite in one and the same movement.

A reading formation, in other words, peers into the textual mirror because it can only see itself properly, which is to say whole, in that imaginary space; it is not unified except fictionally/fictively. If it returns obsessively to certain stories, then, the reason must be that they help dissolve those points of resistance to its unification lodged within the reading formation as "displaced" contradictions. But this has a paradoxical consequence. Seeking to confirm its identity, a reading formation seeks out the texts it can invest with the energy of its contradictions to the end of neutralizing them: it searches in fiction's mirror for the imaginary resolution of contradictions it does not admit to having. As a result, the conflicting possibilities sedimented in a text's means of production are activated by/activate the contradictions informing the text's reading formation, even as the text unifies/is unified *by* the reading formation that interpellates it. *The instrument of ideology's imaginary integration doubles as the instrument of its symbolic dissolution.* Reaffirming a reading formation's, and hence an ideology's, "subjective" self-rapport, fiction simultaneously throws into relief a structure of difference constitutive both of ideology and of itself, but visible in neither taken alone. It thus gives the lie to its own fiction of the integrity of ideology's truth; and, in that measure, it speaks the truth in lying.

This joint production of contradiction and unity explains why the fictional non-sense effect is not merely incomprehensible "noise," the product of a historically conditioned technical flaw in literature's signifying system. For when what might seem to be narrative static is beamed back at the discourses activating a text, what was non-sense begins to make a non-sensical sort of sense; the unplotted points falling outside the fictional narrative proper hint that they might be plotted along other narrative lines radically different from, but no less coherent than the ideological master narrative that excludes them. Thus the textual duplicity that, from the fictional (or ideological) subject's point of view, is the recuperation of the narration's "I am lying" by the narrative's underlying truth appears, from an improper point of view, as a distorted allusion to the struggle of mutually exclusive meanings for the same fictional signifiers. What is properly speaking nothing for the reading formation that duplicates itself in fiction becomes a "nothing with a content." This nothing-

become-something, barred from entering the text's coherent consciousness, nevertheless founds it: it is that which the text *has not to
mean* in order to mean what it does. Therein lie the beginnings of a
possible solution to the "mystery of . . . [the] innumerable editions of
'The Lamplighter' and other books neither better nor worse." It remains to work the solution out.

The Limits of the Popular Mind

If the foregoing is even approximately right, then mass
fiction is not the strategic stutter of ideology; the infinite repetitiveness of the popular muse suggests rather that ideology has a case
of voluble aphasia, that, try as it might, it cannot repeat itself properly even in the medium it appropriates expressly to that end. This,
in turn, suggests that ideology cannot properly repeat itself anywhere. But, if so, the incoherence ideology betrays in obsessively
pursuing its elusive/illusive self-rapport in fiction should also be
traceable in ideological discourse per se. At a minimum, ideology's
non-self-rapport might be supposed to signal its presence *in* ideology
"before" its passage into fiction.

One learns to read the signals, however, only with fiction's help,
just as one learns to make (non-)sense of fiction only by examining it
through the grid of ideology. Especially when the aim is to find out
what both fiction and ideology suppress, this calls for a good deal of
hermeneutic circling. In presenting what one has found, however, it
is convenient to start at one pole of the couple "text/reading formation," locating its (only apparently) internal contradictions before
moving on to the other pole. We have more or less arbitrarily chosen
to begin at the pole of ideology. The next chapter, accordingly, sur-
veys a core component of the best-sellers' reading formation, the
mid-century discourse on God, sex, and the (Holy) family. That discourse's contradictions condensed around a theme that did not once
enter the Historical great debate as thesis or even perverse antithesis
(except perhaps in Orson Fowler or *Pierre*), that had no place in
cultural conversation and so can have none in intellectual history
properly conducted: the non-sense of True-Womanly incest. For *improperly* conducted intellectual history, in contrast, this non-subject
of the cultural conversation matters as much as anything that was
actually said. Indeed, in improper perspective, the debate about

woman's status takes on the guise of a running allusion to another debate on the feminine, one which decorum forbade the scribblers so much as to notice, and which nevertheless made the debate proper possible. It is this other debate, located somewhere "between" *Geschichte* and *Historie*, fictional narration and narrated, that we will try to reconstruct.

2

THE FACTS OF LIFE
IN THE 1850s

There is no constraint like that of love.
—Heman Humphrey

What is physical first, what is moral afterward.
—Horace Bushnell

The conscience is congenital.
—Heman Humphrey

Just who read best-sellers in the 1850s we will never know. The available evidence appears, however, to warrant the guess that the fiction factory's clientele included roughly one in ten Americans, the large majority drawn from the ten to fifteen percent of the population who kept servants or slaves. Within these "middling classes," as all but the most privileged of the privileged were rather inappropriately called, readerships seem to have been, notably, female, and then Northern, urban, and young. Thus the typical votary of the popular novel would have been the wife or daughter of a small capitalist, shopkeeper, company official, bureaucrat, or professional living in one of the larger Northern towns. A smattering of artisan families as well as the children of propertied wageworkers may also have patronized the scribblers; but it is safe to say that, in the main, antebellum fictioneers entertained a social and economic elite.[1]

The reading formation embracing this select group was principally shaped by four ideological currents that emerged with sudden force early in the nineteenth century: let us call them womanology, womanolatry, the pedagogy of surveillance, and natural religion. The last three make up the mainstream of domestic ideology. They furnish the subject proper of the best-sellers, which understand themselves to be fictional restatements of the moral and (vaguely) theological discourses that, gathering head in the 1830s, had by

1850 propelled the saintly mother, the lovingly supervised child, and the religion of the heart to the forefront of the middle-class imagination. Womanology maintained an ostensibly separate existence within a set of "scientific" discourses treating "the strange and secret influences" female "organs and functions" exercised on "the heart, the mind, and the very soul of woman." Womanology's fictional register was the improper; it exercised a strange and secret influence on bestsellerdom, which for reasons of propriety ignored it.[2] We will begin by ignoring it as well, so as to attend to the domesticating vision in its would-be purity.

A Freely Obedient Son of Love

Domestic ideology rested on a double perception of the nature of the child: immanently good, children were yet eminently corruptible. Conjugated with the question of infant sexuality, that paradox informed everything the domesticators said. Its history is bound up with the history of American Calvinism in ways we need briefly to consider.

In principle, Colonial and Jacksonian Protestantism shared a belief in natural depravity. The Puritans took the dogma seriously, as everyone knows, and drew the appropriate conclusions about their progeny. Jonathan Edwards considered children "young vipers and infinitely more hateful than vipers." Cotton Mather reminded parents that "your children are the Children of Death, and the Children of *Hell*, and the *Children of Wrath*, by *Nature*. . . . There is a *Corrupt Nature* in . . . Children, which is a *Foundation* of all *Wickedness* and *Confusion*." Puritan educators accordingly conceived childrearing as, at bottom, a process of smashing the satanic toddler's congenital resistance to authority. "There is in all children," in the typical view of one seventeenth-century New England minister, "a stubbornness and stoutness of mind, arising from natural pride, which must in the first place be broken and beaten down."[3] The soul of Puritan pedagogy was therefore the interdict. This is nicely illustrated by the fact that Bay Colony courts could *execute* children for disobedience.[4] The penalty did not need to be imposed to make its point: only the threat of terror could assure the law a permanent upper hand over children's innate wickedness.

This approach to child discipline was geared to the general mode of social control in the Colonial era. As in "Classical" Western Europe, authority in early America was satisfied to compel the bodily submission of those who defied it; it did not presume to tamper with people's souls.[5] Indeed, for orthodox Calvinists, individuals could be inwardly transformed by no human agency, that of the individuals themselves not excepted. Only God could remake the inner man; only the arbitrary supervention of His grace could convert the objects of authority into its eager lieutenants. The law mandating capital punishment for especially naughty children was therefore typical in its extremity: serving notice that the social order could annihilate its enemies, it simultaneously pointed to the internal limits worldly authority was powerless to overstep. It epitomizes the spirit of the laws under Puritanism: a claim to absolute power on the one hand, a confession of impotence on the other.

The Victorian opponents of this vision of things would train their fire on its pedagogical implications, in particular on the constraints it imposed on religious education. For the Calvinist God tied the educator's hands as He did the magistrate's: Puritan children could not be brought up to be Christians. Their elders might beseech them to seek salvation, and warn them of the consequences of failing to attain a state of grace. Beyond that, they could only stand and wait.[6] The result was not merely a good deal of anguished handwringing, but also a liberating exemption from moral responsibility: though the Saints were powerless to save their progeny, they might by the same token watch them go to the devil with a clear conscience. Thus the arch-Calvinist Nathaniel Emmons could deliver a funeral oration for his son which calculated with austere objectivity the likelihood that the young man might be spending eternity in Hell: "He lived stupid, thoughtless and secure in sin. . . . But whether he did ever heartily renounce the world and choose God for his supreme portion cannot be known in this world. . . . It is more than possible that like others on a sick-bed, he built his hopes upon a sandy foundation."[7]

Emmons spoke these words in 1820. He was out of step with his time. In Jacksonian America, few middle-class people shared his sense of the limits of parental responsibility, and even fewer the serene resignation it inspired. The common reaction to Emmons's detachment (at least among the affluent) would have been horror mixed with disbelief. God gave bourgeois parents a new mission in the post-Calvinist era: they were "to watch over, guard, and restrain"

their children "with an unwearied assiduity."[8] Passive observation
was in full retreat before active *surveillance*, the cutting edge of a
pedagogical method the shock troops of reform had been urging on
America since the 1820s. The reformers' ambition grew with their
success. By 1856, an expert could write that children "should never
be left alone much, and in large boarding schools, a dim light
[should be left] burning in an extensive sleeping room, so that, without disturbing their slumbers, nothing may be performed unseen. In
the bath and privy an equal scrutiny should be observed, and, when
other means fail, some authors recommend the pupil sleeping in the
teacher's bed."[9]

Undoubtedly, this passage represents an enthusiastic variation on
a common theme. But that it should occur at all is eloquent testi-
mony to the change that overtook childrearing with the advent of
the domesticators. The overriding tendency of Jacksonian pedagogy
was to abolish the distance Calvinism put between power and the
child; metaphorically, at any rate, the post-Puritanical master had a
moral obligation to go to bed with his charge. The emotions under-
pinning a child's relation to power shifted accordingly. Heman
Humphrey went to the heart of the matter in his *Domestic Education*:
"there is no constraint like that of love."[10] Interdict was to yield to
perpetual *loving* surveillance. At least in theory, the exercise of authority and the cultivation of emotional dependence would henceforth go hand in hand.

The effects of this shift emerge nowhere more clearly than in
nineteenth-century pronouncements on punishment and its ends. If
the Colonial delinquent kissed the chastening rod to signify his submission to a higher will, his Republican successor kissed it because
she loved it. Under the domestic dispensation, punishment that
alienated culprits from the law defeated its own purposes: modern
parents applied the rod not to stress the awful remoteness of power,
but to induce their offspring to identify with the powerful. A child
must be raised in such a manner, Humphrey declared, "that he cannot be disobedient without a feeling of self-condemnation." Bronson
Alcott took the principle further than most of his contemporaries,
but his conclusions indicate the overall direction of their project:
"harshness and restraint, fear, and interdiction . . . where the laws of
affection, order, and conscience generally prevail, will not be often
required . . . [properly raised,] the child becomes a law to himself."[11]

A law to himself: it was with an eye to mass-producing such conveniently "self-interpellating" subjects that the authority prepared to execute wayward youngsters was replaced by one prepared to sleep with them. The domesticators had grasped that a society embarked on the transition to industrial capitalism wanted more comprehensive methods of social control than the Colonial ruling class had needed. What Foucault calls the "entry of life into history"—that is, "the entry of phenomena peculiar to the life of the species into the order of knowledge and power, into the sphere of political techniques"—was on the American agenda. Only through the politicization of the biological, as Foucault perhaps insufficiently stresses, could the bourgeoisie meet its growing demand "for the controlled insertion of bodies into the machinery of production." The upshot, at the level of daily routine, was the proliferation of "regulatory and corrective mechanisms" indispensable to a "normalizing society . . . the historical outcome of a technology of power centered on life."[12]

Here are the main coordinates of the shift we have rapidly sketched. The pedagogy of surveillance was the "regulatory and corrective" mechanism par excellence: it was the chief means by which the Jacksonian middle class disciplined *itself*, a rarified form of the discipline the bourgeoisie would impose on the working class in the latter half of the nineteenth century.[13] Alcott's model child was the showpiece of the revamped technology of power, a self-correcting mechanism that loving surveillance had carefully adapted to the norms of an industrializing society. In contrast, the young Puritan viper, with his merely negative relation to the law, was the virulent stuff of which Luddites were made. Catharine Sedgwick knew where the improvement lay: self-government, she said in *Home*, provided "the only effective and lasting government—the only one that touches the springs of action, and in all instances controls them." Doubtless old-style conversion also produced such "freely obedient son[s] of love," as Max Weber's famous study argues.[14] But it produced them far too haphazardly for a normalizing society's needs. With the transition from farm and countinghouse to factory, a resource as valuable as free obedience had to be secured by statistically more reliable means than the Puritan God could provide. Election gave way to normalization because only the love of constraint promised the control "in all instances" that Jacksonian social engineers dreamed of.

The thing that made young Puritans vipers was precisely the force that eluded such total control: original sin. Liberal Protestantism therefore had a powerful inclination simply to strike the doctrine from its ledgers, as its growing distaste for the notion of infant depravity attests. But there were countervailing tendencies. They proceeded from the association of depraved nature with the inferior social elements—notably, Negroes, Indians, Irish immigrants, the urban masses, and, in a crucially qualified sense, women. If retaining the original conception of original sin handed labor power too unreservedly over to an angry God's whims, abolishing it outright threatened to eliminate a convenient otherworldly check on the "promiscuous masses," whose prospective hegemony appeared even less appetizing than God's.[15] Ultimately, the lower orders too would have to be normalized—that is, made over into laws to themselves; but until they were, they had to be subjected to laws laid down by their betters, and "broken and beaten down" if they presumed to resist. The reformers' mistrust of the doctrine of original sin thus ran up against a gender-, race-, and class-determined need to preserve the old system of restraint, fear, and interdiction, together with the theology that underpinned it.[16] The bourgeoisie negotiated the resulting doctrinal impasse by striking a historic compromise with itself. It legitimized liberal heresy with the proviso that the heretics concoct a normalizing strategy that would keep egalitarian impulses, and hence the masses, in bounds.

The cautious cultural revolution that ensued developed along two converging paths, one more or less Calvinist, the other more or less heterodox. From positions well outside the Calvinist camp, a mixed bag of nonconformist intellectuals—rationalists, spiritualists, Millenarians, Unitarians, Transcendentalists, etc.—launched a frontal assault on the doctrine of original sin and, especially, infant depravity. Such outspoken iconoclasts stood in the vanguard of a broader cultural trend which rallied, more prudently, around a cult of the child. From the first decade of the century onward, a throng of popular writers gradually unrolled on the collective brain vaguely Wordsworthian visions of infancy as a state "which speaks to us of heaven; which tells us of those pure angelic beings which surround the throne of God, untouched by sin."[17] The sensibility responsible for effusions of this order was already, if one may hazard the phrase, objectively anti-Calvinist. Whatever its precise theological status, the notion that (their) children were born depraved was rapidly sinking into irrelevance for growing numbers of Americans, taking their loyalty to the faith of their fathers with it.

Significantly, the cult of infant innocence also took its toll among the avowedly orthodox. From the "alleviated" Calvinist Lyman Beecher, who early in the century polemicized against the idea of infant damnation, to his liberal son Henry, whose best-seller *Norwood* (1867) effected a muddled synthesis of Calvinism and Transcendentalism, a long line of mainly Congregationalist and Presbyterian thinkers struggled to square orthodox principles with the increasingly child-centered culture of the Victorian middle class. The strategies varied. But they mandated a pedagogical *technique* that held constant from writer to writer, and which was, tellingly, the same "regulatory and corrective" surveillance anti-Calvinists also advocated. Heman Humphrey, a conservative Congregationalist, is a representative figure here as elsewhere. His *Domestic Education* dwells on children's "native depravity" and the futility of human efforts to "conquer the stubborn will of the sinner"; yet it also grants infants a "moral instinct," and, as we have briefly seen, urges on parents typically modern methods of domesticating it. We can skip over the intellectual acrobatics Humphrey et al. performed in both extolling and deprecating efforts to save naturally depraved young souls with inborn affinities for the good.[18] The salient point is that even for the conservative religious establishment of the 1830s and 1840s, the requirements of the normalizing order dictated a marriage of convenience between a Calvinist vision of human nature and post-Calvinist methods of disciplining and directing it.

The marriage was not destined to last. Between 1830 and the Civil War, the unprincipled alliance between Calvinism and the pedagogy of surveillance unraveled. The techniques designed to foster identification with authority prevailed over the theory that stressed authority's essential otherness; a less than rigorous post-Calvinist theology was then patched together to sanction the ascendancy of the new techniques. Key to the transformation was the doctrine of "Christian nurture," which postulated that "spiritual regeneration is seldom effectually accomplished, unless when . . . the active principle of Christian virtue is gradually introduced [in early childhood] to work like leaven in the character."[19] With the enunciation of this theme, the new pedagogy came of age: that it continued for a while to wear quasi-Calvinist garb simply testifies to its tactical good sense.

Christian nurture found its best advocate in the Congregationalist minister and theologian Horace Bushnell. Retaining a more or less orthodox conception of original sin, Bushnell nevertheless rejected what his Puritan forebears saw as its major corollary, the idea that salvation was none of man's doing. Mainstream Protestantism thereby effectively revoked God's monopoly on the production of Christians; redemption, Bushnell proclaimed to receptive middle-class congregations, could be cultivated by everyone at home.[20] More: the steady growth of pious feeling in small children was decidedly preferable to sudden conversion. God Himself had declared His preferences in this matter: placing infants "in the womb of parental culture," He pledged Himself "to them and their parents, in such a way, as to offer the presumption, that they [might] grow up in love with all goodness, and remember no definite time when they became subjects of Christian Principle."[21] The nursery was no longer a vipers' nest; it had become a garden of goodness that, properly tended, would yield a celestial harvest. Salvation had been secularized. Through Bushnell, the new "Calvinism" served official notice of its subordination to the normalizing order.

The entry of life into history, in fine, was by mid-century driving original sin to the outskirts of bourgeois American culture.[22] Battered by the iconoclasts, politely ignored by most middle-class believers, the doctrine had suffered even at the hands of apologists like Bushnell, who defended it in principle while neutralizing its major practical consequences. But the nineteenth century saw more than original sin's disorderly retreat before the genteel juggernaut of "Unitarian sentimentality."[23] Unable to overlook its inferiors' natural depravity, yet unwilling—given its democratic commitments—to deny that it shared a common humanity with them, the bourgeoisie had grudgingly to retain something *like* original sin even in its own conception of itself.[24] The rearguard action Calvinism fought in the pages of a Humphrey or Bushnell was one result. More to our purposes is the fact that, as original sin retreated, it went underground, to reemerge transmuted in the nineteenth-century discourse on sex. It would survive there principally as a radical hesitancy: for Victorian sexologists, sex was and was not sinful, and sin was and was not original.

Natural Religion

As the fortunes of original sin withered, nature's, logically enough, bloomed. While antebellum ideologues were reclaiming the once godforsaken American West, now the garden of the world, troops of reformers were discovering that what was natural about man furnished equally fertile ground for the husbandmen of the Lord.[25] What was natural about man was in the first instance his body. Like the soul, it could, in the post-Calvinist view, be nurtured to near-perfection. More: to nurture the body *was* to nurture the soul, "souls [being] formed by nutrition, by absorption and assimilation, as well as bodies."[26] By 1850, at the latest, one or another version of the idea had been firmly implanted in the middle-class mind; the three decades before the Civil War saw a luxurious flowering of moral discourses on the physiological, cultivated by a burgeoning army of theologians, phrenologists, health practitioners, sexologists, feminists, home economists, temperance crusaders, and medical men. For this new breed of writer, health reform, moral hygiene, and heaven were increasingly intertwined; waxing eloquent on the symbiosis of body and soul, the enthusiastic reformer often ended by confounding them.[27] Thus "the entry of life into [U.S.] history" manifested itself as the grafting of the soul onto the spiritualized body— a phenomenon we will call "natural religion."

The distinction between body and soul persisted, of course. At one level this simply means that all but the most ardent reformers continued to distinguish flesh and spirit even as they crossbred them. More important, however, was the fact that the high priests of natural religion reinscribed the body/spirit opposition onto the body alone. The spiritualized flesh thus became its own opposite: it was now both perfectable nature and primally blasted nature, a "fragile treasure" "to be cared for, protected, [and] cultivated," as well as an inherited liability permanently threatening to drag one down to perdition.[28] The antinomy sprang from the same class contradiction that made mainstream Protestantism balk at eradicating original sin: the bourgeoisie's precious body was also the refractory nature it shared with the humblest of those it exploited. The implicit promise of natural religion—that nature could spiritualize itself—harbored an implicit threat as well: quite simply, that the body of society could do without the class at its head.

That disquieting possibility was not usually spelled out.[29] It made itself felt indirectly, as a philosophical crux within the new theories of education. Post-Calvinist educators educed natural goodness: they could bring out children's virtue because children were already virtuous. Yet the very idea of a pedagogy presupposed that children were not so virtuous that they could do without their educators: educing the natural love of constraint inevitably involved constraining nature. The logical conclusion seemed to be that spiritualizing human nature was a matter of playing it against itself. Education must be a matter of enlisting children's innocence in the crusade against their corruptibility. The dualism this gave rise to vexed vaguely Calvinist theories of childrearing no less than avowedly heterodox ones. The heterodox stumbled up against Rousseau's question: how could the aboriginally pure be corruptible? Quasi-Calvinists faced the same problem in inverted form: how could the naturally corrupt learn purity?

The spiritualization of the body offered an elaborate resolution of these dilemmas. The pedagogy of surveillance was the *practical* correlate of that discursive resolution, its realization-as-technique. The orthodox conception of original sin was its chief casualty. But recasting the paradoxes of Christian idealism in the language of the flesh meant more than straightforwardly translating them. The rewriting added a dimension: in its physiological inflection, the dialectic of sin and purity could be articulated with the dialectic of male and female. The result was neither a simple equation of one sex with innocence and the other with sin, nor a symmetrical distribution allotting each its share of each. Matters were, rather, arranged in a way that made woman the supreme signifier of both purity *and* corruption; the resulting fusion of opposites enabled the domesticators to negotiate a wide range of social contradictions. The glue that held this intricate discursive construct together was provided by a personage who attained unprecedented notoriety in the bourgeois epoch: Man the Masturbator.

The Love that Binds

The most conspicuous sign of the body's new-found significance in American culture was that male sexuality spurted from the periphery of Colonial moral discourse toward the vital center of Republican concerns. The 1830s were rocked by an eruption of literature on male orgasm.[30] It took the form of frantic warnings against the calamitous consequences of masculine "incontinence," a problem the eighteenth century usually winked at. Tracts and even whole books devoted to the subject continued to pour off American presses through the 1850s. They were the lifeblood of a complex economy linking excessive ejaculation to the (potentially lethal) depletion of male energies, the degradation of white women, and the prospective decline of Anglo-Saxon Protestant civilization. One crime in particular concentrated within itself all these subversive possibilities: for the ministers, moralists, and doctors who led the struggle for social purity, male masturbation was Public Enemy Number One.

The crusaders against the solitary vice dwelt on its deadly physiological effects. "Self-abuse," the Consulting Surgeon on Spermatorrhoea warned in his alarming report on the disease, "destroys the body . . . the destruction is not accomplished all at once; slowly but most certainly, the Onanist distills a poison into his frame that will inevitably, if not relieved by timely aid, lead to death." But the onanist wrecked more than his frame. Enfeebling the body, masturbation also assailed the mind: because "the nervous substance and the seminal fluid" were "essentially the same thing," the chronic masturbator was "in imminent danger of becoming Insane, or at least of weak Intellect," or else of "pass[ing], with great rapidity, through mania, into downright idiocy, and into partial or complete impotence." Indeed, to the surgeon Homer Bostwick, it seemed "safe to say, that of all the cases of incurable insanity, a large majority are caused by involuntary seminal emissions, or by masturbation."[31] Needless to add, this compound offense against natural law also violated the moral order. Thus Catharine Beecher could slide gracefully from a statement of the principle that children "must always submit their will to the will of God" into the following psychobiological homily, in which the effects of masturbation on mind, body, and soul are neatly conflated:

Few mothers are sufficiently aware of the dreadful penalties which often result from indulged impurity of thought. If children, in *future* life, can be preserved from licentious associates, it is supposed that their safety is secured. But the records of our insane retreats, and the pages of medical writers, teach, that even in solitude, and without being aware of the sin or danger, children may inflict evils on themselves, which not infrequently terminate in disease, delirium, and death.[32]

Via self-abuse, then, orthodox principle was disseminated into liberal religion. The physiological sin whose wages were death, masturbation gave original sin a genital habitation and a new and natural name. Three things type it as natural religion's version of the primal fault. It was preeminently the child's vice; it was, manifestly, a *natu-*

ral depravity, so much so that it could take hold at the tender young age of two;[33] and it was, in the judgment of medical men as of moralists, a virtually universal practice—at any rate, a virtually universal *male* practice.[34] But if masturbation provided the hinge between Calvinism and natural religion, it did so in a double sense: it separated as it joined them. Unlike its orthodox analog, *this* form of natural depravity had a natural enemy: woman. Through her, the divided body could redeem *itself*. Woman's natural purity, the domesticators insisted, made man's degeneracy accessible to the remedial techniques of the normalizing order.

For the domesticators, woman was above all the "educator of the human race," her tenure guaranteed by a cult of true womanhood that formed the backbone of domestic ideology.[35] The cult of true womanhood dovetailed with a cult of the home, woman's "Garden of Eden," the paradisal place "where truth [could] show herself unveiled, and peace . . . dwell unmolested"; the true woman's affinity for peace, truth, and home proceeded directly from her "meek and lowly spirit," the unmistakable sign of her piety and superior—because Christ-like—moral nature. This "natural love of home and its duties" engendered awesome responsibilities. The first of them was the physical and spiritual reproduction of mankind. It was therefore the moral mother—"God's appointed agent of MORALITY"—who represented the acme of true womanhood. In her revered person, the themes of woman's reproductive calling, predisposition to holiness, love of the domestic, and educational mission ("*mother* is another word for *teacher*") were linked and validated.[36]

One can multiply Victorian restatements of this constellation of themes ad nauseam. Sarah Hale, a leader in women's struggle for higher education and editor of the popular *Godey's Lady's Book,* put it this way:

> The outward world, for rugged toil designed,
> Where evil from true good the crown has riven,
> Has been to Man's dominion ever given;
> But Woman's empire, holier, more refined,
> Moulds, moves and sways the fallen but God-breathed mind,
> Lifting the earth crushed heart to hope and Heaven.[37]

The Reverend John Todd, whose vicious misogyny is a matter of scholarly record,[38] had a similarly lofty conception of woman's calling: "She has a mission—no higher one could be given her—to be the mother, *and the former of all the character of the human race . . .* She

is the queen of the home, its centre, its light and glory. . . . Our
mothers train us, and we owe everything to them. Our wives perfect
all that is good in us. . . . Woman is the highest, holiest, most precious gift to man."[39] "Earth," the radical feminist Margaret Fuller
cooed, "knows no fairer, holier relation than that of a mother."
"Who does not feel," the conservative Maria McIntosh chanted,
"how [woman's] warm affections and quick irrepressible sympathies
fit her for these labors of love?" Even the Seneca Falls Convention
joined the chorus, noting complacently that "man . . . accords to
woman moral superiority."[40]

Granting woman moral superiority squared the circles of natural
religion; womanolatry endowed one half of humanity with the capacity to save the other. The redemptive moral mother, accordingly,
completed the living argument offered by Alcott's "law to himself":
womanolatry plus the pedagogy of surveillance equaled the theology
of Christian nurture. Indeed, true womanhood and salvation by
Christian nurture were so intimately associated that the *analogy* between a mother's love and God's was often only a breath away from
dissolving into their straightforward amalgamation. "She becomes to
our hearts almost as the saints in heaven," breathed the Reverend
William Eliot, his reverence called forth by inexhaustible memories
of mother's redemptive goodness. "God loves the mother for what
she is," on George Weaver's understanding of divine autoaffection;
"she is a reflection of himself." "The family state," observed Harriet
Beecher Stowe and her sister Catharine, "is the aptest illustration of
the heavenly kingdom, and in it woman is its chief minister." But it
was left to yet another Beecher sister, Isabella, to fashion the divinest
image of woman's "mission next to divine":[41]

> *To my conception* [emphasis added] a mother is the only being in this world
> who . . . approximates the divine nature. So feeble in comparison is the
> father's relation to the child, so lost in her higher and diviner relation,
> that it is in the experience of many a mother, whether recognized by
> herself or not, that from the moment of blessed annunciation to heavenly
> birth, she, like the Virgin of old, has known no father to her child save
> the Holy Ghost.[42]

One would be hard pressed to say it better than Isabella. If masturbation was domestic ideology's Original Sin, moral motherhood was
its Incarnation.

But it was incarnation with a difference. In keeping with the principles of natural religion, feminine purity had to be ordained to its holy work by nature itself. That is, the redemptive power *over* human nature had to proceed from *within* human nature. Assigning "THE GOD-APPOINTED EDUCATOR" an innate affinity for religion was a common way of arranging this. Woman, Eliot knew, was "led to a religious life by the natural tendency of her affections." She was "called to the ministry of salvation," Sarah Hale felt, "[because] her nature was of purer essence, and more in harmony with the things of heaven than man's." "Her natural heart," pontificated George Weaver, "is in harmony with the great cardinal principle of Christianity." "The female," medical science agreed, "is naturally prone to be religious."[43] The age needed, however, a more palpable sign of woman's naturally supernatural status than the witness of the womanolators. Domestic ideology obligingly produced one in the guise of female passionlessness.

The doctrine of female passionlessness is judiciously summed up in the observation that "strong [sexual] passions, save in exceptional cases, at certain times, and in advanced stages of dissipation, as little disturb the category of the human as they do that of the animal female."[44] Like masturbation phobia, this was a nineteenth-century shibboleth roughly contemporaneous with the Second Great Awakening. It reversed the Colonial belief that Eve's daughters were particularly prurient creatures whose appetites had to be curbed by the masculine forces of order. By mid-century it was the dominant view among writers of marriage manuals and other advice books, and perhaps among medical men as well.[45] It intersected and fused with the belief that femininity implied special virtue: woman was, the phrenologist Orson Fowler energetically reminded his innumerable readers in the 1840s, "constitutionally" "more virtuous and less passionate" than man.[46] Thus was forged the master link in the discursive chain binding the moral to the physical, and nature to its naturally anointed savior.

Specifically, it bound the secret sinner to his maternal guardian angel. The masturbatory son begot the moral mother; it was altogether appropriate that the pioneering reformer Sylvester Graham (of cracker fame) should close a jeremiad against the unmanly habit with the prayer that the "females of our blessed country remain pure in themselves, and exert a purifying and exalting influence on the other sex." A monitor as pure as masturbation was poisonous had, Graham knew, to be interposed between the young man and his penis. Who better positioned to stand watch at the "gushing mouth" of the "crater" than the ethereal "guardian of home, the presiding divinity of earth's 'holy of holies'"?[47] In the antimasturbatory mother, the "gospel of thrift in semen" found its madonna.[48] Only the embodiment of sexlessness could be trusted to regulate the male body's relation to its own sex. William Eliot made the point with exceeding delicacy; but, for those (of either sex) who had ears to hear, the message was plain:

> O, if we could but understand the depths of a mother's love . . . the days of our early life would be stained with fewer sins. . . . If we could but understand how heartless it is, for the sake of some transient pleasure, some worthless dissipation, for the indulgence of a whim or the gratification of ungoverned temper, to send the pang of grief to that loving heart . . . we should be more careful in our pleasure. . . . If not for God's sake, nor for Christ's sake, yet for your mother's sake, hold back your hand from sin![49]

But what made the sinner want to spare mother that pang of grief? Why did the ungoverned body crave her good government? If the campaign against self-abuse was not to fly in the face of normalizing fundamentals, something more than the aggrieved mother's "no" had to curb the onanist: the man-child had to acquire a natural love for a constraint he would otherwise simply chafe under. What ensured that he would was his *passion for his passionless mother*. The affair between antimasturbatory mother and her auto-erotic son, the normalizers' paradigm of true love and perfect union, was the driving force behind efficient moral education.

The seeds of this lifelong romance were sown during the process of purification through surveillance that was, through the man-child's early years, primarily mother's lookout. The true woman's passionless sexuality played a critical role in sparking and sustaining the affair. In *Perfect Men, Women, and Children in Happy Families*, Fowler explains this to American motherhood rather more candidly than most: "Your loving [your sons] makes them love you as a female which *chastens* as well as evolves their manhood. They must love some female as such. Say practically, by loving or chastising them, whether it shall be you purely, or harlots sensuously."

In fact, filial love was to be pure *and* sensuous, as Fowler, turning now to the sons, proclaims: "*Every Son, 'Behold thy mother!'* Make love to her, and her your first sweetheart. Be courteous, gallant, and her knight-errant, and your nearest friend and bosom confident. Nestle yourself right into her heart, and her into yours."[50]

Dr. Bostwick had already indicated how one nestled right into the maternal heart: by frankly and freely confessing one's shortcomings to mother. To illustrate the point, he cited the testimonial of a forty-five-year-old degenerate with "dried-up testicles" who learned his lesson too late: with his last breath, this unfortunate revealed to his mother that he was dying of self-pollution and begged her "to use all her efforts to prevent his young brothers from indulging in this worst of all bad habits." The moral is plain: had the masturbator told his jilted "bosom confident" of his "temptations" and "weaknesses" earlier in life, he might have been spared his tragic fate.[51]

Whence the son's passionate love for his mother, "the seed from which" would later "grow a grand tree of love."[52] The masturbator submitted to regulation, as said a moment ago, because he passionately loved his mother; he passionately loved his mother, Dr. Bostwick encourages us to add, because she kept on regulating him. The man-child made mother his "first sweetheart" because his *real* first sweetheart was his penis, which his mother and monitor kindly protected from the harm he would otherwise do it. Loving mother, then, the masturbator continued to love his own body: filial devotion stemmed naturally from the autoaffection whose misguided manifestation was autoeroticism. The man-child's ennobling passion was spiritualized onanism. The domesticators could imagine no more exalted emotion than this. There is no love, Humphrey might have said, like that of constraint.

Not that the moral mother constrained her charge to stop masturbating. Nothing but the "internal ruse" of domestic ideology leads one to think that.[53] If mother's real function had been to manacle her masturbatory charge, she would soon have found a natural ally in Fowler's harlot, who also offered an alternative to the worst of all bad habits. The reason the alliance was not concluded—officially, in any case—was that masturbating under maternal surveillance *domesticated* sex, exactly what the harlot could never hope to do. To put it the other way around: if "God's appointed agent of MORALITY" could intervene in the "spermatic economy," it was because young men stayed home and masturbated.[54] Masturbation was the mainstay of the system that sought to wipe it out. Self-abuse propped up a regime of supervised sin whose public face was the regime of supervised salvation womanolators preferred to celebrate. Not for nothing did domestic ideology decry masturbation as the *universal* (male) vice: there was no surer way of making every mother an agent of morality, and every mother's son a sinner sinning under the domesticating eye of purity.

For good reason, the love of constraint can double as a figure for incestuous desire. As loving mother was the man-child's roundabout way of loving his own body, so loving his own body—as he continued to do "despite" mother's vigilant surveillance—was his roundabout way of loving mother. Because mother came between her son and his penis, to masturbate, under the domestic dispensation, was to find oneself secretly violating her. But the domesticators' system was predicated on the universality of male masturbation, and consequently on the universality of a symbolic desecration of maternal purity. Again, by a useful paradox, there was no escaping the pleasurable toils of the system by learning *not* to masturbate, since the only way to learn this was to put mother in the place of one's first sweetheart. Incestuous desire constrained incestuous desire: auto-erotic man faced a Hobson's choice between one or another version of incest.

Adult heterosexuality remained faithful to its origins. Fowler again: "It is that same faculty [amativeness] which attaches the son to his mother, and the husband to his wife. . . . Constituted to prize the masculine above *all* price, [mothers] are of course thereby fitted to develope by culture that in their sons, which they love in their husbands. Fathers, too, reciprocate this affection with their daughters."[55]

If women loved in their husbands what they cultivated in their sons—"new representatives of the husbands"—then they loved being the objects of an incestuous yet pure passion engendered by their supervision of the not-so-secret vice. As for the husbands, they were to "regard [women], *everywhere* [emphasis added], as a mother or sister."[56] (We will attend to fathers and daughters later, with the scribblers' help.) Though the mid-century reformers never said it, and probably never knew it, this was the key to their conception of marriage as of motherhood. The key to the key was provided by the other major form of undesirable male orgasm: husbandly incontinence.

Incontinence was variously defined: sex more than once every seven or ten days, more than once a month, more than once every three years, or, generally, sex for purposes other than procreation.[57] But whatever the precise definition—and the subject aroused such heated controversy that, according to William Alcott, the intrepid Sylvester Graham was nearly crucified for broaching it[58]—the experts reached a consensus on two essential points. First, excessive amativeness was almost always the husband's fault and invariably brought his wife to grief. Second, it was but the continuation of autoeroticism by other means:

> What is the difference between this expenditure of the sexual element, and that caused by solitary indulgence? Is this solely for sensual gratification? So is that. Is this in its nature purely sensual? So is that. Is this one a *solitary* indulgence? So is the other; for the wife is passive, and has no more passional enjoyment than if she were a corpse. All who have attempted to establish a distinction between the two have failed.[59]

What was more, this "unnatural and monstrous expenditure of the sexual element" was just as baneful as its autoerotic twin; it was "hardly possible to name an evil which appertains to the former which does not also characterize the latter."[60] The evils it bred ranged from strife, deformity, infant mortality, idiocy, and insanity to dyspepsia, rheumatism, gout, apoplexy, and business failure. Indeed, reading the most advanced reformers, mid-century man may occasionally even have found himself wondering whether his "hymeneal excesses" did not contribute even more than had his solitary ejaculations to the "ever-deepening, ever-widening, ever-rolling river of human disease, suffering, and pollution" threatening to inundate Western civilization.[61]

The equivalence between an "excessive indulgence in self-abuse and venery" was crucial[62]; it extended the regime of supervised sex past marriage, while guaranteeing the continuity between antimasturbatory mother and passionless wife. For woman, of course, was charged with preserving "connubial chastity," which Graham, invoking Jeremy Taylor, defined typologically as "the circumcision of the heart, the cutting off all superfluity of naughtiness, and a suppression of all irregular desires in the matter of a sensual or carnal pleasure."[63] Harriet Beecher Stowe gives us an idea of how this delicate hymeneal operation might have looked in actual practice. A decade after marrying Calvin, she could write him:

> What terrible temptations lie in the way of your sex—till now I never realised it—for tho I did love you with an almost *insane* love before I married you I never knew yet or felt the pulsation which showed me that

I could be tempted in that way . . . for I loved you as I now love God . . . and as I have no passion—I have no jealousy . . . If your sex would guard the outworks of *thought*, you would never fall.

Calvin was painfully aware of his terrible pulsations: "I try to be spiritually-minded, and find in myself a most exquisite relish, and deadly longing for all kinds of sensual gratification."[64] What held for Calvin held for millions of others, for "matrimonial prostitution," like solitary fornication, was "almost universal."[65] Obeying the wife who reined in his excessive amativeness, the dutiful husband obeyed an avatar of the mother who had curbed his solitary sinfulness. Disobeying, as he inevitably did, he violated his own mother as well as his children's. It was the sanctioned method of continuing to try to be spiritually minded—one all the more efficacious when it succeeded in failing. The "freely obedient son of love" could look forward to eternal salvation because his indestructible pulsations ensured that the husband and father would never grow up.

That Victorian wives mothered their husbands is a familiar enough observation. But its ramifications have been largely ignored, or else assimilated to universalist schemes of Freudian inspiration that miss the historical shift Freud himself helped bring about. Men have, perhaps, been marrying their mothers since Oedipus; but it was only around 1837 (in the United States, at any rate) that they began marrying paragons who, teaching them not to copulate, recalled the Madonna-like mothers who had taught them not to masturbate. The domesticators' way of recognizing this was to effect a discursive "desexualization" of marriage so thorough that the reciprocal relation between incest and the bourgeois family could be treated as a sort of open secret. As William Alcott very openly observed, "[marriage] is a revival or renewal of the family love, with something superadded. . . . Its leading design is to secure a brother or sister as a help-meet . . . it is designed to complete the education of the parties—to form a brotherhood or sisterhood for life."[66]

A "renewal of the family love" designed to "complete the education": marriage gave the pedagogy of surveillance a new lease on life, resurrecting the holy family of one's lovingly monitored childhood. "With something superadded": marriage was also the holy family desecrated, incest perversely authorized by amative man's original sinfulness. But this is only part of the story. Inadvertently, the domesticators assigned incest a second genealogy, one dependent on a much less flattering notion of what the true woman was truly like. Even that uncompromising champion of American womanhood, Orson Fowler, could not help but acknowledge—via indignant denial, to be sure—that something about God's moral agent was open to doubt: "She impure? Then are angel loves. Wrong to *feel* or *express* this God implanted sexuo-maternal instinct? and that right out frankly?"[67]

Let us go on to see what provoked this storm.

Sovereign and Subordinate

There are two interpretations of American womanolatry in general circulation. According to the one, America took its exaltation of the True Woman seriously. According to the other, it didn't. Taken alone, both are misleading. Taken together, they function as a kind of divining rod that points straight to the subterranean source of Fowler's agitation and thence to the contradiction commanding Victorian America's reading of the scribblers.

What has been said so far suggests that the domesticators faithfully translated the diluted Calvinism of mid-century into the language of body and gender, producing a profane scripture centered on the bourgeois holy family: an alliance concluded between woman and God, presided over by the saintly mother, and directed, in some sort, against the sinful man-child. Leslie Fiedler's is perhaps the most compelling statement of the position that middle-class America took the myth it had thus devised for (the) gospel:

> The Sentimental Love Religion challenges the fundamental Calvinist belief in natural depravity; for it teaches that women, woman in general and some women in particular, are absolutely pure; and that their merely human purity can do Christ's work in the world: redeem corrupted souls from sin. In America, especially, the use of women as symbols of piety and purity led to an unfortunate series of misunderstandings. With no counter-tradition, cynical or idealizing, to challenge it, the sentimental view came to be accepted as quite *literally* true, was imposed upon actual woman as a required role and responded to by men as if it were a fact of life rather than of fancy.[68]

The result, according to Fiedler, was an emasculation of culture that perversely fostered its hypermasculinization. Clipped of her sexuality, the chastened American maiden had to clip *Homo ameri-canus* of his; condemned to perpetual boyhood by a "snow maiden" turned castrating mother, the hapless sons of the New World sought refuge in all-male preserves and a sexless homosexuality that compensated the loss of the "adult heterosexual love" their more mature European brethren enjoyed. Thus the domestic ethos put the whole of American culture under the boot of the God-like True Woman—who was, Fiedler sighs, not really a true woman at all.[69]

The theory invites an obvious objection: social power in Victorian America was a male monopoly. We need look no further than the domesticators for the proof: precious few of the divine woman's devotees presumed to question the necessity of her subordination to man. On the contrary, most took pains to establish that "the elevation of woman on the one hand" derived from "her natural inferiority on the other." If the contradiction troubled them, the only indication was their eagerness to deny that it *was* a contradiction: domestic discourse is rife with womanolatrous defenses of feminine subjection. They are organized around a few basic themes: purity, childishness, emotionality, spirituality, and weakness, all natural female attributes. "Woman," in George Weaver's typical formulation, "is the love-element of humanity . . . because love is timid and yielding, she has ever shrunk from the contest of power with her companion." "Her intellectual force," preached Dr. Meigs, "is different from that of her master and lord." "Woman as a sex," Harriet Beecher Stowe pointed out, "ought not to do the hard work of the world, either social, intellectual or moral, [because] there are evidences in her physiology that this is not intended for her." "True feminine genius," the popular essayist Grace Greenwood argued, "is ever timid, doubtful, and clingingly dependent; a perpetual childhood." Feminine piety must be understood in this context: "religion is exactly what a woman needs, for it gives her that dignity that best suits her dependence." Maria McIntosh only spelled out what everyone knew when she noted that the difference between women and men was rooted in the natural order, which in turn reflected divine law: "every creature ha[s] a great work to do in the great laboratory of the universe . . . for its own peculiar work each [is] specially adapted by its organization." One could deduce from the Good Book itself the political implications of this division of labor, "ordained in Paradise, when God said to the woman, 'He shall rule over thee.'" It followed (for McIntosh, on the next page) that the problem of equality between the sexes was a false problem: *"Different* offices and *different* powers—this is what we would assert . . . leaving to others the vain question of equality or inequality."[70]

Separate but equal, then—yet fundamentally unequal, by divine dispensation and natural law. Thus a McIntosh could endorse the gender hierarchy by invoking the natural difference between the sexes and point to the same difference to disallow the question of the gender hierarchy. Again, woman's piety, which justified her ascendance over man, also attested to her simplicity, which established her necessary *dependence* on man. Indeed, one could probably show that every virtue the domesticators vaunted in affirming woman's moral supremacy also counted as a weakness legislating her social subordination. Horace Bushnell baldly stated the operative principle: "the highest virtues," he intoned in his influential polemic against women's suffrage, "belong to the subject conditions." The womanolators' reverent praise of "that best half of our race" was, it would seem to follow, only a devious means of reinforcing its oppression.[71]

Should we, then, explain the True Woman's double status by dusting off the old charge of Victorian hypocrisy? Ann Douglas's *The Feminization of American Culture* does essentially that. The masters of the marketplace, as her reformulation of the classic indictment goes, banished virtue to the hearth so as to get and spend unhindered; their women played along by pretending to find at home virtues capable of mitigating the evils of capitalism. Not for a minute did either party dream of changing existing social arrangements. Quite the contrary: women and the womanolators constituted a loyal pseudo-opposition that dutifully rendered unto Caesar in return for hegemony over a cultural space hermetically sealed off from the arena where men jousted in earnest for real power. Sheltered by their impotence, Victorian society's domestic critics could cultivate a decorative regret over capital's daily rape of values they claimed to cherish. In Douglas's unambiguous formulation, the American "lady" (with her ally the minister) "agreed to put on a convincing show and to lose." Hypocrisy, in this case, was the debt virtue paid to vice. The domesticators' cringing compromise with the mighty reduced a potentially tough feminist critique of "masculine," "laissez-faire industrial expansion" to the infantile form of "sentimentalism," for which, we are informed in an oracular aside, "there is no known substitute in a capitalist country."[72]

On at least one major point, Douglas's argument would seem to be squarely counterposed to Fiedler's. His emasculators accept womanolatry's view of woman as "quite *literally* true," responding to it "as if it were a fact of life"; Douglas's feminizers know they are putting themselves on. Douglas, as a result, finds it only too easy to explain how a "feminized" culture could have accommodated a society run by men. Domestic discourse, as she reads it, is shot through with blatant inconsistencies and embarrassed silences; they are its way of genuflecting before the bloody altar of real power, of guiltily admitting that sentimentalism stands in flagrant contradiction to terribly unsentimental social realities.[73] In contrast, the author of *Love and Death* is forced to look for contradiction, if anywhere, *between* a coherent domestic creed on the one hand ("fancy") and a divergent reality on the other (the *real* "facts of life"). Yet Douglas's and Fiedler's arguments are linked precisely where they are counterposed. Equating contradiction with hypocrisy (dishonesty, sham, fakery, rationalization, and show are among the labels she attaches to sentimentalism), Douglas simply rediscovers the gap she finds between ideology and reality *inside* ideology, which is thus opposed to itself as, for Fiedler, monolithic "fancy" is opposed to social "fact"— as, for Henry Nash Smith, "fantasy" is opposed to the dark "truth of romance"; as, for the dialectical school of scribbler criticism, the scribblers' "sense of female vocation" is opposed to their veiled "dissatisfaction and despair." Proclaiming woman's "ascendance" along with her "dependence," Douglas's sentimentalizers effectively admit their own mendacity; Fiedler's act theirs out by unhappily living their lie. For Douglas as for Fiedler, accordingly, analyzing mid-century ideology boils down to debunking it. The anti-feminizers' common aim is to expose the infantile fantasies of Victorian ideologues, with an eye to reinstating the adult truth in its rightful cultural place.

It is a style of analysis which necessarily proceeds as if one could winnow what was "for show" from what was "for real" in (Victorian) culture. But one can't. "The sentimental view," Fiedler says without quite grasping the implications, was "accepted" by its blinded partisans as "quite *literally* true." Precisely so. One has only to add—with Douglas, but bearing Fiedler's lesson in mind—that its metaphorically castrated *male* partisans "quite literally" continued to rule the sentimental roost. Far from being masculine power's (castrating or self-mutilating) other, "feminized" culture provided the instrument through which a class-based, racist, and misogynous power spoke, the creed through which it codified itself and naturalized the social order. But then domestic discourse can have been neither a pious fraud women practiced on themselves at the behest of a pharisaical male bourgeoisie, nor the wool it pulled over the eyes of America's cringing castrati. If it castrated, the castration in question was the kind that empowered. If it was fakery, it was fakery of a very sincere sort: much more than a diversionary tactic, it made a large part of the sweeping strategy of diversion that was mid-century bourgeois ideology. In a word, America's domestic show was for real; and the most important of the real things it showed was that sovereignty and subordination were not only not incompatible, but, indeed, indissolubly wed. If the domesticators could quite unhypocritically defend their self-contradictory position, the reason is that nature had already embodied it for them in their favorite authentic exhibit: naturally sovereign, naturally subordinate, chastened and chastening woman.

In sum: domestic discourse could contradict itself and yet maintain an imaginary integrity because its key term, "woman," elided two counterposed notions under a single signifier. The challenge, then, is to understand how the domesticators forged this self-contradictory unity and why woman was interpellated as its self-identical subject. To find out, we must briefly quit the "Empire of the Mother" for the scientific domain where the womanologists held sway.

A Moral and a Sexual Creature

Womanology (its practitioners did not, of course, use the term) was the scientific study of the weaker sex. Its most significant postulate, for our purposes, was that woman's purity was shadowed by a potential for depravity even greater than man's: "The best things perverted become the worst. Take from the air we breathe, one of its component parts, and a single breath of it causes death. Take from woman's character her love and practice of virtue, and her presence becomes death to the soul."[74]

The whore, that is, lurked in the madonna. The womanologists named the reasons: the female of the species, Dr. Meigs succinctly noted, was "a moral, a sexual, a germiferous, gestative and parturient creature." If she was especially moral, and, potentially, especially depraved, it was because she was especially sexual: Woman's "intellectual and moral perceptivity and powers are feminine as her organs are. . . . The medical practitioner has, then, much to study, as to the female, that is not purely medical—but psychological and moral rather."[75]

Yet study collapsed the psychological and moral back into the "purely medical." As the data accumulated, it confirmed that woman's mind communed directly with her viscera, and that the most feminine organ dominated the exchange. Scientifically speaking, it was the "instincts connected with ovulation" which endowed woman with the "gentle, affectionate, and nurturant" character indispensable to moral motherhood.[76] But not only good things emanated from the "inner court of the temple of the body." Pathology and psychopathology showed that woman's diseases—mental as well as physical—stemmed "either directly or indirectly, from the womb, the organ of love and maternity." Even "very slight modifications" of that organ could have catastrophic consequences.[77] Pure or impure, in sickness or in health, the womanologists' woman remained the prisoner of (her) nature.

The female within the female appeared most dramatically at puberty. It was then that a girl's "judgment" began "to be swayed by a heretofore unknown attribute, the newborn element of the nature, the capacity for, the desire of, the delight in, maternity." So swayed, the always trembly female nervous system became especially "tremulous," occasioning "vague emotions, of an instinct that seeks some object—it knows not what." Girls negotiating the perils of puberty were therefore particularly susceptible to disease. Since their minds were so thoroughly dominated by their bodies, puberty also brought an increased susceptibility to immoral influence. At this delicate juncture, "acquaintance with the opposite sex, particularly if extended so far as to become a reciprocal affection," could easily arouse the "dormant passion." "*Once aroused*," it could and certainly did "exercise a potent influence on the female organization"; a closely researched study of prostitutes proved it. So sensitive was the adolescent miss, indeed, that one stray gaze might destroy "pure morality" forever; for the human female, no matter how "naturally pure," was "easily and largely susceptible of perversion." The best prophylaxis was "instruction and advice given in the quiet of the domestic circle" "so soon as a child can talk and walk"; but even this was no infallible guarantee of natural modesty. Sometimes none but

the most extreme measures could avert a female's "downward departures": womanology found its logical culmination in clitoridectomy, introduced in the late 1850s, and "female castration" (ovariec-
tomy), practiced from the 1870s on.[78]

We have already encountered the discursive equivalent of clitoridectomy: female passionlessness. Harping on this proof of
woman's spirituality, domestic ideology betrayed her sexual vul-
nerability; the verbal clitoridectomy operated by the womanolators
was a defensive maneuver, a denial and by the same token an anxious admission that God's agent of morality was as "sexual" and "germiferous" as she was moral. But the admission was, so to speak, ex-
cised even as it was made; germiferous sexuality could not be
admitted into the sanctified domain of womanolatry without fatally
endangering the essential dogma of feminine purity. In what sense,
then, was womanology "in" womanolatry at all?

To borrow a term from Michel Pêcheux, womanology "traversed"
it. That is, it silently assured crucial connections between notions
that the womanolators claimed to link up on other, usually "self-
evident" grounds. Better: which they linked up in such a way as to
black out—in Pêcheux's terms, to "forget"—womanology's determining role "inside" their own discourse.[79] The proposition womanology most notably underwrote by thus traversing a discourse that
"forgot" it was the illogical—but ideo-logical—dogma that woman's
moral superiority implied her social inferiority.

To be sure, there was nothing secret about the findings of the
womanologists. Not only were the doyens of domestic discourse not
ignorant of them; domesticators and womanologists were sometimes
the same people. The domesticator did not, then, suppress the scientific data on woman in order to put disagreeable medical realities out
of his mind; he *managed* them in such a way as to keep infinitely
more disagreeable moral realities from ever entering it. One in particular was perfectly inadmissible, because at odds with the first principles of domestic discourse, and yet altogether indispensable, because the very basis of domestic woman's double status. The
necessary and intolerable implication of the secret pact between
womanolatry and womanology was that the affair between moral
mother and masturbatory son was initiated by the lusty female animal. That is, Fielder's Sentimental Love Goddess was also Douglas's
impostor: not, however, because she wished to mutilate her beloved
man-child, nor yet because she only played at curtailing his preroga-

tives—but because, in defiance of the celestial law she herself embodied, she longed with all her heart to copulate with him.

For the reasons sketched in Chapter 1, we can establish that highly improper thesis only by making the literary detour that is the main business of this study: one has to interrogate domesticators and scribblers *together* to extract a full confession of their common secret. But at least two anomalies in domestic discourse as such provide a clue as to what the domesticators had to hide—to begin with, from themselves. One (we will come back to it) is the natural unnaturalness of masturbation. The other is the gap that appears when womanolatry is measured against the claims of the natural religion that ostensibly underpinned it.

Natural religion, we said, diverged from Puritan orthodoxy by proclaiming the tendential unity of nature and spirit. Human nature, in the post-Calvinist view, could be nurtured gradually heavenward; the body offered the nurturers a natural access route to the soul; the spiritualization of nature was itself a natural process. Consistency demanded that one be naturally—indeed, bodily—directed to one's place in the new scheme of salvation. Man was. Autoaffection in the most primitive sense lured him onto natural religion's pivotal scene. Masturbating under the domestic dispensation, the man-child sowed the seeds of his incestuous love for mother; his attachment to that sublime and sublimating being ripened into love of her Holy Ally, God. Thus was the original sin of onanism converted into the means of man's redemption. The originally sinful male body could grow over into its spiritualized opposite because grace routinely became flesh in Everyman's domestic Madonna.

But we have yet to inquire into the natural motivation of the other actor on the (anti)masturbatory scene. What prompted woman to spiritualize man's carnality? According to the doctrine of female passionlessness, it was precisely not carnal desire; woman had over man "that degree of power which the mind exercises over the body" because her body did *not* make immoral demands on her spirit.[80] Clitoridectomizing her in the cradle, the domesticators secured an all-important objective: "absolutely pure," as Fiedler puts it, neutered woman could do "Christ's work in the world." Yet assigning her this lofty function on the basis of her always already spiritualized anatomy resurrected the very problem natural religion had set out to bury. With no natural urge drawing her toward her masturbatory/copulatory ward, woman threatened to become what Calvin's God had been, a transcendent power who redeemed nature from a position outside it. Because her body was spiritualized, was a body wholly spirit, the mere fact that she had one did not suffice to bond her spirit to the (man-child's) flesh, did not suffice, in other words, to *naturalize* the passionless mother's passionate devotion to her lecherous son. There womanolatry failed natural religion. The deficiency had to be made good somewhere else: if God's agent was not to sabotage the very theology she incarnated, she, no less than the man-child, would have to be called to her place in the normalizing order by nature.

A scientific observation of Dr. Acton's shows how domestic ideology "resolved" the resulting dilemma, backhandedly alloting woman her dram of desire even as it clitoridectomized her: "the best mothers, wives, and managers of households know little or nothing of sexual indulgence. Love of home, children, and domestic duties are the only passions they feel." That is, the best mothers acquired the rights to "passion" at the cost of "sexual indulgence." Their *sexual* passionlessness thus assured, the mid-century could unblushingly name the first object of their *household* passion. Washington Irving expressed the most sacred sentiments of his age when he ejaculated, "Oh! There is an enduring tenderness in the love of a mother to a son that transcends all other affections of the heart."[81] Between them, Irving and Acton locate the stratagem that lent domestic ideology its contradictory consistency. The domestication of woman's natural desire doubled as its (de)sexualization. Passionlessness secured the incestuous reorientation of the American Eve's passion. One begins to see why Fowler sprang so hardily to the defense of woman's "God implanted sexuo-maternal instinct": here was the fissure where womanology breached womanolatry, the open border between passion and passionlessness. Fowler only blurted out what the Actons and Irvings said without meaning to, and what the domestic economy of natural religion absolutely required. The moral mother obeyed her body after all.

Womanology, then, provided the missing link between the corruptible female flesh and woman's high spiritual calling. Every masturbator's mother had once been a daughter at school, had been imperiled by the (un)natural animal instinct that sought some object it knew not what. Preserving womanly purity required that the daughter turn her back on that nameless Thing and that the wife have as little to do with it as possible. But preserving *manly* purity required that the mother seek it out, thus revealing it to be the same object her masturbatory son also blindly groped for. The daughter's damnable instinct was redeemable, and redemptive, insofar as it would one day bind the mother to the little man at home: the incestuous female animal had to be smuggled into the domestic sanctuary—woman's "Garden of Eden"—under the skirts of the "ethereal guardian" who guarded it. Purity maintained an interior link to the grossest immorality; Victorian woman embodied not passionlessness, but *passion*(lessness).

Passion(lessness), not the secret sin, names the domesticators' real secret, an internal ruse so clever that even its perpetrators were duped by it. They readily saw, with the womanologists, that "the best things perverted become the worst"; but they necessarily missed the perverse circumstance that the best things *were* the worst, that the fair sex owed its natural superiority to the "foul unnatural crime" of incest.[82] What they missed was, needless to add, right under their noses. The fifth column boring its way through the chthonic regions of "Woman's Empire" was manned, if not directed, by the domesticators themselves; their discourse revealed that fair was foul, and foul fair, in the very realm "where truth show[ed] herself unveiled." For not only did womanly truth unveil herself at the scene of man's suicidal crime; she also left her prints on the murder weapon, which she, and not the bumbling man-child, loaded with its murderous charge. Man mangled himself under the evil influence of the outside agitator always already stationed in domesticity's sanctum sanctorum. "God's appointed agent of MORALITY" was also working for the other side.

The vigilant Dr. Edward Dixon was one of the few who caught her out. Young America's "excessive sexual excitability," he excitedly informed the nation in 1847, had an "incredible" etiology—incredible, yet all too true. The concealed wellspring of chronic spermatorrhea lay buried in voluptuous mama's innocent breast; the American mother's habit of artfully "prolonging the period of suckling" was destroying the American Adam. Any (meta)physician "inclined to philosophical inquiry" might easily verify Dr. Dixon's findings:

Several times [have I] been a personal witness of the fact, that the approach to the breast of the mother was productive of complete turgidity of the sexual organs; and I have been assured that this at times, was followed by every appearance of the nervous exhaustion, attendant on the completion of the act of coition: when I say that I have also received the assurance that these feelings were reciprocated, and often excited designedly by these means, I hope it is unnecessary to remark, that such actions could only have been resorted to by persons of a truly bestial temperament.

To be sure, the crimes committed by such she-devils hardly implicate moral mothers. But Dixon's investigations did not bear exclusively on the bestial. The great "wisdom and truth" he read on the "sacred page of nature" was that the *ordinary* female animal partook of the nature of the beast: "Can we say, however, with truth, that nursing is not prolonged to favour voluptuous impressions, to a certain extent, even in the mother whose mind is comparatively pure? I fear not."[83]

Is it any surprise, then, that many an infant male was bedeviled by unremitting priapism, never more acutely than when being dandled in his mother's lap?[84] Can one wonder at the "hopeless condition of the mass" of mid-century American males, subject to the incendiary influence of "smothered passions" "from the cradle to the grave"? Especially from the cradle: for, whenever self-abuse might begin to rage in the narrow empirical sense, it was *mother's* smothered passions that had always already set it to smoldering. But we know this already, for we have read Orson Fowler; the doctor's insight, if not his attitude, is also the phrenologist's (proving that domestic ideology's crackpots saw deepest into domestic ideology's cracks). The one and the other unerringly put his finger on domesticity's incestuous navel. That Fowler revered while Dixon reviled the incestuous Madonna's "sexuo-maternal instinct" only accentuates the oscillation that made mid-century domesticity tick. America's perdition, no less than its salvation, must be chalked up to the "passionate adulation of doting mothers."[85]

Whence a telltale instability in the relation between the male sex and (mother) nature. We have noted the implicit equation between, on the one hand, masturbation and original sin, and femininity and grace on the other; but we have noted too the age's discomfort with the very idea of original sin, not to mention the ideological problems connected with branding (white) *men* as the original sinners. For "it was certainly not the intention of nature" to deprave; "does it seem then, on a first glance, unphilosophical," inquired our (meta)physician, to identify "that passion, which is acknowledged to be the

strongest . . . of all others belonging to our nature" as the foun-
tainhead of man's depravity? On balance, the domesticators seemed
to feel that it did not. But they also felt rather strongly that it did.
Alongside the implicit equation of male sexuality with the primal
fault, therefore, they put another neatly reversing it. Thus Dr. Bostwick, mindful that masturbation often began to rage at the age of
two, trumpeted that, in the realm laid waste by the "seminal diseases," "the depraved passions of a fallen race appear to run riot
with resistless force"; this did not prevent him from blasting the universal vice as an "unnatural habit" "contrary to the laws of nature,
and of nature's God." Graham was persuaded that "man, in a pure
state of nature, would . . . have no disposition to exercise [the sexual]
function to any injurious excess"; Wright, that "where there is no
violation of *natural* law, there is no disease, no sin"; Sanger, that
masturbation was "perverted indulgence of the natural instinct."[86]
There is no need, however, to multiply examples. What do the awful
physiological scourges visited on the incontinent demonstrate, if not
that nature and sin were natural enemies?

But then so were man and woman. Not for the reason that mother
wouldn't let the man-child do what he wanted—though her antimasturbatory ardor might seem to say so—but because *she made him
do what she wouldn't let him.* The natural enemy of depraved nature
embodied the natural force that depraved nature. It was, perhaps,
her greatest contribution toward redeeming the natural man: his secret sin could be denaturalized because it could be secretly re-
naturalized and assigned its ultimate source in the female breast.
With an altogether illuminating illogic, Augustus Gardner showed
how the domestic enemy—more precisely, the domesticated female
animal—could be quietly saddled with the burden of this ponderous
dialectic:

> There is a natural prurience in the human mind, that loves to contem-
> plate wickedness, and demons, and enormities. This [masturbation] is
> one of them. The habit once formed, it is kept up in after life, as a
> sensuality—and then comes its dangers and physical disabilities. As sug-
> gested already, the animus is not from within. When the vice is com-
> menced, nature is yet tranquil, no internal fires are raging, no imagina-
> tions stir the brain, no stimulus comes from the well-turned ankle, or the
> graceful form of one of the opposite gender. The youth is simply led into
> this wrong-doing as he would be seduced into robbing a watermelon
> patch or a peach orchard.[87]

Evidently, universal sin is both original and derivative. There is "a natural prurience in the human mind": the seeds of wickedness must lie within. But "nature is yet tranquil" when youth begins robbing the peach orchard; the urge to masturbate must come from without. Coming from without, however, it should remain powerless to touch the inner man—a hypothesis borne out by the fact that, initially, the masturbatory "animus" sets no "internal fires" to "raging," that the novice onanist "intends," as Fowler tastefully puts it, "no more wrong than in eating."[88] What, then, lends "self"-pollution its permanent and soul-corrupting power? What makes the young man "keep it up"? Something must *retroactively* turn outside into inside, boyish "habit" into prurient "sensuality," tranquil nature into the well-loved demons of natural wickedness. The one "animus" sufficiently powerful to work the change radiates, naturally, from the "graceful form" of the female animal. Only feminine "stimulus" can genuinely "stir the brain," belatedly filling masturbatory form with its sinful content. Though originally committed by man, the original sin originates with woman. (Male) nature, in the end, is more sinned against than sinning; *female* nature puts the peach orchard East of Eden.

Gardner was by no means the only domesticator to hint that America's man-corrupting animus emanated from "the graceful form of the opposite gender." But few of his sane contemporaries—the Dixons and the Melvilles aside—ever dreamed of saying that it emanated from the moral mother ("is there a mother who would place temptation in the way of her son?").[89] One has to say it for them: even before the unmanly "vice" was "commenced," the "graceful form" that belatedly *made* it a vice was already on hand.[90] The moral agent responsible for the remission of the man-child's sins was also the temptress responsible for his sinful emissions.

This would have been bad enough if it had only involved mother's innocently seductive *form*. But, as we have briefly seen, it involved something more. The general run of domesticator did *not* see this, however briefly; in Pêcheux's sense, mother's excesses were precisely what he or she forever "forgot." Yet what scandalized Dr. Dixon and warmed the cockles of Orson Fowler's heart also haunted the homiletics of innumerable others not blessed with their acumen. It was that dormant, tremulous emotion which slept in the inner court of the temple of mother's body, that household passion which prompted her to unveil her truth in her domestic Garden of Eden, that enduring tenderness and quick irrepressible sympathy which bound her to Father, son, and Holy Ghost—all this, and a thousand other things besides. A thousand things that finally added up to one: mother transformed innocent "habit" into sinful "sensuality"—*and thence into salvation*—because she craved a partner in forbidden passion.

The original sin of filial onanism, then, derived from the *even more original* sin of maternal incest. But it was unthinkable that a mother should take up her saving mission in hopes of seducing her son. That unthinkability "solved" post-Calvinism's main theological dilemma. The apparent contradiction in man's nature—his natural inclination to commit an unnatural sin—could be relocated in woman's; but, since woman embodied passionlessness, to relocate the antinomy was to cancel it. Better: since woman embodied *passion*(lessness), to relocate the antinomy was to "cancel" it. The dormant passions slumbering within mother's graceful form were not dead; they survived as the improper register of domestic discourse, the register consigned to silence by "cultural conversation"—and so *made audible*. And they survived, especially, as their principle effect: woman's superiority implied her subordination because moral motherhood implied incest.

Incestuous woman had, then, to be subjected to the moral law she embodied. As the innocent child had to be cured of his congenital corruptibility, so God's moral agent had to be preserved against the immorality festering within her own flesh. But transposing the paradox into the feminine register transformed it. The way woman was subjected to the law shows how. "There is no constraint like that of love": the normalizers' cardinal principle held for woman too. It meant, however, something different in her case. Autoerotic man, as we have seen, had to be constrained to love incestuously. Woman loved incestuously by nature: *she had to be constrained to love constraint.* What more convenient arrangement than to appoint the object of her forbidden passion—the man-child—the Law-Man who constrained her? Natural feminine frailty, not Victorian hypocrisy, made Man the Masturbator Man the Master. Precisely that which guaranteed the true woman's femininity—the fact that she was "constituted to prize the masculine," and especially her autoerotic son, "above *all* price" (see p. 52)—also required that the power to tame the female animal be placed in the masturbator's hands. The mid-century liked to say it quasi-Biblically: woman had to learn to kiss the chastening rod.[91]

Kissing it chastened her incestuousness. But her incestuousness made her kiss it. The rod that awakened the forbidden desires of the daughter at school doubled as the rod that interdicted them. Incest, (female) nature's supreme challenge to the law, also furnished the best means of bending female nature to the law. "Sexuo-maternal instinct" ensured that the *female animal* would remain passionately devoted to the phallic master who constrained the *moral mother* to be purely passionless. As incest was the problem, in short, so was it the solution. Thanks to woman's (un)natural interest in her man-child's penis, the burden of original sin could be transferred from mastur-batory man to incestuous woman; but, thanks to man's natural mas-tery of naturally frail woman, this original sin too motivated its own forceful conversion into sinlessness. Therein lay post-Calvinism's un-spoken "resolution" of the contradiction between natural depravity and natural goodness. Feminine incest simply elided the difference. Not only was woman innocent and corrupt at once: her corruption sustained her saving innocence. The female's inborn incestuousness, her con-genital fault, formed the secret place where sin and sinless-ness joined, where the law (il)legitimately coupled with transgres-sion.

That, at any rate, is the improper tale we mean to (re)construct by conjugating domesticators and scribblers. But the tale to be (re)con-structed does not concern itself with (im)moral mothers seductively suckling their turgid male tots. It concentrates on incestuous daugh-ters/sisters who love their phallic fathers/brothers, and thus on men who "culture and develope the natural attachments of the female character."[92] It concentrates, that is, on the "moral and sexual crea-ture" in the making—and on the make. Writing about the daugh-ters, the scribblers identified incest as the future mother's vice and the mother of the vices. And they identified it as the mother of the virtues as well, as the intolerable and indispensable condition for training agents of morality. Sexuo-maternal instinct in its formative stages: that is what scribblers and domesticators improperly con-spired to tell their readers about.

Every Ass(ociation) Must Have a Head

The story scribblers and domesticators told about sex was "traversed" by a story about class, so that the axiom that woman's

superiority entailed her subordination reflected the notion that democracy implied class hierarchy. But the mirror relation involved
was a strange one: the "political" principle mirrored appeared most
conspicuously in the "nonpolitical" discourse that mirrored it. In a
society regarding itself as (at least tendentially) classless, the contradiction between the universalist claims of bourgeois democracy on
the one hand and its narrow class character on the other made itself
heard mainly by proxy. At least in the North, domestic discourse was
the main proxy. Superior yet subordinate woman represented the
masses to, and in, the classes: her sovereign yet subjugated status
legitimized that of the majority in the eyes of the elite she belonged
to. A lady inscribed the privileges of her class on her own body.[93]

Her subjugation, we have argued, found its ultimate ideological
justification in her secret affliction. But no one said so. Or, rather,
everyone did, by saying that her nature dictated that she defer to
man. The self-evident *naturalness* of the gender hierarchy could then
be silently invoked to sanction the idea of natural hierarchy as such.
Accordingly, a good deal more than the orderly relation of the sexes
followed from the unspoken premise of woman's flawed nature. Catharine Beecher's authoritative *Treatise on Domestic Economy* began by
indicating just how much more:

> [In a Christian, democratic society] there must be the relations of hus-
> band and wife, parent and child, teacher and pupil, employer and em-
> ployed, each involving the relative duties of subordination. The superior
> in certain particulars is to direct, and the inferior is to yield obedience.
> Society could never go forward, harmoniously, nor could any craft or
> profession be successfully pursued, unless these superior and subordinate
> relations be instituted and sustained.[94]

This is a by no means unique overture to mid-century discourses
on gender. An analogy gratefully taken for granted made for a
smooth transition between "the relations of husband and wife" and
its correlates—most notably, the relations of "employer and employed." But the analogy went further than was commonly noticed.
It went, indeed, beyond analogy. One might go so far as to call it an
incestuous bond: the relations of production could reproduce themselves only by pairing off with the gender relations that (re)pro-
duced the relations of production. In the absence of that doubling,
the (re)productive economy threatened to disintegrate, undomesti-
cated "liberties" to "degenerate into licentiousness."[95] Beecher's de-

fense of fundamental democratic principle therefore invoked the politics involved in founding families:

> [Except for children,] in a truly democratic state, each individual is allowed to choose for himself, who shall take the position of his superior. No woman is forced to obey any husband but the one she chooses for herself; nor is she obliged to take a husband, if she prefers to remain single. So every domestic, and every artisan or laborer, after passing from parental control, can choose the employer to whom he is to accord obedience, or, if he prefers to relinquish certain advantages, he can remain without taking a subordinate place to any employer.[96]

The freedom to choose one's master—that was the cornerstone of a "truly democratic state." It was the privilege which, above all others, gave women, and by extension the "employed" as well, their "peculiar interest in Democratic Institutions."[97] But the right to choose one's master implied, for the worker as for woman, the right to choose no master at all. One danger of democracy was that too many might avail themselves of the privilege, until there were "rulers enough for a hundred republics, but not . . . a single good *subject*."[98] "Every association must have a head," Beecher affirms, echoing de Tocqueville; yet the principles of *democratic* association threatened to decapitate American society: [in Europe] "the lower orders [are] more dependent, and more subservient to employers. . . . in this country . . . everything is moving and changing. . . . There are no distinct classes."[99]

How, then, was the individual's freedom to choose a master, or to forego one, to be reconciled with "the relative duties of subordination"? How, conversely, was one to forestall a dangerous "reaction" of "our unparalleled political freedom, upon our domestic relations"?[100] In the latter case, woman's ruling passion provided the answer: the base desire that legislated her natural inferiority also guaranteed that she would naturally desire to be (over)ruled by her proper lord and master.[101] In the case of the lower orders, matters were not so clear. Regrettably, the "head" of the social "association" often had to address the body in the language of "harshness and restraint"; for the "promiscuous masses" had a tendency to forget that "the principles of democracy" were "identical with the principles of Christianity," and that the "primary idea of Chrisitanity [was] obedience to, and reverence for, the proper authority."[102] But if one needed, from time to time, to remind the uppity of the "advantages" they might "relinquish" along with their wages, the repressive technique involved was flagrantly at odds with modern principles. In the guise of domestic ideology, a more gratifying vision of mass discipline presented itself. Rooted in the home truth that the preservation of proper authority was "the primary idea of the family,"[103] it gave the symbolic equivalence between woman and "the lower orders" full value: as the female animal was bound to the Law-Man by an excess of love, so, in the bourgeoisie's bolder fantasies, were the masses bound to the classes that exploited them. Thus the great problem posed by democracy turned out to contain its own solution. The childlike, irrational, and potentially unruly—in a word, the womanish—People could be ceded sovereignty in the political sphere for the same reason woman could be granted it in the moral one: here as there, the apparent desire for mastery was at bottom a desire for Master. The masses' vital instincts, not their unreliable reason, would subject them to the constraints that allowed society, like the family, to "go forward harmoniously." The bourgeoisie would not have to beat down, nor even to woo, the classes whose labor power it depended on; it faced the far more pleasant prospect of curbing their desire for a more perfect union with their betters, of properly distancing itself from its too ardent underlings. Modern statecraft too could turn on "soliciting and refusing" a "socialized" form of incest.[104]

Harriet Beecher Stowe may have understood this better than her sister. Not the least of Uncle Tom's tragedies is that, in a just universe, the devout slave would have made a devoted wageworker; his passionate yet passionless devotion to little Eva is a plea for the constraint of love in productive as well as in race relations. Most scribblers made similar pleas in similar accents; Tom is only the most famous of a host of fictive plebeians—faithful darkies, but also tramps, street urchins, hired hands, even mildly criminal sorts—constrained to rapt obedience by love for masters and, especially, mistresses. It is, however, unnecessary to dwell on such peripheral personages. They are, in the end, glosses on the novels' true-womanly heroines; they remind us that the "imaginary solution" of class contradiction appears in scribblerdom, not *alongside*, but *as*, the incestuous dialectic. In the fondest dreams of the middle class, woman kissed the chastening rod on behalf of unnamed millions. Though the thesis lies beyond the scope of this study, the teeming millions are surely the ultimate reason woman had to kiss the rod in the first place.[105]

Passion(lessness), (im)Propriety, (w)Holeness

Turning to the subject of (the) domestic sex, we have hardly been diverted from the subject of the divided subject. For the "presiding divinity" of domesticity was the divided subject par excellence. She was rendered whole, and holy, by virtue of her subjection to God and man; she was subjected to Him/him by virtue of the unholy desire wholly excluded from her virtuous self. The operation left a hole at the center of her being that enabled as it undid the fiction of her wholeness. Woman's condition was—exemplarily—(w)holeness.

"Woman's fiction" reflected woman's condition. Source of meaning-effects it could not possibly, as fictional subject, mean, the divided text had its closest likeness in the divided sex, source of an incestuous passion with which the sex had nothing to do. Passion(lessness) was the analog of (im)propriety. But, as with the relation between gender and class, more was involved than analogy. For it was in bestsellerdom that domestic woman's identity was most effectively forged: woman's fiction was largely fabricated in "woman's fiction." Yet if domestic discourse secured its imaginary coherence in the domestic novel, the domestic novel, for its part, reflected the fictitious coherence of domestic discourse. Through its fictionalization, in other words, ideology acquired the unifying power that unified scribbler fiction. The best-sellers produced ideology's fictitious integrity as they *re*produced it.

But the mirror structure involved was not as simple as that. For the scribbler heroine not only made part of fiction's (re)production of domestic ideology; she also *represented* its reproduction. Holding up to ideology a mirror in which it could see itself whole, the best-sellers also showed it a figure in the mirror who figured both the wholeness of the whole mirror image *and* the process of its mirroring. They did not, then, simply represent the ideology that interpellated them; representing the interpellation of a representative subject, they also represented their own relation *to* ideology. Better: they *related* that relation. Making the true woman incarnate the cohesiveness of the domesticating vision, they recounted, naturally enough, the making of the true woman: they turned on her ongoing incarnation of domesticity's truth, which was simultaneously their *own* incarnation of it. Thus the fictional true woman had a double vocation: representing truth, she also represented truthful representation.

She might therefore be likened, not only to the scribbler novel as such, but specifically to the moment of narrative unfolding we have called the "narration." Perilously suspended between tremulous daughterhood and moral motherhood, the child-woman embodied that endlessly renewed possibility of straying whose equivalent was narration's endlessly renewed "I am lying." Yet woman was as naturally constrained to represent true womanhood as narration is constrained to represent fiction's "cohesive and coherent" truth. The scribblers arranged to impose both constraints at once. "Woman's fiction" represented narration's subjection to its narrated by (re)presenting the fiction of the true woman: the narrative of the dubious daughter's subordination to firm Fatherly law doubled as the narrative of scribbler narrative. Enacting *in* a story the imposition of truth they enacted *as* a story, the scribblers told the tale of their own self-rapport.

But they also exposed woman's fiction for the imposition it was; and, in so doing, they gestured at their own misrepresentation of ideology's interpellation of bestsellerdom. They had to: to show the "female of the species" coming into the truth she embodied, the scribblers were obliged to hold open the possibility of her falling off from it. But the fair sex's "downward departures" could not be properly represented. Not, as one might imagine, for reasons of decorum: the scribblers were past masters at allusively circumventing their own prudishness. The "best thing perverted" could not be properly represented for the far weightier reason that its proper representation shaded off into the improper. As we will see, the scribblers habitually signaled the possibility of woman's moral decline by ominously alluding to their heroines' "passion." A venerable literary legacy, from Genesis to *The Quaker City*, offered to make the allusion an allusion to incest. Proper Victorian readers could by no means take up the offer; but neither could they reject it outright. For the unwholesome female urge that made domestic ideology whole also knit together the domestic novel. The forbidden passion that made the second sex want to represent its divine truth was the same demon that drove the scribbler novel to represent its. The domestic heroine embodied her whole text's intolerable and enabling condition: representing representation, she also represented the domestically unrepresentable.

Thus the founding weakness of domestic ideology gave domestic fiction a language in which to confess its own. Interpellation, whispered the best-sellers, was incestuous. The child-womanly subject submitted to the ideological Subject out of an urge for forbidden union that the Subject forbade. Passionless woman was ruled by her ruling passion, domesticity by dark forces it could not domesticate; woman suffered the division imposed by the domesticators' dual mirror structure in the impossible hope of attaining a wholeness her subjective status put out of reach. The fantasy that motivated her subjection likewise motivated woman's fiction's. Whether its Subject be conceived as domestic disourse, History, or God in His Heaven, the scribbler novel too was joined to the Source of its truth by a bond that gave its truth the lie; its aspiration for "self"-rapport was a child-womanly longing to be one with the unattainable One that fathered it. Woman's fiction's truest confession was that it was not what it was: it said that the sex which was not one, like the text which was not one, became one, like any subject, only fictitiously.

A text so divided, the scribblers would more or less openly concede, could never be healed. Woman, they self-contradictorily insisted, could. The treatment they prescribed was one that simultaneously proscribed incest and rewrote it in acceptable form: chastening. There was no holier word in the whole of scribblerdom.

3

HIS SISTER'S KEEPER:
Susan Warner's *The Wide, Wide World*

Being natural self-knowledge, knowledge of self on the basis of nature
and not on that of ethical life, [the relationship of husband and wife]
merely represents and typifies in a figure the life of spirit, and is not spirit
itself actually realized. Figurative representation, however, has its reality
in an other than it is . . .
   The feminine element, therefore, in the form of the sister, premonizes
and foreshadows most completely the nature of ethical life. She does
not become conscious of it, and does not actualize it, because the law of
the family is her inherent implicit inward nature, which does not lie open
to the daylight of consciousness, but remains inner feeling and the divine element exempt from actuality. The relationships of mother and
wife, however, are individualized partly in the form of something natural,
which brings pleasure; partly in the form of something negative, which
finds simply its own evanescence in those relationships . . . In a household of the ethical kind, a woman's relationships are not based on a
reference to this particular husband, this particular child, but to a husband, to children *in general*,—not to feeling, but to the univeral. The
distinction between her ethical life . . . and that of her husband consists
just in this, that it has always a directly universal significance for her, and
is quite alien to the impulsive condition of mere particular desire. . . .
   The brother, however, is in the eyes of the sister a being whose nature
is unperturbed by desire and is ethically like her own; her recognition in
him is pure and unmixed with any sexual relation . . . This relationship at
the same time is the limit, at which the circumscribed life of the family is
broken up, and passes beyond itself.

—G. W. F. Hegel

   Heroines of domestic fiction suffer horribly, as a rule.
Sooner or later, they start to wonder why one should have to. Somebody is always on hand to tell them. Gerty Amory, protagonist of
Maria Susanna Cummins's *The Lamplighter*, raises the issue early on,
after just barely emerging from the rigors of a childhood that makes
David Copperfield's look like fun. Gerty is about fifteen when she
pauses to review her catastrophic past. When she was eight, her
wicked stepmother gorily boiled her pet kitten alive, felicitously sum-

ming up the first chapter of a cataclysmic career spanning malarial
Rio, the London underworld, and the Boston slums. Her impecu-
nious guardian Trueman Flint and her bosom friend/quasi-lover
Willie Sullivan have recently put a categorical point to chapter two,
Trueman by expiring after a debilitating illness, Willie by weighing
anchor for India. Readers uninitiated into the Stygian world of
scribblerdom might suppose that picking her way through this catalog of horrors would have won Gerty the right to complain some.
Cognoscenti will know better. For, by prevailing standards, Gerty's
represents an entirely unexceptional coming of age, which is why it
is fitting that, after caterwauling briefly over her own "childish
griefs,"[1] the heroine shapes up and shifts her plaint into the third
person—the more fitting as the unfortunate whose shoulder she is
crying on, the saintly Miss Emily, has suffered far more spectacularly
than Gerty, having, for example, been tragically blinded by a former
lover (Gerty's long-lost father, as it turns out) who reached for the
acid instead of the smelling salts at the cathartic moment of an always dramatic relationship. Here, then, are Emily and Gerty putting
female troubles in perspective, in a recital of *The Lamplighter*'s version of what might be called the scribbler catechism:

> "And so, Miss Emily, since I see that you and Willie have troubles, and
> that tears will come, though you try to keep them back, I think the world
> is full of trials, and that everybody gets a share."
> "It *is* the lot of humanity, Gertrude, and we must not expect it to be
> otherwise."
> "Then who can be happy, Miss Emily?"
> "Those only, my child, who have learned submission; those who, in the
> severest affliction, see the hand of a loving Father, and, obedient to his
> will, kiss the chastening rod."
> "It is very hard, Miss Emily."[2]

No one will ever state more succinctly than these two the central
issues in the mid-century mass novel. Indeed, it is scarcely an exaggeration to say that the whole corpus of scribbler scholarship boils
down to the handful of arguments contained in Gerty's and Emily's
chat. Traditionalists contend, in essence, that the scribblers were of
Emily's party; revisionists counter that they adhered secretly to
Gerty's; the dialectically minded consider that they were of both parties at once. But not only do Emily and Gerty give us half a century
of proper criticism in embryo; more to our purposes, they also stake

out the embryo's phylogenetic limits. The critics may be at log-gerheads as to what domestic fiction means, but they are in perfect and so unspoken agreement with Gerty, Emily, and one another as to what it does *not* mean: for example, that the hard, chastening rod Emily's theodicy attributes to the loving Father is the sacred equivalent of that other hard, chastening rod biology and the gender system conjointly bestow upon father. Briefly, not-saying this non-meaning is what makes scribbler criticism proper. Nina Baym, whom we will continue to cite whenever we need to pull things back into proper perspective, decants all the commentary in which the Father's rod is just the Father's rod: "in woman's fiction . . . purity was so taken for granted that it was ignored."[3] Indeed; that Miss Emily can deliver her homily without once smirking at Gerty proves it. And as anyone who has read *The Lamplighter* knows, it is easier to imagine the Virgin Mother smirking at the archangel than it is to imagine Miss Emily smirking at anybody.

It would, however, be a bit hasty to conclude that in domestic fiction "[God's] nature . . . transcended gender," much less that the scribblers "produce[d] a feminist theology in which the godhead is refashioned into an image of maternal authority."[4] For the chastening rod en-gendered the Father even if "woman's fiction," Emily-like, turned a blind eye to His sex. More: it was precisely through its pure blindness to God's sex that domestic fiction granted itself the purity it took for granted. The true woman's fiction—the fiction of the true woman—consisted in neither seeing nor saying what "woman's fiction" fairly flaunted: the reciprocal relation between woman's suffering and her sexuality, the unholy alliance between the female animal and her highly sexed Maker.

Emphatically, this is not to suggest that purity was an artful blind for a shameful sexual insight. Miss Emily would be indignant—and rightly so—if she heard that what she was "really" talking about was sex. The opposite is the case: sex was precisely what she was *not-talking* about. Still more precisely: what she was not-talking about was incest. In all probability, incest was the furthest thing from her mind when she exhorted Gerty to love their common Father, or when, years later, she married her (Gerty's) beloved father, the searing but maladroit lover of her (Miss Emily's) youth. For the improper critic, that purblind love stands as a trenchant warning: it cuts short all speculation to the effect that woman's fiction has secretly appropriated its own impropriety, that it is ridden with a guilty awareness of its own incestuous underside. But if this necessitates treating the scribblers' ignorance with the profoundest respect, it by no means obliges one to adopt Miss Emily's vision of things.[5] Improper criticism, at any rate, tries not to: scrutinizing textual functions the novels and their critics quite properly scotomize, it asks how woman's fiction managed to cohabit with the impurity it shut out, how the loving rod could be *both* the sexless Father's *and* the sexy father's. For the mid-century reading formation (whose [de]forming presence we will be taking for granted from now on) did indeed take the scribblers' unmanning purity for granted: in the 1850s, domestic fiction was as pure as it was purely incestuous. The resulting pure duplicity is the object of the practical criticism that follows.

Mothers, Old Gentlemen, and Better Friends

To the two principal offenses solicited and refused by domestic ideology—incest and onanism—there correspond, broadly, two character types in domestic fiction. The first is the congenitally flawed child-woman who commutes passion into passion(lessness) at the prodding of God and a man. The second is the debilitated yet potentially masterful male who conquers an unmanly habit with the help of a sovereign and subordinate child-woman. Improperly regarded, the simpler scribbler texts attend only to the etiology of passion(lessness), while the more complicated treat both woman's primal fault and man's derivative failing. Since woman's fault *is* primal, it seems appropriate to begin an examination of domestic fiction by analyzing a novel in the first category first. None is more instructive than the tearjerker heading up the parade of 1850s bestsellers: Susan Warner's *The Wide, Wide World*.

Like all the best-selling novels of the decade (with the partial exception of *Uncle Tom*), *The Wide, Wide World* is dedicated to the proposition that kowtowing to authority makes for happiness in this world and bliss in the next. It develops the idea in a domestic Bildungsroman that chronicles the chastening of its heroine, Ellen Montgomery, by a representative assortment of authority figures, chief among them the hero, Ellen's "adopted brother," John Humphreys. For hundreds of pages, God and/or John give Ellen a rough time: after a wrenching separation from her mother, she is treated hardly by her crotchety Aunt Fortune, adopted by a saintly young lady who dies, subjected to a severe if salutary drilling by John, and then, after she falls in love with her drillmaster, forced to leave him for British relatives who manhandle her à la Aunt Fortune. According to a familiar pattern, Ellen's submission to all this purgatorial unpleasantness fits her for the paradisal pleasures of religion's happy reign. But bending to the Father's will also yields her "unspeakable joy" of an earth(l)ier sort. As the novel closes, it is delicately intimated that, after "three òr four more years of . . . discipline"—significantly, after the end of *The Wide, Wide World*—the lucky heroine gets to marry her "brother."[6]

Discourses commending docility generally feature rebels, and Warner's is no exception. But Ellen's rebelliousness is of a cast rarely encountered outside scribblerdom; it bears a confusing resemblance to excruciating obedience. The confusion sets in with the novel's opening scene. The prepubescent heroine has just learned that her bankrupt father will be sailing off to Europe in hopes of recouping his fortune. On doctor's orders, his invalid wife will reluctantly go with him. Ellen is to be left behind in the United States. Deprived at a blow of parents and prospects, the dutiful orphan designate utters not a word of protest. She cannot, however, keep from crying, and "passionately" at that. But not for long. Upbraided by her mother, the heroine quickly reins in her childish passions: "Ellen was immediately brought to herself by these words [of reproof]. She arose, sorry and ashamed that she should have given occasion for them; and tenderly kissing her mother, assured her most sincerely and resolutely that she would not do so again. In a few minutes she was calm enough to finish making the tea." (14)

The next day, the devoted daughter declares herself even more plainly:

> "Why mamma: — in the first place I trust every word you say — entirely — I know nothing could be truer; if you were to tell me black is white, mamma, I should think my eyes had been mistaken. Then everything you tell or advise me to do, I know it is right, perfectly. And I always feel safe when you are near me, because I know you'll take care of me. And I am glad to think I belong to you, and you have the management of me entirely, and I needn't manage myself, because I know I can't; and if I could, I'd rather you would, mamma." (18)

This is as perfect a pledge of allegiance as ever model heroine spoke. But, like every instance of female perfection in the scribblers, it has the defect of its virtues: it glows with the same misplaced passion that makes a girl cry over losing her mother.[7] Mrs. Montgomery's restrained reception of Ellen's filial loyalty oath indicates why her daughter's attitude is both just right and all wrong: "My daughter, it is just so; — it is *just* so: — that I wish you to trust in God. He is truer, wiser, stronger, kinder, by far, than I am, even if I could be always with you; and what will you do when I am away from you?" (18)

Here, in few, is the semi-orthodox lesson the further course of *The Wide, Wide World* will impress upon us: Ellen must forsake mother and follow Him. Her will to impotence must be retained, yet reoriented. But how are her childish affections to be transferred from mother to the Father? The Sovereign she owes fealty to has always been "with" her; Mrs. Montgomery has surely been true, wise, and kind enough to enjoin her daughter to seek Him; yet this paragon of a parent, though armed with the Christian truth, has not succeeded in breaking and beating down the instincts alienating Ellen from God. Even her unflinching declaration of her own preferences for the Father fails to wean Ellen of her powerful weakness for her mother:

> "Mamma," said Ellen . . . with an indescribable expression, "do *you* love him *better than you do me?*"
>
> She knew her mother loved the Saviour, but she thought it scarcely possible that herself could have but the second place in her heart; she ventured a bold question to prove whether her mother's practice would not contradict her theory.
>
> But Mrs. Montgomery answered steadily, "I do, my daughter." (38–39)

Just as steadily, Mrs. Montgomery names the evil power she is impotent to overcome. It is because her daughter's heart is "hardened by sin" that Ellen adamantly prefers her mother to her Savior. Heir to Eve's fault, with "passions . . . by nature very strong" (11), the child-woman is naturally incapable of "loving him *best*" (38).

Or so it seems to her anxious parent. But Mrs. Montgomery's is perhaps a one-sided view of the prim-Eval passion agitating Ellen's bosom. The very heart that so obdurately spurns the Father may yet be softly yearning for its true Lord and master, and merely marking time with a maternal substitute for some paternal object it knows not what (cf. p. 60). If so—if Ellen's spontaneously "feminist theology" is only an infantile error—then her mother can safely consign her to the wide world's mercies, trusting precisely to her child's maligned passion to find the strait way to one "truer, wiser, stronger, [and] kinder." Because Mrs. Montgomery is true, wise, kind, and infirm, we have reason to suppose that such emotion as may tip Ellen toward Him will be stirred to life by what her invalid mother manifestly lacks: muscle. Should that turn out to be the case, Mrs. Montgomery's imminent (and, we feel sure, permanent) departure from the scene will have been, for her daughter, precisely a point of spiritual departure: a sign that Providence sunders little girls from mothers the better to acquaint them with woman's natural part. That part, and its (im)proper counterpart—in Miss Emily's muscular metaphor, the Father's chastening rod.

As if to test the hypothesis, Mrs. Montgomery dispatches Ellen on a dry run into the wide, wide world, represented, in this instance, by the nearest dry goods store. Fighting nameless fears and forebodings, "confused, and almost confounded" by the "moving crowd" all around her, the heroine promptly encounters a personage who gives her nebulous anxiety terrifyingly solid form. It is the bold, ill-bred, and ill-humoured clerk Saunders. A glance at his disagreeable eyes convinces Ellen that "she need not expect either kindness or politeness from him," and her child-woman's intuition is right on the mark: refusing to do his clerkly duty by Ellen, Saunders tricks, mocks, insults, and finally abandons her, leaving his victim "struggling with her feelings of mortification," "her face . . . on fire, her head . . . dizzy." She stands there traumatized, unable to stir. Fortunately, a kindly old gentleman happens along, and, after acquainting himself with the mistreated girl's tale, gives her no longer so cocky tormentor the tongue-lashing he so richly deserves. Because the miscreant knows this is "a person that must not be offended," he complies, crest-fallen, with the order to serve Ellen as he ought. The heroine melts with gratitude toward the kindly old gentleman. Joyously she goes forth from the store with her protector, who sees her straight home (45–49). There, over the child-lady's uncomprehending head, he declares meaningfully to her mother: "I assure you, ma'am, if I had had no kindness in my composition to feel for the *child*, my honour as a gentleman would have made me interfere for the *lady*." And he draws the ominous moral: "There are all sorts of people in this world, and a little one alone in a crowd is in danger of being trampled upon." (50–51)

With these words the old gentleman unwittingly echoes his author, who entitles the chapter recounting Ellen's maiden mishap "A peep into the wide world." We have had a preview of *The Wide, Wide World*, cast as a premonitory review of "this world" and what it holds in store for "little ones" like Ellen; notably, monsters like Saunders, ready and willing to "trample upon" the *lady* in a *child*. But if that fate, as the "Peep" shows primly but grimly, attends the child-woman just around the corner, so too does the surest means of warding it off: with the proper sort of bodyguard, Ellen may yet negotiate little-ladyhood intact. The Saunders affair is thus an inauspicious beginning and the foretaste of a happy end; John Hart knew what he was doing when he picked it to represent Warner in his anthology of U.S. women's fiction.[8] Yet these hair-raising pages promise us Warner's finale as much by differing from as by anticipating it— better, anticipate it *by* differing from it. As climax, the Saunders episode would be sadly defective; and, though he saves the day, the defect lies with Ellen's savior. His insufficiency is that he is insufficiently like the savage he saves her from. For the shopman offers to perform the cruelly necessary task whose needfulness Mrs. Montgomery has freshly impressed upon Ellen. *Saunders sunders*—or, rather, he would if he could. The old gentleman, in contrast, reattaches Ellen to her mother; through his protective person, *incest insists*. The miracle to be wrought by a Better Friend will consist in overcoming the difference between these two operations. The old gentleman is not the man for the job: he is not made of stern enough stuff to "confound" the passions allusively exposed in the "Peep." We cannot, however, flesh out that point before examining other of the men in Ellen's life. For the moment, then, let us simply say that her first champion is too old. For readers schooled in scribbler nuance, the description that introduces him suffices to trace his limits: "It was an old gentleman — an odd old gentleman too, [Ellen] thought; one she certainly would have been rather shy of if she had seen him under other circumstances. But though his face was odd, it looked kindly upon her." (48)

Odd, old, and kindly: together, the adjectives neuter Ellen's benefactor, clearly no match for the worst the wide world has to offer. The Saunders episode confirms this, despite appearances. Tactfully, it signals that the old gentleman speaks too loudly, and does not (even when in a great passion) carry a big enough stick. He rages at Saunders—"'You know better, you scoundrel!' retorted the old gentleman, who was in a great passion"—where the truly potent hero would, bridling his rage, dispassionately dispatch the brutal bully;[9] and, while he plies the chastening rod stoutly enough to scotch the snake, he fails to quash him, as appears years later when this inveterate enemy of womankind is resurrected to work further evil. The situation, of course, precludes his administering a more thoroughgoing humiliation, but that is part of the point. Real heroes find themselves in different situations.

In short, our dry-goods store savior is a surrogate. Mrs. Montgomery has steeled us for that disappointment by declaring, in words that acquire their full resonance only in the wake of Ellen's misadventure, who all surrogate saviors are surrogates for: "him without whom you can do nothing" (22). Supplementing her sanctioned view of matters with another, the "Peep" discretely hints that the old gentleman is also doubling for a manlier Messiah, one equipped—let us provisionally say—permanently to suspend the sexual threat old gentlemen can only fend off. The Omnipotent, one gathers, is incapable of guaranteeing Ellen safe conduct without more potent male help. Praising "Him," we begin to suspect, Mrs. Montgomery said more than she knew. Or else she knew more than she said.

Certainly she said more than that a Christian girl's patrimony entails matrimony. In the improper context the Saunders episode begins to weave, Ellen's mother's hymn to Him evokes something one might better call patrimatrimony. What that is, Mrs. Montgomery, the old gentleman, and Ellen's vile tormentor cooperate to show us—by showing us, from a standpoint the young heroine cannot yet share, what it *will not have been*. It will not have been more perfect union with mother. Looking prophetically toward Ellen's future, perfect guardian, the "Peep" also draws the eye back toward the congenital imperfections of his aboriginal stand-in, inviting one to notice that (invalid) mothers are even less qualified than old gentlemen to take His place. It is, we cannot but conclude, tragically appropriate that Ellen's is going away to die. In her own sanctified idiom, Mrs. Montgomery says just that: "'O, my child, my child! if losing your mother might be the means of finding you that better friend, I should be quite willing—and glad to go—for ever.'" (23) Going forever, the Better Friend's locum tenens trails the obvious question in her wake. What about father?

Father leaves much to be desired. His glaring absence from the Saunders scene suggests as much; as if this called for prompt clarification, the next chapter trains the spotlight on Ellen's should-be protector. It is, appropriately, the only chapter in which he figures; appropriately, because, as the chapter is there to show, Captain Montgomery is AWOL even when he reports for action. Like his wife or the old gentleman—but with considerably less excuse—Ellen's father defines a space he cannot fill. We already know that he has plunged his womenfolk into their present woe by going bankrupt. Now it is hinted that his failure stems from unmanly self-indulgence: "Captain Montgomery was abroad [on *Sunday*]; and he had been so, — according to custom, — or in bed, the whole day." (56) Even solvent, a man enfeebled by such vitiating practices is hardly likely to make a satisfactory husband or father. Without delay, the Captain demonstrates that he is neither. Breaking in at 10 P.M. on his ailing wife's Sabbath repose, he discloses that he has unilaterally arranged for Ellen to be shipped off at six the next morning, forbids Mrs. Montgomery to wake and bolster her for the shock of their imminent parting, and then falls callously asleep: "The captain, in happy unconsciousness of his wife's distress and utter inability to sympathize with it, was soon in a sound sleep, and his heavy breathing was an aggravation of her trouble; it kept repeating, what indeed she knew already, that the only one in the world who ought to have shared and soothed her grief was not capable of doing either." (60)

Even more conspicuously than the old gentleman, then, Captain Montgomery is standing—or lying—in for an absent "only one in the world." His wife's emotional deprivation is also his daughter's. The immediate indication is that this paternal zero can move Ellen neither to tears nor to spontaneous confession, which is to say, according to a protocol Warner has already begun to lay down, that he can play no positive part in shaping her soul. In the presence of soul-shapers, friendly or otherwise, the heroine is given to weeping.[10] As to her confessional urge, we have the evidence of her relationship with the old gentleman, in whose company "her tongue ran very freely, for her heart was completely opened to him. He seemed as pleased to listen as she was to talk; and by little and little Ellen told him all her history." (51)

With the Captain, in contrast, Ellen is tight-lipped:

"How did she bear it [the news of her impending departure]?" asked Mrs. Montgomery when he returned.

"Like a little hero. She didn't say a word, or shed a tear. . . . "

Mrs. Montgomery sighed deeply. She understood far better than her
husband what Ellen's feelings were. (62)

The as yet absent "only one" will, evidently, find no rival for
Ellen's affections in her father. But that does not diminish the Captain's importance, it grounds it. For the Captain engenders his
daughter's desire precisely by leaving so much to be desired. His
happy unconsciousness, fruit of his spiritual bankruptcy, feeds her
passion for her mother in ways the little girl can hardly appreciate,
but that we can hardly fail to: unable to open Ellen's heart or loosen
her tongue, the Captain compels her to solicit her mother for the
satisfaction of all her natural needs. The family threatens, in consequence, to escape the command of the fatherly, and Ellen's rebel
heart the loving correction of the Father; mother and daughter are
menaced with a liberation no true woman can want. Because she *is* a
true woman, Mrs. Montgomery responds valiantly, battling like a
Trojan to keep the paternal front from caving in. That she is debarred by her own true-womanly logic from manning the post the
Captain deserts does not make her any less formidable a Christian
soldier; her heroism consists precisely in leaving his position perilously undefended, while begging Ellen to beg Heaven to leap into
the breach. The Captain's gaping breaches thus become a pivotal
factor in Ellen's spiritual odyssey, and this at the critical moment
when her journey through the wide world is about to begin. Looking
back, as it were, through them, we see that the Captain has been
pivotal from the first; absent center of the practice pilgrimage that
has already led Ellen from one father-manqué to the next, his nullity
founds the series that promises to converge on the Infinite. That,
perhaps, is why *The Wide, Wide World* opens by almost reverently
(un)veiling papa's failings. "'Mamma,'" Ellen launches the novel by
asking, "'what was that I heard papa saying to you this morning
about his lawsuit?'" The reply images the doom the Captain's appall-
ing negligence hastens: "'I cannot tell you just now. Ellen, pick up
that shawl, and spread it over me.'" (9) Yet when the invalid finally
does put a caption under her morbid tableau, she spurns the easy
chance to damn her husband for prematurely digging her grave—to
say nothing of the temptation to give fatherhood as such a bad
name. Her tendency is rather to exculpate her worst enemy on the
grounds that he is but her Better Friend's accomplice: "'You know,
my dear, that I am not apt to concern myself overmuch about the

gain or the loss of money. I believe my Heavenly Father will give me what is good for me.'" (11)

Who, then, is the Better Friend better than? Should we say, with recent critics, that Mrs. Montgomery is her own Best Friend, that she conceives her "Heavenly Father" as a superlative version of her matronly self? The suicidal logic she espouses tends toward a different conclusion. She points to it when she sells her mother's ring to buy her daughter a Bible. Cashing in the maternal legacy to promote the Father's Word, she symbolically converts her mother as she would hope to convert her daughter; liquidating her mother's "trinket" (29) to cover her husband's liabilities, she becomes her own Better Friend . . . by championing the Friend Who liquidates *her*. In the process, she willy-nilly identifies Him with His earthly travesty: the "holy alliance" that weds her to "the source of all power" annuls her invalid self, while aligning the *Captain's* murderous impotence with the doings of the Omnipotent.[11] To be sure, Captain Montgomery is at best an accessory to murder; after all, it is his heavenly Ally Who sends his wife to her final reward. But that, of course, is the point. The Better Friend is not merely better than Mrs. Montgomery; nor is He nonspecifically—uncomparatively—better. The Better Friend is a *better friend than His bumbling lieutenant, the Captain*; He is a General Signifier of the fatherly, Who, as its overarching, infinite limit, integrates even the most negligible and negligent of papas into the paternal army. Thus it is that Warner engenders Ellen's (other)worldly savior, deriving Him without Whom she can do nothing from an invalid mother and a paternal cipher. Her next task is to bring Him into *The Wide, Wide World*.

She claims to do so against the resistance put up by Ellen's natural passion. It is a perplexing claim. For if the first fruit of Ellen's passion—her all-absorbing love for her mother—is indeed "natural," then the love that will bind her to her Better Friend must be less so. Naturally the narrative does not want to concede this. Nor does it have to, directly, since it can tacitly refer Ellen's excesses to the Captain's deficiencies: if father were worthy of his archetype, Ellen would not love mother to distraction. This, however, only bares a deeper dilemma, implying that if the Captain had properly secured the affections of his family, Ellen's passion would have chained her to him, its natural male object. By a logic Sigmund Freud was to make notorious, unperverted natural passions produce perverse results.

It is therefore good—indeed, providential—that Ellen's family circle is so unnaturally breached. Her father's failings force a kind of
fortunate fall from the familial Eden, driving the future orphan out
into the world in quest of her natural liege Lord. Does this make the
love she will eventually bear Him natural or unnatural? The answer
is both, and in a double sense. Insofar as it fulfills her patrimatrimonial desire for (a) father, it will be natural, and therefore,
like incest, unnatural; but it will be unnatural, and therefore, like
true religion, natural, to the extent that it *supplements* her desire for
father with a *super*natural desire for the Father. It is this natural
unnaturalness, the shifting foundation of female passion(lessness) as
of patrimatrimony, that constitutes the improper burden of *The
Wide, Wide World*—and Ellen's burden in it.

Strange Familiar Gentlemen and the Com-mutation of Passion

The Wide, Wide World puts the theoretical question of
Ellen's relations to the Father in the down-to-earth terms of evangelical practice: how is the child-woman to be made to love Him? It
answers, with apparent ingenuousness, that she was made to love
him—and then proceeds, as we will see in a moment, to elevate the
homonym into a synonym. But it also shows, as we saw a moment
ago, that she loves mother with a depraved passion that threatens to
deprive her eternally of Him. The relation between these two moments is the riddle of *The Wide, Wide World*. If Ellen's devotion to the
Father derived naturally from her attachment to mother, redemption would emerge as the baseborn child of sin. If the Father displaced Ellen's mother by fanning the flames of a competing congenital passion—a parallel, but more powerful, desire for Him—then sin
and redemption would be as sister and brother. Both alternatives are
unthinkable. There is only one other. Ellen must be denatured in
order to be saved.

But, rejoins natural religion, she must be denatured *naturally*.
Ellen is accordingly subjected to a natural conversion process whose
effect is less to denature her than to endow her with a second nature: patiently, her passion is written over by Scripture until she desires the Only One capable of delivering her from her desire. This
obscures the family tie between sin and salvation; it fails to obliterate

it. For if the power to rewrite her now comes from without, still, she must desire to be righted by it; if the rectified version of Ellen is to be a version, precisely, of *Ellen*, something of her original desire must survive its conversion. What makes the simultaneous repetition and redemption of her prim-Eval self possible? What reconciles the necessity that her passion perish with the equally urgent necessity that it persist?

In principle, the answer is grace. In practice, it is a sexually stimulating regime of Christian nurture: Christian com-mutation. Com-mutation gracefully mobilizes the logic of the constraint of love: it brings the child-woman round to loving the Father only insofar as he (re)rights her con-genital fault. But only her fault inspires her love of Him. She cannot, in consequence, properly love Him at all: Christian com-mutation is, strictly speaking, impossible. That impossibility begets *The Wide, Wide World*. Prolonging the climactic moment of Ellen's conversion forever, it ensures (pace St. Paul) that *her* master's charge will never be at an end. With good reason: should the master ever stop righting—should Ellen come to love the Father con-genitally—the wide world itself would end, and end most abominably. Here, then, are the elements of Ellen's coming of age: eternal writing and abomination, incest and the Word. The Better Friend's sacred mission is to forge their (un)holy alliance.

Incest first meets the Word on the symbolic boat that transports the (un)fortunate Ellen to her paternal Aunt Fortune's.[12] Hardly has she embarked than her unmotherly chaperone Mrs. Dunscombe (oblivious, despite the name, to the deficiencies of her own God-given headgear) pokes fun at Ellen's perfectly decent, if mildly frumpish bonnet. Dunscombe's gratuitous sadism sends the "lightning of passion" crackling through her temporary charge's "every vein" (66). Devastated, the little girl shoots off, and buries herself below decks. Hours later she is still disconsolately alone, lost in imaginary intercourse with her mother ("'Who is there to teach me now? O! what shall I do without you?'" [68]). It seems as though the whole wide world were against her; but, if only because we have seen the chapter heading—"'Strangers walk as friends'" (5)—we know better. *Salvation is coming in the person of the stranger.*

The stranger in some sense caps the sequence Mrs. Montgomery initiates by going forever. In some sense, because he is not quite man enough to master Ellen in the end; he does not (perhaps only for lack of time) confound her as thoroughly as he ought. Otherwise he is everything a better friend should be, and prefigures in his few hours with the fledgling heroine her interminable relation with her main mentor and master John. Which is to say, above all, that he prefigures the fusion of *The Wide, Wide World*'s religious and sexual dynamics, just as both are beginning to gather head. The operation is effected simply enough. The stranger's charms plead his cause; he pleads the Father's; his pleading the Father's cause is passed off as the greatest of his charms. Schematically, it is just what will transpire between Ellen and John, with a single difference immediately apparent but hard to pin down: let us call it the more thorough (de)sexualization of Ellen's encounter with the stranger. It is unimaginable that the prepubescent heroine should enter into an erotic relation with this model "gentleman," doubtless old enough to be her father.[13] Because it is unimaginable, it can happen before our very eyes: expertly, the strange gentleman seduces Ellen for Christ. Her passionate grief provides him his opening:

> At length, a gentleman . . . happened to look, as he passed, at [Ellen's] little pale face. . . . he stopped just in front of her, and bending down his face towards hers, said—"What is the matter with you, my little friend?" . . . There was no mistaking the look of kindness in the eyes that met hers, nor the gentleness and grave truthfulness of the whole countenance. It won her confidence immediately. All the floodgates of Ellen's heart were at once opened. She could not speak, but . . . burst into one of those uncontrollable agonies of weeping. . . . He gently . . . drew her to a retired part of the deck . . . then taking her in his arms he endeavored by many kind and soothing words to stay the torrent of her grief. (68–69)

This overture sounds the eternal themes of Warneresque romance. First, the child-woman, forlorn, vulnerable—a figure marking the perpetual possibility of her possession by another, a standing, or rather sitting, invitation to a seduction. Then, a strange gentleman. The word itself signals that Ellen's invitation is about to be taken up, for in Warner's lexicon "gentleman" automatically carries a sexual charge (the proof is that elsewhere it has to be carried off with modifiers like "odd" or "old"). Between the child-woman and the gentleman, a mating ritual that immediately finds its essential form, that of the *examination*. Examination in a double sense: inspection ("bending down his face towards hers"), but also interrogation ("What is the matter with you, my little friend?"). The ambiguity of the question bespeaks the ambiguity of the gaze that prefaces it. Solicitous/inquisitive/inquisitorial, the stranger will set things to rights (what is the matter with you, what is your trouble) by ferreting out what is wrong with Ellen (what is the matter with you, what is your fault). But, in *The Wide, Wide World*, these two tasks are one. Hence the *un*ambiguity of the gaze and the question that articulates it: as plainly as Saunders's vile eyes declare his evil intent, so there is "no mistaking" the "truthfulness" of the stranger's "whole countenance." The effect too is as unmistakable in the one case as in the other. Indeed, it is more or less the same. The examination overpowers and opens (here, "the floodgates of Ellen's heart"), leaving its subject in "uncontrollable agonies" before her examiner. With a look and a penetrating question, the stranger becomes a familiar.

He exploits this instant intimacy to reright Ellen according to Scripture:

"You love your mother better than you do the Saviour?"

"O yes, sir," said Ellen, "how can I help it?"

"Then if he had left you your mother, Ellen, you would never have cared or thought about him?"

Ellen was silent.

"Is it so? — would you, do you think?"

"I don't know, Sir," said Ellen, weeping again — "o, sir! how can I help it?"

"Then Ellen, can you not see the love of your heavenly Father in this trial? He saw that his little child was in danger of forgetting him, and he loved you, Ellen; and so he has taken your dear mother, and sent you away where you will have no one to look to but him: and now he says to you, 'My daughter, give *me* thy heart.' — Will you do it, Ellen?" (70)

"Will you do it, Ellen?"—there is the question *The Wide, Wide World* turns on. It is definitively answered only at the other end of the novel, when Ellen eagerly agrees to "do it" for her "brother" John. The strange familiar gentleman's preliminary plea names the major condition for John's eventual victory: the loving Father must "hinder" His daughter's "enjoyment" of her mother (70), must lure the sinfully passionate girl-child into the Paternal arms. The familial metaphor shades off into another; masterfully articulating the desire of the Father, the stranger slips naturally into the role of the father. The familiar tone of his discourse would by itself suggest the analogy, but the text tactfully insists on it, now calling the stranger Ellen's "grave protector," now arranging for him to call her "my child" after repeating that she is Christ's:

"And were there ever sweeter words of kindness than these? — 'Suffer the little children to come unto me, and forbid them not'. . . . Do you wish to be his child, Ellen?"

"O yes, sir — if I could."

"I know, my child, that sinful heart of yours is in the way." (73)

"I know, my child . . . ": leagued with One Who knows Ellen's inmost self even better than she does ("he is here, close to you, and knows every wish and throb of your heart"), her deputy father questions her not to procure information, but to procure Ellen—to confirm his natural right to plumb the depths of her soul. It is a penetration she ardently desires, or, rather, desires to desire. Only the flesh is weak (Ellen's, but perhaps also the stranger's):

"Shall I put you in mind, Ellen, of some things about Christ that ought to make you love him with all your heart?"

"O yes, sir! if you please." (71)

This commendable will to submission convinces the stranger that "his little friend" is not simply leading Christ on ("and he thought he saw that she was in earnest"). Heartened, he presses His suit with a hymn to Him:

"Open my heart, Lord, enter in;
Slay every foe, and conquer sin.
Here now to thee I all resign, —
My body, soul, and all are thine." (75)

The hymn brings the Father only partial success, since Ellen, though she "long[s] to," cannot quite assent to the last couplet: her "completely melted" heart still somehow resists the passage of the Word. But the "father" fares better: we are given an earnest of the eventual triumph of the Former in Ellen's unconditional surrender to the latter. Hardly has the familiar gentleman begun to examine her than he "takes her in his arms"; as he plies his probing questions, she perches on his knees; after some further evangelical exhortation, she sleeps with him: "She dropped her head against the arm of her friend and fell fast asleep. He smiled at first, but one look at the very pale little face changed the expression of his own. He gently put his arm round her and drew her head to a better resting-place than it had chosen." (77) The pair's physical and spiritual communion crests in a thrilling embrace:

"I must go," said Ellen, standing up and extending her hand; —
"Good-bye Sir."

She could hardly say it. He drew her towards him and kissed her cheek
once or twice: it was well he did; for it sent a thrill of pleasure to Ellen's
heart that she did not get over that evening, nor all the next day. (82)

In fact, Ellen never gets over that thrill of pleasure, the ambivalent
joy of yielding to the Lord and master who purges her of one
(un)natural passion by awakening another still more (un)natural.
The kiss is prologue; it gives her the taste of a consummation she
most devoutly wishes ("Shall I . . . ?" "O yes, sir! if you please") but is
as yet incapable of accomplishing ("O, if I could! — but I don't know
how"). Poor Ellen will never quite learn how: hence the abiding thrill
of that aporistic embrace, whose irresolvability it is the improper
business of the rest of *The Wide, Wide World* to draw out. But her
gentleman friends have already intimated what sort of drama is
coming: the odd old one obscurely, the strange familiar one oscularly. *The Wide, Wide World,* their foreplay foretells, will revolve
around com-muting her incestuous passion; and com-muting it will
be a matter of soliciting and refusing a daughterly kiss—forever and
ever.

Brothers and Sisters and Something Superadded

The air of romance that wafts enticingly through *The
Wide, Wide World's* hundred pages of prologue grows considerably
thicker in its central episodes, dominated by Warner's hero John.
We meet him toward the middle of the novel and instantly recognize
him for the savior Ellen has long sought unawares: the no longer
absent "only one in the world," the secular authority nonpareil, the
hyperpotent protector with a privileged relation to Omnipotence.
Mrs. Montgomery could wish her daughter no better (worldly)
friend. One could hardly blame her for wishing something more.

Or could one? John is, after all, Ellen's brother, or rather
"brother." The novel takes pains over this "fraternal" relationship. It
is established even before John makes his entrance, when his un-
sullied sister Alice adopts Ellen as her "sister." It is pointedly rees-
tablished when Ellen meets John:

"John," said Alice, "this is my little sister that I wrote you about —
Ellen Montgomery. Ellen, this is your brother as well as mine, you know."

"Stop! stop!" said her brother. "Miss Ellen, this sister of mine is giving us away to each other at a great rate, — I should like to know first what you say to it. Are you willing to take a strange brother upon her recommendation?"

Half inclined to laugh, Ellen glanced at the speaker's face, but meeting the grave though somewhat comical look of two very keen eyes, she looked down again, and merely answered "yes."

"Then if I am to be your brother you must give me a brother's right, you know," said he, drawing her gently to him, and kissing her gravely on the lips. (274)

From this moment forward we are relentlessly reminded of Ellen's and John's "consanguinity" ("I will not let you forget that I am your brother, Ellie," vows John on p. 348, proving in this, as in all else, as good as his word). The last reminder comes in the novel's penultimate paragraph, the one that—"for the gratification of those who are never satisfied"—coquettishly publishes our siblings' banns. Grown to womanhood, we gratifiedly read there, "Ellen did in no wise disappoint her brother's wishes" (569).

What it means to be John's sister we can deduce from his relationship with Alice. It is, to put it mildly, intense. Here is how she receives the budding divine when he comes home from divinity school at, significantly, Christmastime:

Alice started to her feet with a slight scream, and in another minute had thrown her arms round the stranger and was locked in his. Ellen knew what it meant now very well. She turned away as if she had nothing to do with what was going on there. . . . And then she stood with her back to the brother and sister, looking into the fire, as if she was determined not to see them till she couldn't help it. But what she was thinking of, Ellen could not have told, then or afterwards . . . [Alice's] usually calm, sweet face was quivering and sparkling now, — lit up as Ellen had never seen it, — oh, how bright! (273–74)

Brother and sister locked in one another's arms, with a supernumerary "sister" (not) looking on: this is *The Wide, Wide World*'s primal scene. If Ellen turns shamefacedly away from it, "as if she had nothing to do with what was going on there," it is because she really *is* locked out of the fraternal embrace: she can never ever become John's sister. The fact that she becomes his "sister" insists on the exclusion. It serves as a nagging reminder that *her* relation to John rests on an "as if" that makes it a simulacrum of the connatural bond between John and Alice, an imitation that must forever fall

short of the real thing. But the real thing is an imitation too: Alice
can quiver in John's arms to her heart's content, but that is all she
will ever get to do there. The potential for full and natural union
between brother and sister can only be realized via the *un*natural
union of "brother" and "sister." The novel's primal scene thus derives from a scene that derives from *it*: John and Alice's prefatory
embrace rehearses the future coupling of John and Ellen, which rehearses the impossible coupling of Alice and John. The Warneresque ménage à trois is a pair of counterfeit pairs in search of their
real—and impossible—original.

Relations in this unstable triad are derivative in another sense:
they reduplicate—with "something superadded"—the ménage à
trois that was the Montgomery household. This calls attention to itself above all through Alice:

> "Miss Alice," said Ellen after a long time — "I wish you would talk over
> a hymn with me."
> "How do you mean my dear?" said Alice rousing herself.
> "I mean, read it over and explain it. Mamma used to do it sometimes
> . . ."
> "I am afraid I shall be a poor substitute for your mother Ellen. What
> hymn shall we take?" (238)

The suggestion that Ellen's "sister" is substituting for her mother
encourages us to read her "brother" as her ersatz father. No doubt
innocently, Alice invites us to notice how Ellen's facsimile family repeats and completes its defective model. The contrast, no less than
the similarity, speaks for itself. The novel never tells whether Alice
outdid Mrs. Montgomery at talking over a hymn; it is too busy demonstrating how much more serviceable she can be when it comes to
taking over a him. Plainly, Ellen's second mother's advantage is her
John: first, because Ellen can share him; second, because he is worth
the sharing.

Ellen must feel the difference from the moment John takes his
sister in his arms. That initial eye-opening embrace between her future foster parents contrasts poignantly with the Captain's snoring
indifference to his sighing spouse, his "happy unconsciousness" of
her deepest conjugal needs: John plays out with Alice a domestic
scene Ellen missed at home. By identifying with her "sister" and second mother, then, Ellen can vicariously couple with a lovable version
of the Captain. Her (non)relation with her dormant father is retroactively made over into a kind of incest degree zero, an effect ampli-

fied by the symbolic damping of the distinctions between Ellen, Alice, and Mrs. Montgomery. The patrimatrimonial undertones swell to a crescendo with the emergence of a final parallel between Ellen's families old and new: both disintegrate. Having consoled her over the definitive departure of Mrs. Montgomery, Ellen's second mother follows her prototype to the grave.

Exiting, she bequeaths Ellen John ("dear Miss Alice said Miss Ellen was to take her place" [448]). But the continuing existence of the flesh-and-blood Captain threatens drastically to devalue the bequest. As long as her father is bifurcated into a repulsively real and a seductively symbolic variant, Ellen's relation to her spiritual "brother" must remain imperfectly patrimatrimonial. If God awards her only a "brother" in compensation for a dead mother—while leaving her saddled with a fatherly dud—He will hardly have "ma[d]e up to [her] more than all [she] has lost." (57) She must *lose* her father in order to gain him; nothing else can prevent the qualitative difference between the godly "brother" and the all-too-human father from rupturing the continuity of *The Wide, Wide World*'s male line. This, perhaps, is why Warner now reduces her defective father figure to the absolute zero he always potentially was. In the thick of the Alice-John drama, Ellen's surviving biological parent fades insubstantially away, disappearing, we are casually informed, at sea. Yet, though Warner remorselessly drowns father, she also tosses him a life preserver: he is sea-changed into something that can be superadded, as a kind of enriching paternal strain, to "brother." The defunct Captain thus raised to a pure paternal function, one masterfully assured by John, Ellen can regale the patrifratrimatrimonial desire she will never suspect she had: she can take her first rival's place in her rejuvenated father's arms by taking her second rival's place in her "brother's."

The Wide, Wide World hands her the victory without making the slightest allusion to the fray. Dying the ethereal death reserved for the saintliest scribbler virgins, Alice sweetly clears the field for John and his "sister" while the latter hovers decently in the background. This is Warner's second and final take of the primal scene:

> "Are you happy, Alice?" whispered her brother.
> "Perfectly. This [John's last-minute arrival on the scene] was all I wanted. Kiss me, dear John!"
> As he did so, again and again, she felt his tears on her cheek . . . kissed

him then, and then once again laid her head on his breast. They remained so a little while without stirring; except that some whispers were exchanged too low for others to hear, and once more she raised her face to kiss him. A few minutes after those who could look saw his color change, he felt the arms unclasp their hold; and, as he laid her gently back on the pillow they fell languidly down; the will and the power that had sustained them were gone. *Alice* was gone. (440–41)

Her going unites the symbolic siblings in an embrace that presages their coming union, while recalling that introductory clinch between John and his sister:

With an indescribable air of mingled tenderness, weariness, and sorrow, [Ellen] slowly rose from her seat and put both her arms round [John's] neck. Neither said a word; but to Ellen the arm that held her was more than all words; it was the dividing line between her and the world — on this side everything, on that nothing . . . he held her still, and looking for a moment at the tokens of watching and grief and care in her countenance, he gently kissed the pale little face, adding a word of endearment which almost broke Ellen's heart again. Then taking her hand they went down the mountain together. (443–44)

Patrifratrimatrimonially considered, Alice's conclusion is eminently logical. Her death eliminates the impossible possibility that she might couple with her brother; it also realizes it, and that twice over. First, Alice's unilateral *Liebestod* transports her to realms where nothing will ever again sunder her from John ("'we have,'" he once prophetically consoles her, "'an eternity to spend together!'" [406]). That she dies a *sister* but not a *wife* means, then, not only that she dies forever secured against the possibility of incest, but also that the possibility of incest is forever secured by her dying; no bothersome brother-in-law will be vying with brother for Alice's attentions in heaven. But this eternal suspension of the forbidden passion is attended by obvious impracticalities. Ellen's convoluted relations to her relations provide the down-to-earth alternative. Coupling with his "sister," John couples with his sister this side the grave; shielded by those invisible inverted commas, Ellen embraces the father she never really had. Alice's supreme sacrifice seals an unspoken covenant: it promises an authorized transgression of the interdict on whose inviolability *The Wide, Wide World* turns. The siblings' deathbed embrace is the dress rehearsal for the unplayable scene Mrs. Montgomery, the Captain, the strange gentleman, even Saunders have, each in his/her own way, taught Ellen—and us—(not) to look for.

The Sister's Seduction

John and Ellen having gone down the mountain together, one might expect that Warner would precipitously marry them off. Instead, one finds John protractedly chastening his charge. Since well before his sister's (un)timely demise, the young divine has been drilling her understudy; indefatigably, he keeps it up afterwards, fixing chastening as the sole mode of intercourse between "brother" and "sister." We must, then, renouncing romance, satisfy ourselves with pedagogy—and this to the very end of *The Wide, Wide World*.

There is an easy explanation for the exclusion of eros from Warner's tale. John's "sister" is scarcely thirteen when his sister breathes her last; to become a true woman, she needs more "time, 'that rider that breaks youth'" (11). In orthodox perspective, then, the second stage of our passionate pilgrim's progress simply gives her the time she needs. And, of course, the training. Mrs. Montgomery and Alice have schooled Ellen in the rudiments of Christian theology; John will now initiate her into its practical applications. But the continuity masks a quiet revolution. The infantile instinct binding Ellen to her mother(s) had to be unambiguously rechanneled toward the Better Friend. In contrast, the passion that makes John's "arm" mean more "than all words" will be dammed up without being diverted, quelled and yet retained in its original intensity. Prolonging Ellen's Christian education, her last mentor simultaneously reverses it: transferring her affections to the next world, he transfixes them to their (im)proper object in this one. There is no constraint like that of love; John Humphreys wields living proof of Heman Humphrey's dictum.

The constraint of love, as the strange familiar gentleman has shown, is imposed principally by the masterful gaze. John deploys his the moment he lays eyes on his "sister":

Meeting the grave though somewhat comical look of two very keen eyes, she looked down again, and merely answered "yes" . . . Ellen's eyes sought the stranger as if by fascination. At first she was in doubt what to think of him; she was quite sure from that one look into his eyes that he was a person to be feared; — there was no doubt of that; as to the rest she didn't know. (274–75)

About the potency that shoots from those fearsome orbs, Warner wants us to be quite as sure as Ellen. She therefore lets us eavesdrop on this exchange between a man who knows John and a woman who obviously doesn't:

"I do not know precisely," he went on to the lady he was walking with, "what it takes to rouse John Humphreys, but when he *is* roused he seems to me to have strength enough for twice his bone and muscle. I have seen him do curious things once or twice!"
"That quiet Mr. Humphreys?"
"Humph," said Mr. Howard,—"gunpowder is pretty quiet stuff so long as it keeps cool." (318)

Indubitably potent, then: Ellen did not miss her guess, the mastering gaze never lies. But potency has many faces; small wonder that Ellen, after facing Saunders, should be wary of the gunpowder in her He-man's glance. Her suspicions are, however, promptly allayed—or lulled—by a second overpowering look, "the look of love" John shoots at his (then still hale) sister Alice. Though aimed at his sister rather than his "sister," it wins the latter's undying regard at first sight: "from that minute Ellen's mind was made up as to the doubt which had troubled her" (279). She is never once tempted to change it.

John sees to that. Reassuringly, he presses his optical might into the service of the pedagogy of surveillance, lovingly devoting his super-vision to comprehensive supervision. It is comprehensive indeed. One can hardly exaggerate the divine's clairvoyance. There is no hiding from big brother: "Of one thing [Ellen] was perfectly sure, whatever [John] might be doing, — that he saw and heard her; and equally sure that if anything were not right she should sooner or later hear of it." (461) There is no hiding one's thoughts from him either:

Ellen blushed exceedingly. "I do believe, Mr. John," said she, stammering, "that you know everything I am thinking about." (317)

"Why," said Ellen, laughing and blushing, — "how *could* you guess what I was thinking about, Mr. John?" (321)

"[John] always knows what I am thinking of," [Ellen said], "just as well as if I told him." (414)

This preternatural prescience makes it unnecessary for John to pry. Like the strange familiar gentleman, he nevertheless pries with a vengeance. Though he has all the answers, John is forever questioning Ellen. His aim, like his predecessor's, is to make her see that she is *questionable*. He begins in earnest at a Christmas party at which Ellen, succumbing to a momentary temptation, cheats at a children's game. A public confession notwithstanding, she remains oppressed by the onus of her sin, and steals off to an empty room to grieve over it unassisted. But she is not alone. Hardly has she shut the door behind her than she senses a panoptical presence. It is John, who proceeds to conduct *The Wide, Wide World*'s first full-length examination:

> "Running away from your brother, Ellie!" said he kindly; "what is the matter?"
>
> Ellen shrank from meeting his eye and was silent. "I know all Ellie," said he, still very kindly, — "I have seen all; — why do you shun me?"
>
> Ellen said nothing; the big tears began to run down her face and frock. (295–96)

Eve would have recognized the scene. But it takes a turn that would have pleasantly surprised her. Quite unlike Jehovah, John queries his quarry solicitously, not punitively:

> "I want to talk to you a little about this," said he. . . . "Will you let me ask you a question or two?"
>
> "O yes. . . ." (296)

"O yes": having lovingly constrained that pledge of full cooperation, John sets out to extract the confession of unworthiness that is "all the answer he wishe[s]" (297). To expedite matters, he hands down this mild but damning verdict, unwittingly sustaining the strange familiar gentleman's: "'You will wonder at me perhaps, Ellie,' said John, 'but I am not very sorry this has happened. You are no worse than before; — it has only made you see what you are — very, very weak, — quite unable to keep yourself right without constant help.'" (296) And he goes on to pronounce this chastening sentence: "'Be humbled in the dust before him — the more the better; but whenever we are greatly concerned, for our own sakes, about other people's opinion, we may be sure we are thinking too little of God and what will please him.'" (297)

There is no need to spell out that what pleases God pleases John, that he has taught Ellen how to please him in teaching her how to please Him. She responds by signifying that she is eager to please, that is, to be humbled in the dust before her "brother": "'I am very sorry,' said poor Ellen, 'I am very wrong.'" According to the established pattern, she should now reap a token of the ultimate earthly reward for her self-abnegation: her master should afford her "the thrill of pleasure" that his acknowledgement of her tractability would bring. But here John breaks precedent, affording the miscreant no opportunity to embrace her one-man judge and jury. It falls to his sister to bring the scene to its climax: "As Alice came up with a quick step and knelt down before her, Ellen sprang to her neck, and they held each other very fast indeed. John walked up and down the room" (297).

The constraint of love, it appears, mandates the restraint of love. To say so is to only to repeat our frustrated question: why should *The Wide, Wide World*, instead of galloping toward its patrifratrimatrimonial climax, insist on incessantly chastening its nubile child-woman? But we are champing at the bit, proving only that we too deserve a "strong check" (416) of the sort John periodically administers his "sister." To be sure, what he *says* in defense of his permanent arraignment of Ellen is hardly enough to bridle our impatience. Where is the logic, he spurs us rather to ask, of humbling a little girl in the dust because she is "very, very weak"? John, however, sees more than he says. Indeed, he sees all. He does not need to read *The Wide, Wide World* to know that Ellen's weakness is yoked to "passions . . . by nature very strong." Nor does he need to say that the mightiest of those animal passions is a very, very strong weakness for her "brother." The novel's elementary structures say it for him, in accordance with a principle he helpfully explains: "When two things have been in the mind together, and made any impression, the mind *associates* them; and you cannot see or think of the one without bringing back the remembrance or the feeling of the other." (479)

We cannot, for example, see or think of Ellen's chastening without bringing back the remembrance of the family affair. That the two are so memorably *associated* is an accident of the child-woman's experience, an accident which yet constitutes the main axis of *The Wide, Wide World*: the examination illuminates, as Fichte might have put it, her family history's divine pedagogy, while her family history, in turn, illuminates the pedagogy of her divine. Against the backdrop of the family affair, the immoral impulse curbed in the examination emerges as the female animal's rampant con-genital passion. Taming her with question and gaze, John enacts Warner's rendition of the incest taboo; harrying instead of marrying her, he acts out the deferral of love that is the law of *The Wide, Wide World*. Not by accident is it his chastening rod that forestalls the unseemly hastening of our "siblings'" nuptials. Sisterly deference to the rod and the deferral of fratrimatrimony are different versions of the same chastening thing.

Yet woman is not chastened by discipline alone. Only love can constrain her to defer to the rod that restrains her. John has firmly grasped this (Heman) Humphreyesque truth: *his* rod is a "happy mixture of pointedness and kindness" (415). Hardly has he begun to wield it than it "has wound round Ellen's heart, and constrained her to answer immediately" (477) all the humbling questions he puts to her. Indeed, her "brother's" loving strictures—unlike, say, her "sister's"—carry the irresistible authority of *natural law*: "what [Alice] asked of her Ellen indeed *tried* to do; what John told her *was done*" (351). The heart that, "hardened by sin," has rebuffed her heavenly Father joyfully embraces the living Word as proffered by John. Only under *his* rod does she come to cry "'O how love I thy law,'" does she learn to love with her whole sin-hardened heart the power that denies her her heart's desire:[14] "Of one thing [Ellen] was perfectly sure, whatever [John] might be doing, — that he saw and heard her; and equally sure that if anything were not right she should sooner or later hear of it. But this was a censorship Ellen rather loved than feared." (461)

What makes her love it so? It is that John does ocularly what the strange familiar gentleman did oscularly: he thrillingly indulges the lawless impulse he checks. The Law-Man's all-seeing gaze is double-barreled. To penalize Ellen, John looks her down, as here: "'Why?' said Ellen, the crimson of her cheeks mounting to her forehead. But her eye sunk immediately at the answering glance of [John's]." (415) This "reproof," we are told, "went to the quick." But not cuttingly: though it makes Ellen cry for an hour, she "join[s] with it no thought of harshness or severity." For John commutes every sentence he executes in the very act of executing it; looking Ellen down, he also looks lovingly *into* her. The gaze that enforces the law effects a coupling outside the law: the penetration the child-woman provokes by being bad is the optical version of incest. Forever stemming his patient's passion, Ellen's spiritual physician is also forever pandering to it; the pedagogy of surveillance *is* the family affair. What has been said about Ellen's brewing her mother's tea therefore applies nicely to John's sensual censorship too: "this ritual does not merely promise fulfillment; it offers consummation in the present moment."[15]

But, if the punishment of Ellen's desire doubles as its accomplishment, John risks being hoist by his own petard. One need only invoke his *associative* law to implicate him in incest: as one who "always knows" what is in Ellen's mind, is the Law-Man not guilty of countenancing—more, of instigating—the female lawlessness he so emphatically interdicts? Without, of course, acknowledging the accusation, Warner does her best to rule it out of court. John, she shows us, censures Ellen only because Ellen wants him (to); moreover, the passion that makes Ellen want him (to) is precisely what he censures. But such evidence damns the divine quite as definitively as it exonerates him. The ocular firepower that "completely subdues" the little girl's frailty (415), the penetrating interrogatories she "never [thinks] of trying to evade" (469), the "higher style of authority" that "reach[es] where [others] could never attain" (538)—are these so many manifestations of the constraint of love, or so many proofs of an act of prior restraint? Reaching Ellen's unattainable place, does John's irresistible authority—by virtue of its very irresistibility—not constrain his "sister's" love in the most forceful sense of the word? And how, indeed, must we judge the divine Word, if incest meets with the secret sanction of the divine who meets it with such stringent sanctions?

There is a line of questioning that threatens to turn the wide world upside down. But the higher authorities have no easy way of quashing it. The sensual/censorious question is too valuable a disciplinary tool to be scrapped for the sake of sheltering the Law-Man from evil imputation; the Warneresque Grand Inquisitor can no more relinquish the prerogative of the interrogative than he can admit that his pedagogy amounts to child molestation. As if in response to this fundamental dilemma, the novel compulsively rehearses its traumatic beginnings; it sends Ellen out on a second solitary sally into the wide, wide world. There, in a stormy replay of the Saunders scene, Warner not only reopens the question of Ellen's questionability; she also reads it back into the very origins of *The Wide, Wide World*. It is the Law-Man's main chance to abrogate his own *associative* law. He turns it to violent advantage.

Chiding, Chastening, Chastising

We now know how much is riding on John's repression of his sinfully passionate "sister": he staves off nothing less than incestuous apocalypse by staving Ellen off. But it hardly seems that he needs the rod to do it. In a pedagogical program founded on the constraint of love, muscular chastening ought to yield to a gentle motherly chiding, the human powder keg to that "image of maternal authority" bestsellerdom's more sanguine critics discern in the scribblers. Why, then, does John's distinctly paternal-fraternal "bone and muscle" (318) remain so salient a feature of Warner's anatomy of power? *Why doesn't the chastening rod wither away?*

The answer is that only heroic prowess can keep girlish weakness from becoming woman's—and the wide world's—ruin. *The Wide, Wide World* rams that lesson home in an episode in which potency bares its other face: violence. Potent violence finds its pendant in something that, one might think, should have perished with the Puritans: breathless child-womanly terror.

Two men in *The Wide, Wide World* inspire that chastening emotion: Saunders, the villain, but also John, the hero. Saunders's beastly behavior in the dry goods store indicates well enough what makes *him* so frightful. Thus, though one may be shocked, one can hardly be surprised when, (un)expectedly resurfacing years after his inaugural humiliation, the rebarbative shopman waylays Ellen and falls to molesting her pony: "His best way of distressing Ellen, he found, was through her horse; he had almost satisfied himself [by whipping it a little]: but very naturally his feeling of spite had grown stronger and blunter with indulgence, and he meant to wind up with such a treatment of her pony, real or seeming, as he knew would give great pain to the pony's mistress." (400)

If Saunders's villainy comes as no surprise, neither does the fate he is meted out: one knows, after all, about the gunpowder in John's soul. Now the militant Christian explodes into action. Riding up out of nowhere, he catches the recreant flagrante delicto, demands that he unhand Ellen's mount, and, when the impassioned blackguard offers to resist by brandishing the "club end" of his "sapling whip," collars and sends him sailing "quite over into the gulley at the side of the road" (401). With this the snake is foiled for good. But it takes his retraumatized victim an age to recover her aplomb:

> She had no words, but as [John] gently took one of her hands, the convulsive squeeze it gave him shewed the state of nervous excitement she was in. It was very long before his utmost efforts could soothe her, or she could command herself enough to tell him her story. When at last told, it was with many tears. "Oh how could he! how could he!" said poor Ellen; — "how could he do so! — it was very hard!" (401)

It is a time-honored tableau: the villain quavering at his rival's feet, the virgin quivering in her savior's arms. One might regard it as sufficient justification of the hero's muscle: Saunders's recrudescence, in that perspective, would be potency's best defense. It is an eminently proper reading: heroic violence vanquishes villainous vileness, preserving the virgin from violation.

But John's law of *association* authorizes less conventional arrangements of the figures in this group portrait. One can, for example, associate the antagonists with a view to highlighting the *resemblance* between them. Saunders's eyes, in particular, look like John's: the second Saunders scene, glancing back at the first across the grueling interval of the examination, insists on the affinity between the master's gaze and the monster's glare. The common feature that puts them "in the mind together" is the confounding "impression" both leave on Ellen: fear dwells in her response to being pedagogically eyeballed by John (she "shrank from meeting his eye"; "her eyes sunk immediately at the answering glance of John's") as to being sadistically sized up by Saunders ("the most disagreeable pair of eyes she had ever beheld . . . she could not bear to meet them, and cast down her own"). We have seen enough of John's pedagogy to appreciate the associative logic of Ellen's anxieties. What the vicious clerk tries to do to her on the road, the virtuous clergyman does to her at home: John too penetrates her, punishes her, works his will on her weakness. Indeed—a circumstance his detractors have eagerly seized on—John has even anticipated Saunders by "chastising" (376) a defenseless horse.[16] Warding off the rapacious shopman, in a by now standard view, Ellen's protector shields her from a version of himself; the energy informing both the hero's heroism and the villain's villainy appears to alternate between saving the heroine and savaging her. The reason benevolent male violence crushes malevolence, it would seem to follow, is to maintain a precarious distinction between itself and its dark double.

Warner would not have endorsed the suggestion. Yet it is not, in our sense, an improper one. Standing helplessly to one side while the mighty vie to work their will on her, shrinking back from the vi(ri)le eyeballing minister and monster both treat her to, Ellen quails conventionally before a conventionally generalized male lust. Secret sharer in Saunders's crime, John helps set off the child-woman's lustrous purity by making part of its naturally lascivious male foil.

But the luster is deceptive: Ellen embodies a purity that is also the sheerest duplicity. Innocent, she is also guilty as sin. We will, then, reshuffle our trio once more, putting Ellen in the mind together with Saunders in token of her unlawful association with her fellow sinner. She herself confesses her collusion in the crime attempted against her. As her savior prepares to hurl Saunders into the pit, his gathering wrath puts the fear of the Lord into *her*. Breathlessly, she betrays her identification with the reprobate:

> "We will dispense with your further attendance," said John coolly. "Do you hear me? — Do as I order you!"
> The speaker did not put himself in a passion, and Mr. Saunders, accustomed for his own part to make bluster serve instead of prowess, despised a command so calmly given. — Ellen, who knew the voice, and still better could read the eye, drew conclusions very different. She was almost breathless with terror. (400)

The point of John's deterrent strike is plainly not lost on Ellen. Her breathless terror testifies to her intuition that the chastising of churls carries out the chastening of little girls by other means. Doubtless, her spontaneous sympathy with her mortal foe is only a kind of prim-Eval tic; but the reflex reflects, precisely, an ancient affinity. It is rooted in natural rebelliousness against the Law-Man. Victim and victimizer are associated in their (un)natural desire to break the law: Ellen, by violating the incest taboo; Saunders, by violating Ellen. But it is a condition of *The Wide, Wide World* that Ellen's desire never surface. Her fellow feeling for the outlaw she abhors must therefore be met with *prophylactic* terror, token of an anti-incestuous violence that, given her manifest innocence, is always in excess. Saunders is there to absorb the excess. That is what makes him crucial and negligible at once: theme of a trifling ten pages out of some six hundred, and an ubiquitous, eternal presence in the wide, wide world. The nugatory shopman represents a menace of the first order because he threatens to breach the social citadel at its most vulnerable point—or, rather, to slink in where it is always already breached: at the portal of female sexuality. Ellen is why Saunders must be so terrifyingly chastised.

But if Ellen is a version of Saunders who is a version of John, then John too stands convicted of clamoring at the incestuous gates; the second Saunders incident would only seem to confirm the suspicions we have already laid at the Law-Man's door. Yet there is less John to Saunders than meets the eye. This "brother" (as Saunders dares suggest: "'Not for you, brother,' said Mr. Saunders sneeringly; 'I'll walk with any lady I've a mind to.'" [400]) of Ellen's "brother" can offer her no more than a mock chastening and a travesty of fratrimatrimony; exposed, he turns out to be almost comically short on "prowess." Indeed, the pitiful contrast with John's storied potence all but reduces the masquerader to a version of the con-genitally defective child-woman. It thereby points to the factor distinguishing his bogus prowess from the real thing: namely, his acceptance of the invitation his "brother's" "sister" embodies. The essential difference between John and his fellow horse-beater is that the one curbs, while the other whips up, woman's animal passion. Saunders is the unmale malefactor the Law-Man would become if he yielded to the blandishments his "sister's" weakness proffers. It follows that, in snapping the blusterer's "sapling whip" in two, Ellen's savior scores a double victory: casting out woman's old enemy, he routs the prim-Eval sin whose notorious consequence is the fall of man. Protecting the vulnerable virgin from the villain's seeming strength, he protects *himself*—and the wide world—from the child-woman's lethal weakness.

That her weakness is not defenseless innocence but defenseless guilt we have all the evidence of the family affair to show. But, as if to prevent Saunders's more spectacular delinquency from putting that evidence out of mind, the second Saunders incident is prefaced by a supplementary reminder of Ellen's moral frailty. It comes in the person of her naughty playmate Nancy Vawse. Jane Tompkins has recently heaped praise on Nancy's impoverished, widowed grandmother, celebrating her husbandless self-sufficiency as a worldly emblem of scribbler "Heaven"; she commends the sprightly separatist for achieving fulfillment "without the dependency of childhood, or of most Victorian women."[17] But there is trouble in this paradise; what may be Heaven for the post-menopausal widow is Hell for the prenubile Nancy, an orphan the unendowed dowager has to raise without a John. One can imagine what must become of the unchastened creature. Warner, however, spares one the effort. Whenever Ellen goes out to play with her father- and brotherless alter ego, she comes home sopping, sobbing, and/or soiled. In time, the good girl learns to avoid such contamination; the bad one continues to besmirch herself. Ellen moves Heaven and earth to persuade Nancy to read the Bible and reform, but Ellen is not a John any more than Mrs. Vawse is. Hence one is anything but certain that her blackest visions do not materialize after Nancy permanently and ominously vanishes: "'But Nancy—before you begin to read the Bible you may have to go where you never can read it, nor be happy nor good neither.'" (334)

That unnamed tomb of all feminine hope, Ellen innocently reminds us, is where all girlish waywardness tends. Bound, one fears, for Hell via the whorehouse, naughty Nancy stands as a warning of the mor(t)al risks of autonomous female development. The warning is intended, not least, for the one who issues it. That it unfolds in counterpoint with the drama of John, Ellen, and Alice encourages us to elaborate on Nancy's bad example: the vector that extends from Nancy's actual insubordination toward some unnamed horror has an invisible extension that connects Ellen's potential insurgency to the nameless horror of incest. But for the severe, severing grace of God and John, Ellen would be mired in a morass even fouler than the one her playmate must disappear in.[18]

The events that blaze the way for Saunders's assault prove it. Ellen exposes herself to him while trying to help Mr. Van Brunt, her aunt's benevolent but benighted farmhand. She does to Van Brunt what John does to her, and more or less simultaneously: she chastens him until he takes Christ into his heart. This is at once eminently desirable, and problematic in the extreme. On the one hand, God's moral agent-in-training is duty-bound to evangelize, and, concomitantly, to chasten. On the other hand, whenever she does, there arises the intrinsically perverse possibility of the rod's passing to the distaff side. Sexual order can, therefore, only be maintained (as will appear more fully in the next chapter) if the chastened male, or a proxy, simultaneously chastens his chastener. But Van Brunt, however truehearted, remains a blunt and brutish hired hand; he is in no position to apply the rod to so delicate a creature as Ellen, or to

be represented in that disciplinary capacity by so refined a personage as John. Indeed, he is in no position to apply the rod at all.
On the day Saunders is resurrected, he indicates as much by breaking his leg—by "us[ing] himself up," as Nancy characteristically puts
it, bawdily insisting on his incapacitation.[19]

Van Brunt's fracture is in keeping with his humble social status;
that Ellen should take one "sickened" (386) look at his leg, and then
boldly ride off for help, is therefore no more unseemly than the fact
that she makes him "fit to go to heaven" (389).[20] But this is, for the
reasons just noted, vaguely unseemly. To be sure, the indiscretion
involved is trifling. But it is not therefore inconsequential; for, as
John observes, Hamlet-like, right after vanquishing Saunders: "'Little things often draw after them long trains of circumstances . . . and
that shows the folly of those people who think that God does not
stoop to concern himself about trifles.'" (401)

The trifle in question, Ellen's temerarious assumption of the rod,
takes *its* weighty significance from the long train of circumstances
that precede it. *Their* significance has been spelled out by Saunders's
assorted "brothers." When Ellen's shipboard savior asked his little
friend, "what is the matter with you," he posed, we recall, two questions at once: "how have you been wronged," but also "what is wrong
with you." John's Christmas party verdict sustained the negative
note: this "has only made you see what you are — very, very weak—
quite unable to keep yourself right without constant help." The sentence John pronounces after extracting Ellen from Saunders's
clutches is only superficially different: "But Ellen, you must ride no
more alone." (401) In fact, *she must ride no more alone because she is
quite unable to keep herself right.* Without the help of him without
whom she can do nothing, even her efforts to save a Van Brunt can
drive her straight into the skulking Saunders's arms—or, what is the
same thing but worse, prematurely into his "brother's."

In the end, then, Saunders is Ellen's fault: she is weak because she
is very, very weak. As her powerful weakness solicits her "brother's"
sensual censorship, so too does it secretly long for her "brother's"
"brother" to flagellate her mount. No wonder Ellen is "wrought up
to a terrible pitch of excitement and fear" as Saunders's ersatz whip
flicks over her filly (398). If the fear does not blind us to the excitement, we will find it no more surprising that, as her tormentor
"fashion[s] a very good imitation of an ox-whip" out of his sapling,
Ellen watches "in an ecstasy of apprehension" (397). Always already
relinquished by Van Brunt, the chastening rod has momentarily

slipped from the Law-Man's grip, passing into the hands of his lawless twin. Ellen's terrified delight springs from her intuition that the usurpation portends a violation of the sexual order. That it also portends a violation of *her*, one she craves as much as she dreads, is the logic of sensual censorship and the indelible mark of John's and Saunders's fraternity: with the one horse-beater as with the other, Ellen craves the censorship for the sake of the fratrimatrimonial sensuousness. Shadowing the image of the virgin writhing in the embrace of a fiend is another, more blurred but more basic, that portrays her as her vicious tormentor's ecstatically Vawsian victim.

She was similarly victimized the day of her maiden venture into the wide world. In retrospect, one may perhaps be pardoned for wondering if a little secret doubtfulness does not also attend her role in that introductory engagement with male malevolence. She is, we recall, "confused, and almost confounded" even before approaching the shopman: might this be our initial clue that she cannot keep herself right without constant help? Effortlessly, Saunders works her up to a terrible pitch of excitement and fear: is this complex emotion a precocious, negative manifestation of that trembly girlish instinct that seeks some object it knows not what? If so, the foreboding Ellen feels the first time she sallies forth without him without whom she can do nothing ought not to be pooh-poohed: "But at the very bottom of Ellen's heart there was a little secret doubtfulness respecting her undertaking." (44) Magnified, that trifling doubt suggests that the passionate prepubescent who stands with face on fire under Saunders's mortifying glare is the same doubtful creature who blushes crimson at a chastening frown of John's, the same creature who thrills as the familiar gentleman bares her weakness or burns with ecstatic apprehension as Saunders makes ready to flog her filly. In short, the pattern of Ellen's responses to the vi(ri)le is retroactively invested with its (im)moral meaning by her post-preadolescent encounter with John's bastard "brother." If Saunders is Ellen's fault in the end, he is—so the highly improper verdict—her fault in the beginning too.

The point of blaming the victim is, of course, to exculpate the victimizer(s): if Saunders is Ellen's fault, then her passion cannot be John's. The second Saunders scene thus provides a recapitulative reading of the family affair: it reads the suspicions generated by the examination out of textual court. But those suspicions, we have been saying, color the second Saunders scene itself. John eliminates them with coldblooded violence. Without "put[ting] himself in a passion," he sunders Saunders from Ellen. He sunders himself, that is, both from the naturally (com)passionate child-woman and her impassioned companion in sin. Dispassionately chastising the malevolence that would prey on Ellen's con-genital weakness, he retroactively secures his license to chasten his future bride: the impassive, *chastising* rod proclaims that the *chastening* rod was always unincestuous. The gunpowder in John's soul explodes the blasphemous notion that his "sister's" incestuous self is made in his godly image.

But does Ellen accept her spiritual physician's interpretation? Does she now appreciate the enormity of riding alone, and has she been suitably chastened by the chastising of Saunders? For once, John seems uncertain. He therefore falls back on the admonitory technique that made up the major part of Ellen's Christmas party punishment: he restates his text in *negative oscular terms*. Already, in the person of his unholy "brother," Ellen has been offered the fraternal kiss whose suspended possibility has long held her in an ecstasy of apprehension. That offer was violently revoked, only to be replaced by another not so different; John's victory once in hand, it is his own "brotherly" kiss that comes within Ellen's purview. But he seems not to want to bestow it. Waiting for her reward, the heroine is, for a memorable moment, made to stand with "swimming eyes and a trembling lip . . . Mr. John had forgotten the kiss he always gave her on going or coming." We know why it is so important: "Ellen was jealous of it as a pledge of sistership." And we can guess why John has "forgotten" it: withholding his affection, he gives his "sister" time to remember how close she has come to putting her precious "sistership" at risk. In that chastening interval, the chastisement visited upon Saunders humbles the only miscreant who matters in the dust. Having duly deposited her there, John can bring the episode to its real climax: chastened, expectant, Ellen garners the fraternal kiss "the want of which she had been lamenting" (402–3). She had been lamenting the want of it since the Captain. Now that she has secured it, one can be fairly certain she will ride no more alone.

The Defiles of the Defiling Signifier: the Incestuous Union of Nature and the Word

Writing alone was like riding alone. Warner religiously avoided it: she wrote with God. Indeed, she went so far as to suggest that He, not she, had composed *The Wide, Wide World*. "Thank him for it," she wrote her admirer Dorothea Dix, "I wash my hands of all desert in the matter." Such (un)pretentiousness characterizes scribblerdom from top to bottom.[21] As the domestic heroines efface themselves before their Johns, so their authors efface themselves before their Author. Nor is the gesture confined to the margins of their work; it is enacted *in* their fiction, *as* their fiction. Scribbler novels are self-effacing artifacts: .recounting their heroines' self-effacement, they simultaneously recount their own. Thus the story of the righting of Ellen doubles as one about the righting of writing. But Ellen's education involves more than righting alone. It is also, and not fortuitously, a matter of riding. The critics are quite right to insist on Ellen's spontaneous identification with John's chastened horse: her horse-beater of a "brother" gives her too "a regular [riding] lesson" (341) in more than one sense of the word. To put it bluntly, he rides her—or, more precisely, rides the female animal *in* her. That she "rather love[s]" it links riding, via righting, to (re)writing: Ellen's craving for a riding master all but spells out her author's for a writing master. As the one child-woman loves being overridden by her sensually censorious "brother," so the other longs to be written over by her celestial Father. Warner's magisterial pun, then, conjugates more than the taming of equine and child-womanly passion; it whispers that textual desire too can only be satiated under "religion's happy reign" (553).

Let none accuse our author of verbal excess. However powerful her passion for words, Warner's overriding impulse was to surrender her will to the Word's.[22] She had been trained to it by a long tradition, that of the *typos* or *figura*. Typology, it will be recalled, "establishes a connection between two events or persons in such a way that the first signifies not only itself but also the second, while the second involves or fulfills the first."[23] Invented mainly to facilitate rewriting the Old Testament in the light of the New, the hermeneutics of the *figura* also served, from the Church Fathers to Dante, as a tool for assimilating *post*-Biblical events to the Master Writing of Scripture: "what Dante does, in his journey, Christ *has* done. Dante's descent into Hell, and his release from it, is a typological repetition, a 'subfulfillment' of Christ's."[24] The Puritan divines in whose writings Warner was steeped exploited the *figura*'s "post-Scriptural" potential to the full, above all to write their own history as a "subfulfillment" of the Word. From here it was a short step to finding typological correspondences in natural history too. In a "world slickt up in types" (Edward Taylor), God's cross-references graced every page of the book of His creation.

The Wide, Wide World is slickt up in stereotypes. Here is Warner's *typos*, the mark of her covenant to write, like Dante, "in imitation of God's way of writing."[25] Lest we miss its significance, exemplary characters regularly affirm the wide world's stereotypicality, chiefly by assimilating Ellen's history to the canonical texts it "subfulfills." Showing her that her experience has already been had, they show *us* the aesthetic function of the ugly fault that sets its immutable course: Ellen, they make one see, is a throwback to our first Mother. Taking her Scripturally pre-scripted place in the story of sin prim-Eval, she enters her author's claim to have written a *fiction non-novel*.

It is a problematic claim. Even as he validated it, John Hart pinpointed the problem. *The Wide, Wide World*, he exclaimed in his *Female Prose Writers*, was "one of the most original and beautiful works of fiction of which American literature can boast . . . the only professed novel in which real religion, at least as understood by evangelical Christians, is exhibited with truth."[26] An original fiction that faithfully recites the eternal verities: the formula goes straight to the paradoxical heart of Warner's aesthetic. If the archetypicality of her pilgrim's progress implies the timeless validity of Holy Writ, the mere existence of a *Wide, Wide World* implies that Holy Writ has to be wholly rewritten. "One book like it is not written in an age," declaimed *The New York Times*;[27] this was, whatever the reviewer's intentions, equivocal praise. Had Warner authentically imitated God's way of writing? Or had she impiously foisted off an original as a copy?

Her misgivings over what she (or God) had wrought crystalized as a problem of genre: the novel Hart called a "professed novel" did not in fact profess to be a novel. Like all Warner's novels, it professed to be a "story." Caroline Kirkland might contrast *The Wide, Wide World*'s "respectability" with the degeneracy of earlier novels;[28] Warner knew, like generations of Calvinists before her, that her genre was innately depraved.[29] Small wonder that her sister Anna turned a look of "troubled surprise" on a friend indiscreet enough to call Susan's "novels" by their proper name.[30] But we can cite higher authority than Susan's sister's. At the end of *The Wide, Wide World*, Ellen's "brother" secures her promise to "read no novels" (564). He does not trouble to name his reason.

He does not have to: the reason lies in the name. The novel's *novelty*, precisely, challenges "real religion's" timelessness. Yet the "post-Scriptural" extension of typology implies a capacity to engage novelty that is fully exploited only *by* the novel. The problem was that, by Warner's day, the novel was threatening to put the typological cart before the spiritual horse. Once one pole of the *figura* was planted outside Scripture, in human or natural history, the Biblical letter itself sank inexorably toward the level of the postscriptural. A "world slickt up in types" authorized a "potential symbolization of all natural phenomena" that must ultimately put spiritualized nature on the same footing as the Scripture it verified.[31] The implications, celebrated by Emerson, tormented his sometime student Beulah Benton, a fictional scribbler fashioned in the image of the real ones: "She was perplexed to draw the exact line of demarcation between myths and realities; then followed doubts as to the necessity, and finally, as to the probability and possibility of an external, verbal revelation."[32]

Warner sought to sidestep such pitfalls by carrying the effacement of the scribbler signifier to the limit, by practicing a textual self-abnegation without reserve. Since novel writing, by its nature, blurs the "line of demarcation" between Scripture and scribbling,[33] the *figuras* of the (non)novel must be relentlessly denatured; to present the wide world *sub specie aeternitatis,* and no mistake, the stereotypical had to perform *on its own substance* the act of converting ephemeral nature into enduring spirit. Only by that sacrifice of its own natural part could the scribbler text approach the pure immanence of (if one may be forgiven the pun) a Divine Enunciation. But, as a fiction purged of the dross of its natural signifiers is no fiction at all, this amounts to saying that Divine Enunciation portends obliteration of *The Wide, Wide World.* John says no less. "'I know,'" he tells Ellen, "'that a day is to come when those heavens shall be wrapped up together as a scroll—they shall vanish away like smoke, and the earth shall wax old like a garment; — and it and all the works that are therein shall be burned up.'" (312)

This is, as it were, a self-effacing prophecy. For the John citing John citing Jesus citing His Father[34] is not exactly quoting; *he is the quotation.* "Typologically repeating" the John whose revelations he reveals to Ellen, the divine proclaims the nullity of the (non)novel writing that (re)produces him; recalling the impending annihilation of the wide world and its works, he symbolically undoes the (non)work which is *The Wide, Wide World.* Through her *typos's* representative and redeeming self-sacrifice, Warner offers to absolve herself of the sin of originality.

Yet John *Humphreys* remains his author's creature, *The Wide, Wide World* her creation; the day when they shall vanish away like smoke is not yet. If Warner is to avoid even provisionally impersonating her Creator, the relationship between the author and her creation must be inverted: her creature has somehow to make her *his*. *John* must stand godfather to Warner's (re)production of the Word, and hence, not least, of John. He does so by preserving what he prophetically destroys; he redeems the very nature Divine Enunciation spirits away.

That he can is owing to his status as a doubly privileged *figura*. For John recalls not only the John who comes after Jesus (the John of Revelation, traditionally identified with the John who became a second son to Jesus' mother), but also the John who goes before Him; he thus (ex post facto) prefigures Christ. Especially for Ellen: his are "the hands," Warner says, "of all the most successful" in tending the divine "seed" implanted in her (569). They assume their sacerdotal task, as we have noted, at Christmas, seizing the reins of a plot against Ellen's passion until then conducted by . . . whom? By (representative of all the others) Ellen's stern (aunt) Fortune; by "time, 'that rider that breaks youth'"; by the Writer who pens "the great book of [Ellen's] fate."[35] Nominally, that book is Warner's; by rights, it is the Divine Author's. But not even He writes alone. His text is time's and Fortune's: it is collectively written by all those whose youth-breaking power is summed up and surpassed in John—the rider who rights Ellen's original fault, and thus the writer who (re)writes the great book of her fate. In a word, coming into *The Wide, Wide World* to go about his Father's business, John also takes over his author's. Relieved, under the new dispensation, of the "anxiety of authorship,"[36] Warner authorizes herself to create *The Wide, Wide World* by *de-authorizing* herself. *John* writes in imitation of God's way of writing; his putative author trails after time's rider.

Ellen is what John writes on. He reworks her nature as he reworks his horse's; with a "judicious use of the whip and spur" (377), he forms her into the *typos* she was born to become. Chastening is thus erected into a *figura* of figuration. This is what makes Ellen, in her turn, a privileged *figura*. A type in the making, *she types the (non)novel*— and hence the wide world as well as *The Wide, Wide World*.

Yet the world Ellen types is more than an inert vessel for the Word. The child-woman does not passively reflect the Father; she actively reproduces him. "'There is a friend,'" quotes Alice, after exhorting Ellen to bear with her (aunt) Fortune "manfully," "'that sticketh closer than a brother.'" This delicate allusion (whose immediate source is Widow Vawse, p. 189) to our *imitatio Christi's* limits also stakes out those of the fiction he figures in: it says that scribbling is to Scripture as John's rod is to the Lord's scepter. But has Ellen truly grasped the imitation's limitations? Her response to her "sister" suggests quite the opposite. "'How soon,'" anxiously inquires the heroine, "'is Mr. John going away?'" (321).[37] To be sure, a glimpse into the little lady's fantasy life partially dispels the impression this creates:

> "What was your little head busied upon a while ago?" [John asked Ellen] . . . "Well?"—
> "I was thinking—do you want me to tell you? . . . I was thinking about Jesus Christ," said Ellen in a low tone. (407)

Alongside this soulful confession, however, honesty compels us to range another. It is wrested from Ellen by Mr. Lindsay, a natural relation who, since he himself aspires to become Ellen's father, equally disapproves her devotion to God and to John:[38]

> "What was the matter with you this afternoon?" . . .
> "Must I tell you all, sir? . . . I wish you wouldn't ask me further; please do not!—I shall displease you again."
> "I will not be displeased."
> "I was thinking of Mr. Humphreys," said Ellen in a low tone. (534)

Is the pattern of Ellen's low-toned musings symptomatic? Does she take all too literally Alice's advice to parry Fortune's blows "manfully"? If she "'do[es] sometimes seek [the Divinity's] face very much when [she] cannot find it'" (471), is it because her divine's keeps getting in the way? Doubtless. But to claim that, for Ellen, it is *John* who sticketh closer than a brother would be to claim both too little and too much. It is Jesus Christ, *and* Ellen's "brother."

That is, the child-woman (to spill a secret evident since John began to keep her right at the Christmas party) yokes the Divinity and her divine in a natural *figura* of godhead; she "beholds [God] with reverent desire in the mirrors that reveal him."[39] Thus, even while being written on, Ellen sustains the rider who (re)rights her; (mis)conceiving Jesus as her John, she brings God into the world. (Child-womanly) nature forges the instrument of its chastening: Ellen *makes* her chastener into time's rider. Associating her hero and her Author by prostrating herself before both, she associates herself with her author in (re)creating her Creator.

One might take John's law of *association* as the law of this association. That, however, would be to place *The Wide, Wide World* under the sign of the contingent, and thus the novel. Not accidentally, Warner launches her version of gospel by evoking the perversions this can breed. Had Ellen's mother had better doctors, might her depraved daughter not have forged godhead into an image of maternal authority? But what would become of the (stereo)typological if one's mother came to type the Father? What, on the other hand, ensures that she will not, in the realm of the novel writing that naturally deviates from Holy Writ?

Child-womanly nature does. By the miracle of com-mutation, Ellen is *instinctively* constrained to associate God with familial gentlemen. For her, the Father is, precisely, a father, and His beloved Son a "brother"; she embraces the saving Word because she adores the family member it is figured by. Her girlish weakness motivates the apparently arbitrary bond between the transcendental Signified and its worldly signifier. "'There is something wrong then with you, Ellie,'" says John, when she confesses a chronic inability to find God's face (471). Need we add that, if there were not, her "brother" could never become time's rider? That it is because the child-woman wants him to right her that she embraces the Master Writing of Scripture? That, consequently, her weakness underwrites both religion's happy reign *and* the reigning scribbler aesthetic?

And yet there *is* something wrong with Ellen. She rewrites the supernatural as the familiar/familial because hers are the narrow limits of the wide, wide world; so rewriting it, she inevitably *wrongs* it. Not that she thereby *misrepresents* the otherworldly: the family, Warner knows better than Hegel, "represents and typifies in a figure the life of spirit." But if this familiar figure is not a defective representation, it nevertheless has the defect of being a *representation*: between it and the pure immanence of godhead stands the barrier of "natural relation."[40] The demerit of the child-woman as of the *figura* is to erect that barrier.

Is it Ellen's glory, or her shame, that she can bring down what she erects? Everything rides on the answer—one's assessment, not only of the child-woman, but of the (non)novel too. For the latter, as everybody knows, is preeminently her genre. Indeed, one might go so far as to say that it is her *gender*, rewrought as an aesthetic. Naturally relating the life of spirit, the novel enacts the child-woman's inmost wish to relate naturally to the life of spirit; figuring God as a natural relation, it enables her to engage Him in barrier-breaking natural relations. "'Do not fancy he is away up in heaven out of reach of hearing,'" her gentleman friend once admonished Ellen; "'he is here, close to you . . . and knows every wish and throb of your heart'" (73). It is because He sticketh as closely as this that His daughter can relate to her "brother" as to her Father's Son. And it is because he sticketh *closer* than a brother—as closely as the John the gentleman only prefigures—that she can eventually rise from the rank of "sister" to that of bride of Christ. Which is to say—by a logic in which typology, theogony, and aesthetics coincide—that she can envision one day *becoming her Father's mother*.[41] Warner's, in short, is a natural imitation of God's way of writing, a child-womanly and yet divinely authorized conception of the living Word. The ultimate stake of *The Wide, Wide World* is imaginary Holy Patrifratrimatrimony.

Or else it is incest on the grandest conceivable scale.

What demarcates the improper from the immaculate conception of Divine Enunciation? How is Scripture to be discriminated from the foulest scribbling, the all-embracing Word from the (un)naturally proliferating word, a natural relation to godhead from apocalyptically unnatural relations? Plainly, the Father cannot sequester Himself up in Heaven out of worldly passion's reach, dooming the d——d mob to write alone. Is His sole remaining option to entice woman's fiction toward the thin line of demarcation between the ethereal and the venereal—only to hurl it back into the chastening nothingness figured by Alice's anti-incestuous death? Must scribblerdom join the Humphreys (John and Heman) in deriding womanly writing? Does woman's fiction have no choice but to image its "holy alliance" with the Word as that necrophiliac revel John seems to promise his moribund sister?

Happily, Warner holds out a practical alternative. For her as for Hegel, there exists a natural relation untainted by natural relations: *one* familial figure straddles the line of demarcation between the Word and the world. No need to open the *Phenomenology* to say which one it is. "The brother," Warner has proclaimed the length and breadth of *The Wide, Wide World*, "is in the eyes of the sister a being whose nature is unperturbed by desire," "her recognition in

him . . . pure and unmixed with any sexual relation."[42] That the
sister can mingle with her father's son in "pure," "unmixed" and yet
natural union is nature's way of saving the scribbler aesthetic; "unperturbed by desire," *this* (un)natural bond, than which "no relationship is more pure," guarantees that the *figura* of the *figura* can reproduce God without prejudice to the rod.[43] Cast in its matrix, every
typos bears the stamp of Divine Enunciation. The irreproachability of
woman's fiction's conception of God is figured by the chaste passion
which welds Ellen to her "brother"; that of the spiritual power which
fecundates the figural, in the chaste chastening rod with which John
rights his "sister." Heaven can boast nothing holier than the natural
relation between natural relations at the heart of the fiction non-
novel's natural relation of the Word.

The *Phenomenology* leaves it at that. *The Wide, Wide World* takes a
more dialectical view of the affair. It is encapsulated in the invisible
inverted commas that distinguish Warner's siblings from Hegel's: *her*
natural relations are "natural relations." " 'This person you call your
brother—' " Mr. Lindsay jealously demands of Ellen, " 'do you mean
to say you have the same regard for him as if he had been born so?' "
Replies the heroine, passionately: " 'No . . . but a thousand times
more!' " (530). John, in other words, sticketh a thousand times closer
than a brother. But is this because he is a thousand times the
brother, or because he is, after all, only a "brother"? The little lines
of demarcation are conspicuously absent from Warner's text; the
way she writes it, Ellen's " 'brother' " is simply a "brother." Could one
ask for a clearer sign that the sole difference between super-natural
relations and supernatural relations is, in the final analysis, writing
alone?

But writing, in Warner, makes a *double* difference. The (anti)inces-
tuous writing which is *The Wide, Wide World* is also the rerighting
which makes incest (im)possible by deferring it to the end of the
wide, wide world. To abolish the novel, then, would be to collapse
back into the (im)purity of the undifferentiated Word. The worldly
typos of that preverbal fusion is familiar: it is the unhallowed alliance
of the child-woman and her mother. Its otherworldly *typos* is familiar
too; it is the (un)holy alliance of the child-woman and her Father.
One had better not, then, deride writing: for the duration of *The
Wide, Wide World*, it is the only available means of suspending Unholy Patrimatrimony. Yet the cunning of incestuous reason derides
writing from within the very scene of righting. What, if not writing

alone, breeds the textual perversion that equates the Father's *righting* Ellen with her brother's *riding* her? What, if not the perverse word, permits that conning of reason which—whether the fault be one of genre, or gender, or both—conjugates proper and improper from one end of woman's fiction to the other? Like the child-womanly teapot (cf. p. 103) or the Paternal-fraternal rod, the word too offers consummation in the present moment—even as it defers it to an all-consuming moment that never comes. Womanly fiction's *figuras* disfigure what they figure; the line of demarcation that sunders "brother" from brother, and Father from lover, is effaced by each stroke of the pen that traces it.

But it is also traced by each stroke of the pen that effaces it. That is why one so badly wants *The Wide, Wide World* to end: in the hope that what comes after will indeed "transcend gender," that a merciful God will at last erase the line so frustratingly effaced and retraced by His rod. Is this prospect of liberation John's ultimate Revelation? Or does he simply promise Ellen more of the same, forever? He has "no doubt," he tells her, that people who "love each other" in this world "will know each other again" in the next. This glimpse of the post-apocalyptic throws him and his "sister" into a "long musing fit," prolonged a great while after Alice joins them (313). Is our trio musing about a happier place than scribblerdom, and do they eventually get there all three? One likes to think so. But writing alone will never tell. Nor will anything else in the wide, wide world.

Perhaps the veil will be lifted in Beulah.

4

LIFE WITH FATHER:
Augusta Jane Evans's *Beulah*

Hee for God only, shee for God in him.
—John Milton

A man without religion is to be pitied; but, oh!
a godless woman is a horror above all things.
—Augusta Jane Evans

John Humphreys is everything a man should be. This puts him in a heroic minority, for the typical scribbler hero is only potentially everything a man should be, and can realize his potential for perfection only with the help of a divinely inspired true woman. But the typical scribbler heroine is only potentially a true woman; like Ellen Montgomery, she can realize her true-womanly potential only with the help of her leading man. A symmetrical arrangement, then, a mutual improvement scheme in which the sexes show one another the way to Paradise Regained? Not quite. For hero and heroine move heavenward under the sign of the chastening rod, and only the hero has one. Until it has purified her of her moral flaws, no mid-century heroine can hope to win heroic souls for Christ. The hero has it easier; he can chasten the heroine while still hardened by sin. Indeed, it is often his sinful hardness that does the chastening. The thing that makes John a hero, then, is not his model character, but the more ordinary thing our best-selling heroes all have in common: to a man, they are endowed with the power to bring the female animal to heel. And, flawed or not, they all tend to deploy it the same way: by soliciting and refusing woman's incestuous desire.

Yet fifties fiction neither minimizes man's characteristic infirmities, nor leaves their sexual symptomatology wholly in the dark. Thus scribblerdom teems with male misfits, semiheroic to villainous, whose shortcomings contemporaries would unerringly have associated with onanism. One thinks, to begin with, of the sickly army of scribbler delinquents who slowly distill into their frames a poison that unmans: once and (sometimes) future stalwarts knocked at least provisionally out of commission by compound toxins whose only *pronounceable* componenent is alcohol. But the best-sellers are also studded with troops of sober, upright fellows whose very uprightness points to an equally baneful sort of intemperance. These men are too hard: their prominent manliness is insufficiently tempered by a softening Christian virtue. The most visible consequence is an inclination to bully the fair sex, one that would surely find expression in "excessive amativeness," were the heroines not there to excise the excess. But excessive amativeness, as we have seen, flows naturally from auto-eroticism; more, the one form of incontinence is categorically indistinguishable from the other. The scribblers silently exploit this fundamental equivalence to fine-tune the fine line between manliness and tyranny. Indeed, if they can unsubversively dilate upon woman's savior's defects, it is, at bottom, because the tendentially tyrannic protagonist is the anemic onanist's not-so-distant cousin: a man who, like his more flaccid fellows, cries out for a woman's restraining hand.

Why, then, does the hyperphallic he-man not figure as the incestuous heroine's brother in sin, his barely veiled sexual fault the pendant to hers? The answer, in a nutshell, is that her fault *gives rise to* his. *The Wide, Wide World* illustrates the point: Ellen's weakness, soliciting Saunders's savagery, occasions John's forbidding rigor. But *The Wide, Wide World* is not the best case to cite, featuring as it does its hero's near-faultlessness; it represents what we will hereafter call the "simple domestic plot," to distinguish it from the more common "double plot" in which a still faulty hero is saved by the heroine he saves. The double plot too designates its hero sole keeper of the chastening rod, and, typically, makes the rod too hard into the bargain. But, to rephrase our question, does it not by that very act pronounce him as sexually suspect as the heroine? More: since incest emerges only at the level of the textual "improper," whereas the hero's hardness is a prominent feature of the story, would it not be more natural to give the latter the lion's share of our attention? In a word, does the double plot not solicit a feminist critique of the very gender system the simple plot apologizes for?

It does, of course, witness the recent burst of feminist readings of the scribblers. What we will try to show in this chapter and the next, however, is that such readings find their historical horizon in the mid-century's abiding sense of woman's con-genital defect. The improper tale we have disengaged from *The Wide, Wide World* provides the foundation for whatever other story the scribblers might tell. The double plot may well be *dominated* by the story of woman's domestication of man; it is nonetheless *determined* by the passion(lessness) a certain feminism pragmatically ignores. This is no less true for the fact that the double plot reveals tantalizing glimpses of the masturbatory/copulatory scene in which domesticating woman tames and trains her lustful mate. For that scene too takes its subordinate place within the overarching drama of female incestuousness locked in passionate conflict with male law.

The present chapter examines the dialectic of the female and the phallic in Augusta Jane Evans's best-seller, *Beulah*. *Beulah* pairs its flinty hero with a self-abusive hero manqué, arranging for the heroine to cure this composite deviant of his double deviation. The text thus evokes both standard male failings and the affinity between them. Pragmatic feminism registers the fact in its own fashion by reading *Beulah* as a record of incipient feminist protest. Examining Nina Baym's rendition of the argument in some detail, we try to show that this is a perfectly proper interpretation of *Beulah* and, by extension, of the double plot in general. Then we go on to supplement Baym's proper reading with an improper one.

The Lady or the Tiger?

Broadly, *Beulah* hews to the pattern laid out in *The Wide, Wide World*. The novel chronicles the prenuptial trials and tribulations of its titular heroine, a child-woman who, despite her patent moral and intellectual excellence, needs and gets a powerful chastening. The chastening is presided over, if not quite administered, by *Beulah*'s titanic hero, the steely physician and Faustian philosopher, Dr. Guy Hartwell, M.D. Hartwell comes as close to being an atheist as scribbler savior comfortably can; he is thus a manifestly flawed character, himself in dire need, one would think, of a redemptive chastening. Beulah does in fact chasten him, but only tentatively; his conversion to Christ is just beginning when the novel ends. As if to redress the resulting imbalance, the heroine is called upon to chasten Hartwell's dissipated foil, her "brother" and childhood sweetheart, Eugene Graham, quite as definitively as Hartwell chastens

her. As in *The Wide, Wide World*, chastening sows the seeds of pa-
tri(fratri)matrimony. Hartwell, who is Beulah's *fatherly* guardian at
the start of the novel, becomes her *husbandly* guardian at the end of
it. "Brother" Eugene, who cannot also marry the heroine, does the
next best thing: he fathers a daughter and decides to call her Beulah.

This family romance frames another tale that is, by scribbler
standards, audacious. Alone among the best-selling heroines of her
day, Beulah dares to call the wisdom of religion and matrimony into
profound and prolix doubt; one follows her—if one has the
stamina—as she footslogs her wearying (and sporadically footnoted)[1]
way through the dismal swamp of contemporary freethinking and a
vaguely Fulleresque feminism. Parallel to this intellectual odyssey
there unfolds a *Pilgrim's Progress* of the emotions, during which Beulah does her utmost to break with her beloved (meta)physician: she
forces herself to refuse his repeated offers of adoption and a tempting proposal of marriage to boot. The link between her spiritual
struggles is, on an orthodox reading at any rate, that between bad
theory and worse practice: distancing herself from the true faith
(Methodism), Beulah naturally distances herself from Hartwell too,
sailing so far out upon the seas of unwomanliness and ungodliness
that one might—if one didn't know better—give her up for lost. But
Guy Hartwell is a human lodestone. Accordingly Beulah is, just as
she seems about to drift beyond the point of no return, drawn back
to him, to her true-womanly self, and hence, as it were, to Beulah.
Her personal and philosophical problems are resolved at a blow:
coming home to Hartwell, Beulah also comes home to Christ and the
Word.

Yet Hartwell, we said, is something uncomfortably akin to an atheist. On that count alone, he hardly seems the right sort of Guy(de) to
lead Beulah out of the dark wood of apostasy. His temperament
makes him a still more improbable secular redeemer. Hartwell is
hard, as one notices the moment he enters Beulah's life: "Dr. Hartwell stood on the hearth, leaning his elbow on the mantelpiece, and
watching [Beulah's] slight form as it stole softly to and fro . . . said
abruptly: 'Sit down, girl! you will walk yourself into a shadow.'" (29)

However well-meant the doctor's orders, this is, one knows from
having observed John Humphreys, appallingly bad form. Yet it is
the form all Hartwell's dealings with his girl-child take. When he
barks out his first command, Beulah is twelve; ten years later she is

still his girl or child, and he is still barking. Here is Hartwell propo-
sing to Beulah at the other end of the book:

> "Beulah?"
> "Sir . . . "
> "Oh, don't 'sir' me, child! I want to know the truth, and you will not
> satisfy me."
> "I have told you the truth."
> "Have you learned that fame is an icy shadow? that gratified ambition
> cannot make you happy? Do you love me?" (356)

Here is Hartwell winding up his last proposal but one: "'You are a
mere shadow now . . . I have blamed myself more than once that I
did not suffer you to die with Lilly [Beulah's sister], as you certainly
would have done, had I not tended you so closely. Your death, then,
would have saved me much care and sorrow; and you, many struggles.'" (283)

Even in this case, the irascible doctor's intentions are unimpeach-
able; he is trying to get Beulah to take a vacation. But he displays a
sad ignorance of the great modern truth either of the Humphreys
(John or Heman) could have taught him: there is no constraint like
that of love. Small wonder, then, that Beulah refuses to heed Hartwell; small wonder that she complains bitterly, "he wants to rule me
with a rod of iron" (150); small wonder that she espouses theories
justifying woman's independence of man, perhaps even of God.
Hartwell's imperiousness, arrogance, and habitual (if unintentional)
hard-heartedness leave Beulah no choice but to rebel.

Such, at any rate, are the outlines of an analysis that would make
Hartwell's domineering rod the driving force behind Beulah's apostasy. We will see in a moment how Nina Baym fills them in, constru-
ing *Beulah* as a barely veiled indictment of mid-century woman's oppression. But we need first to insist a bit that Beulah, her author,
and Hebrew etymology alike encourage us to discern in *Beulah* a
very different, Warneresque-Bunyanesque parable.[2] Let us look
again at the opening skirmish between the hero and his antagonist:

> Dr. Hartwell said abruptly:
> "Sit down, girl! you will walk yourself into a shadow!"
> She lifted her head, shook it in reply, and resumed her measured
> tread. (29)

Having traversed *The Wide, Wide World*, we know how much is at
stake in this wordless revolt. The stakes are raised even higher when
Beulah tacitly contests authority's privilege of privileges, the right to
a forthright answer. Hardly has the doctor begun to probe into Beulah's past ("where are your parents and friends?") than the suffering
heroine raises "her hand deprecatingly, nay commandingly, as
though [to say]: 'No more. You have not the right to question, nor I
the will to answer.'" (29)

Hartwell's tactlessness may be lamentable. But he is thirty, a doctor, and trying to help, and nothing entitles a twelve-year-old orphan girl to defy him with commanding gestures or stubborn silences. Moreover, as Beulah has just met him, and as there is
manifestly nothing of the Saunders about him, her impudence cannot be chalked up to the doctor's account; there must be deeper
reasons for it. Now a callous socialite has just prevented Beulah from
visiting her dying sister, whom Beulah's dying father had solemnly
commended to her care, and a number of other things have been
going wrong at the asylum for penniless orphans where Beulah
drags out her sunless existence; but while these circumstances help
explain the little lady's impatient brushoff of the doctor, they are not
its root source. Having gone to school to Warner and the womanologists, we can guess what its root source must be: passion. Turning
back a page or two, to a scene in which Beulah requites the callous
socialite's cruelty in a most unladylike manner, we find that our diagnosis is right on the mark. There is a beast in Beulah:

[Beulah's] look of utter despair gave place to an expression of indescribable bitterness. Springing from her suppliant posture, she muttered with
terrible emphasis—
"A curse on that woman and her husband! May God answer their
prayers as she answered mine!" . . .
It was not surprising that passers-by gazed curiously at the stony face,
with its large eyes brimful of burning hate, as the injured orphan walked
mechanically on, unconscious that her lips were crushed till purple drops
oozed over them. (27)

The rest of *Beulah* bears the stain of those oozing purple drops.
They not only color the passionate if tacit "No more!" that Beulah
thrusts between herself and Hartwell; her subsequent rejections of
his variegated suits, her express reluctance to live on "the bounty of
one upon whom [she has] no claim" (160), and, especially, her self-

imposed exile in the "burning wastes of [metaphysical] speculation" (327) are all refined expressions of the purple passion that makes its maiden appearance here. Beulah spurns Hartwell not out of a commendable protofeminist impulse, then, but out of contemptible pride. The text is thickly scattered with signposts pointing to this orthodox moral. Beulah's "matronly" friend Mrs. Williams, for example, prophetically chides the heroine the first time Beulah moves out on Hartwell: "Don't be hurt, child, if I tell you you are too proud. Poverty and pride make a bitter lot in this world" (78). The next time she packs her bags, Beulah gets much the same advice from the doctor's devout and devoted slave Harriet:

> "Take care, chile. Remember, *'Pride goeth before a fall* . . .'"
> "What do you mean?" cried Beulah, angrily.
> "I mean that the day is coming, when you will be glad enough to come back and let my master take care of you! That's what I mean. And see if it doesn't come to pass." (129)

Especially conspicuous are the hints that Beulah's foray into feminist theory is similarly inspired by the pride that goeth before a moral fall. Hartwell himself repeatedly warns Beulah of the dangers of intellectual autonomy, never more memorably than when the eighteen-year-old heroine is just getting her philosophical feet wet:

> "My child . . . is your faith in your religion unshaken?"
> He felt her fingers close over his spasmodically, as she hastily replied—
> "Of course, of course! What could shake a faith which years should strengthen?"
> But the shiver which crept through her frame denied her assertion, and with a keen pang, he saw the footprints of the Destroyer . . . with an effort he said—
> "I am glad, Beulah; and if you would continue to believe, don't read my books promiscuously. . . . Be warned in time, my child."
> She snatched her hand from his, and answered proudly—
> "Sir, think you I could be satisfied with a creed which I could not bear to have investigated? . . . what have I to fear?"
> "Beulah, do you want to be just what I am? without belief in any creed! hopeless of eternity as of life! Do you want to be like me? If not, keep your hands off my books! Good night; it is time for you to be asleep." (110–11)

That Dr. Hartwell does not reck his own rede hardly promotes confidence in his prescriptions (though, as we will see, it is in Beulah's long-term interest that he not reck it). Moreover, however accurate his prognosis, the treatment he here metes out is as hopelessly unmodern as the un-Humphreyesque pedagogical techniques we saw him applying a moment ago. Still, the dogmatic sleep he urges on Beulah would, as her chronic shivers and pangs foretell, have spared her much weeping and gnashing of teeth. Ellen, who loved to let John censure her reading, could never have "plunged into the gulf of German speculation" (182). Beulah takes the plunge, only to find herself tumbling terrifyingly down a protomaterialist abyss ("if spirit must needs have body to incase it, and body must have a spirit to animate it, may they not be identical?" [181]). Watching her "downward departures," we begin to suspect that, as Hartwell suggested, "promiscuous" reading may indeed conduce to moral decline. The suspicion is immeasurably strengthened when, after Beulah has "toiled in the cavernous mines of metaphysics hopelessly" (327) for a few more years, Hartwell, "à la Parrhasius," holds up before her the devastatingly unflattering portrait of "a tortured Prometheus, chained by links of [her] own forging to the Caucasus of Atheism." Beulah's shuddering response to this interpellation attempt is an admission that her passionate involvement with philosophy has led her where she would not go: "No, no; not that! not Atheism! God save me from that deepest, blackest Gulf!" (228). Promethea should perhaps have kissed the iron rod after all.

Must one therefore categorically condemn her defiance of man and God? Beulah certainly does. As the novel lumbers towards its peripeteia, the Rock of Ages raps on the befuddled philosopher's door in the person of the "incorrigibly unruffled" (313) Mr. Lindsay. He and Beulah are soon discussing all the "leading literary questions"; along the way, the pious man endeavors gently but firmly to show Beulah the folly of her philosophical ways. His efforts climax in the following little homily:

> "There is strange significance in the Mosaic record of the Fall. Longing for the fruits of knowledge, whereby the mysteries of God would be revealed, cost man Eden. The first pair ate, knowledge mocked them, and only the curse remained. That primeval curse of desiring to know all things descended to all posterity, and at this instant you exemplify its existence." (317)

Beulah initially rejects this tactful comparison to Eve, though it sends an auspicious "shudder [running] over her" (317). Yet Lindsay's caveat does not fail of its effect. That very night, "her proud intellect humbled" at last, the no longer baffled Beulah turns "like a spent child" from the last of her metaphysicians (Spinoza, of course); and she turns directly back to "the living God," proclaiming as she weeps "uncontrollably" that "there is no ark of refuge but the Bible." Philosophy, she now sees, has only "mocked [her] hungry soul"; "of myself," is her cry, "I can know nothing!" (320). God has won the battle for Beulah's heart and mind. It only remains for man to conquer the rest of her, and Beulah's capitulation/victory will be complete.

But God's breakthrough on the metaphysical front has already smashed Beulah's resistance on the patrimatrimonial one. "From the moment of her return to the Bible," Beulah prays that the errant Hartwell will return to her, so that she may shepherd him too back into the fold he urged her never to abandon. While he continues "wandering without aim or goal in far distant deserts" (328), whither he has been driven by Beulah's reiterated refusal to "be called by his name,"[3] Beulah confesses to herself that there has always been "one . . . dearer to her than all on earth":

> Finally it became the one intense, absorbing wish of her heart, to see her guardian again. His gloom, his bitterness, were all forgotten; she only remembered his care and kindness, his noble generosity, his brilliant smile, which was bestowed only on her. Pressing her face against [his old dog] Charon's head, she murmured pleadingly—
> "Oh, Father, protect him from suffering and death! Guide him safely home. Give me my guardian back. Oh, Father, give me my wandering friend once more!" (328)

It is six years before the Father answers this heartfelt prayer. Beulah devotes the time to doing penance for her youthful insubordination. She pens a new series of antimetaphysical theological essays "to warn others of the snares in which she had so long been entangled" (327). She makes a pilgrimage to Hartwell's ancestral home, with a view to purchasing and restoring (not renovating!) it. And she rewrites the stormy opening chapter of her (auto)biography, donating five thousand recently inherited dollars to the unfeeling socialite she once bloodily cursed.

All is now primed for Hartwell's return. He therefore returns, and, within seconds of his arrival, affords Beulah her eagerly awaited opportunity to sign and seal her recantation. She jumps on it, and him, "throw[ing] her arms around his neck" and "clinging closely to him" (354). Here is Beulah's moment of sweet surrender:

She felt his strong frame quiver; he folded his arms about her, clasped her to his heart with a force that almost suffocated her, and bending his head, kissed her passionately. Suddenly his arms relaxed their clasp; holding her off, he looked at her keenly, and said—
"Beulah Benton, do you belong to that tyrant Ambition, or do you belong to that tyrant, Guy Hartwell? Quick, child, decide."
"I have decided," said she. Her cheeks burned; her lashes drooped.
"Well!"
"Well, if I am to have a tyrant, I believe I prefer belonging to you."
He frowned. She smiled and looked up at him. (355)

Only two points remain to be cleared up. First, Beulah must signify that she has at last taken to heart Hartwell's prescient warning to keep her hands off his godless books. In effect, she has to affirm that she accepts her appointment as God's agent of MORALITY, and will now try to convert rather than emulate the "avowed infidel" (214) Hartwell redux still is. She is, of course, only too happy to comply:

"Beulah?"
"Well, sir."
"You have changed in many things, since we parted nearly six years ago?"
"Yes, I thank God, I am changed. My infidelity was a source of many sorrows; but the clouds have passed from my mind; I have found the truth in holy writ." (356)

The other thing she must do is sit down, which is what Hartwell wanted her to do in the first place. The novel's final lines freeze her in the desired position:

She laid her Bible on [Hartwell's] knee; her folded hands rested upon it, and her grey eyes, clear and earnest, looked up reverently into her husband's noble face. His soft hand wandered over her head, and he seemed pondering her [Biblically inspired] words.
May God aid the wife in her holy work of love! (362)

In sum: viewed within the frame it builds around itself, *Beulah* emerges as an entirely unironical defense of the iron rod, an advertisement for the patriarchy that castigates feminine rebellion as sinful pride and celebrates submission as the royal road to true-womanly happiness. Should we conclude that Hartwell's hardness doesn't matter, or even that it is part of what *Beulah* glorifies? That would be one-sided. For it is also possible to read this Promethean novel the way Shelley read *Paradise Lost*, suppressing its "moral, virtuous, and pious" letter in order to unfetter its "Byronic" spirit. Nina Baym, who provides the adjectives, also provides a summary that transforms Evans's manifestly "limit-enforcing" romance into a "limit-breaking" manifesto.[4] We take the liberty of quoting Baym's retelling at length, interspersing occasional comments as reminders of the orthodox reading it defies:

Beulah is twelve years old when the story opens . . . saved from a self-willed death only by the intervention of a fascinating older man, Dr. Hartwell . . . [she] grows up in Hartwell's home as though she were his daughter . . . Hartwell is attractive but tyrannical and Beulah is anxious to get away from him all the more because she loves him. And she is tired of dependency. . . . Hartwell cannot really credit such a motive in a woman and is dumbfounded when Beulah positively rejects his formal offer of adoption. [*She rejects it with* "*tears gushing down her cheeks.*" *Warns Hartwell:* "*Mark me, Beulah! Your pride will wreck you . . . Beware, lest, in yielding to its decrees, you become the hopeless being a similar course has rendered me*" *(124).*]

Clara [a friend] . . . tells Beulah how foolish she was to go out on her own. Beulah's response . . . typifies the character and the author . . . "I can stand up . . . I feel humbled when I hear a woman bemoaning the weakness of her sex, instead of showing that she has a soul and mind of her own."

This daring rhetoric is given to the heroine, not that she may later realize its folly, but that she may later make it good. [*Beulah's daring "rhetoric" calls forth this daunting response:* "*All that sounds very heroic in the pages of a novel, but the reality is quite another matter . . . With all your boasted strength, you are but a woman; you have a woman's heart, and one day will be unable to hush its hungry cries*" *(99)*]. Of course she overworks herself; of course she is lonely. "She was very lonely, but not unhappy," Evans writes, and her distinction is crucial. [*Beulah has gone back to Jesus, which makes her happy; she is lonely because one "dearer to her than all on earth beside" is traipsing around somewhere between "palms of the Orient" and "coral crags of distant seas" (328).*]

After a few years . . . Hartwell reappears and makes an offer even more tempting than his last one. He asks Beulah to marry him. . . . He makes it clear that to marry him will be to recant her former position on woman's independence and to submit entirely to his will. Beulah cannot agree to this. [" 'Oh, don't leave me!' She sprang up, and throwing her arms round his neck, clung to him, trembling like a frightened child" (285).] Her refusal sends Hartwell off on four years of wandering in the Orient . . . During these years her religious doubts dissolve. Hartwell's return finds each of them finally ready for the other. For both of them marriage will be a compromise, as it must be; but Hartwell is prepared to compromise at last ["Beulah Benton, do you belong to the tyrant ambition, or do you belong to that tyrant, Guy Hartwell? Quick, child, decide!" (355)], and Beulah no longer equates compromise with defeat.[5]

Plainly, Baym's summary is, in both senses of the word, partial. But that scarcely makes it improper. If her reading of the novel is forced, so is the novel's reading of itself. Baym forces *Beulah* to be limit-breaking; Evans, no less, forces it to be limit-enforcing. Evans imposes a dénouement that defuses the explosive potential of her text; Baym deletes the dénouement in order to show that the text's Byronic impulses cannot really be retroactively squelched. To be sure, Baym has to assign Hartwell a willingness "to compromise at last" that that iron spirit is quite innocent of; but even this interpolation has its justification, since the *potential* for compromise is unmistakably inscribed in the story that leads up to its nonoccurence. *Beulah*, pragmatic feminism shows us, could with perfect propriety end like *The Bostonians*. It just happens not to.

But the pragmatic-feminist rewriting of *Beulah* is chiefly instructive not for what it deletes or adds, but for what it includes and yet suppresses. Beulah, Baym blandly notes, rejects Hartwell's adoption proposal; and then, a few years later, she rejects his "even more tempting" marriage proposal; and then, a few years later, she finds her way to the Father; and then, at long last, she and Hartwell are "ready for one another." Orphan to "daughter" to wife, wayward philosopher to bride of Christ: to call Baym's critical procedure proper is above all to say that she can connect those dots without noticing the picture. It is a picture rather more Byronic than she supposes: it depicts a chastened Beulah coupling contentedly with (God the) father, while a "brother" she has taught not to masturbate looks on. For mid-century readers, whether they knew it or not— and with the exception of people as perverse as Edward Dixon or Herman Melville, they probably didn't know it—this was the compromising scene simultaneously painted and painted over by the text proper. Let us, then, see if we cannot usefully supplement the pious and pragmatic-feminist interpretation of *Beulah* by uncovering that other scene.

A Feeling She Could Not Pause to Analyze

Beulah's descent into the improper begins in a familiar place. Baym zeros in on the main coordinates: a twelve-year-old orphan girl, fighting an advanced case of "spite and anger"; opposite her, "a fascinating older man." One recognizes the "daughter at school," deprived of proper Christian nurture at just the age when a single look might destroy pure morality forever. But the fascinating older man is not as easily classified. He is clearly no odd old gentleman, as an early vision of him in his bathrobe attests:

> To have looked at him then, in his purple silk *robe de chambre*, one would have scarcely believed that thirty years had passed over his head. . . . Mere physical beauty cannot impart the indescribable charm which his countenance possessed. Regularity of features is a valuable auxiliary, but we look on sculptured marble, perfect in its chiselled proportions, and feel that, after all, the potent spell is in the raying out of the soul, that imprisoned radiance which, in some instances, makes man indeed "but little lower than the angels." (42)

How should one regard this demi-angel in purple silk, his potent spell raying out of him? Doubtless the most natural assumption is that he is to become Beulah's "only one in the world." But, however natural, the thought is already tainted with impropriety. By the time one glimpses Hartwell in his robe de chambre, the doctor has invited Beulah to become his little girl: Hartwell "laid his fingers on the pale, high brow, and softly drawing back the thick hair, said earnestly—'Beulah, come home with me. Be my child—my daughter.'" (38)

Should we regard Hartwell as Beulah's father, then? Are his intentions strictly paternal, or might his yet be the look that destroys pure morality forever? Likening him to the angels, the narrator would seem to put him above suspicion; yet there are, we remember, good angels and bad. Hartwell's hardness suggests that he might be a bad one. Particularly ominous is the emotion he displays when the idea of adopting Beulah first crosses his mind. As the scene opens, he is informing the orphan, much more brutally than he needs to, that her brotherly sweetheart Eugene is leaving her for Europe. Beulah quite predictably collapses in the doctor's waiting arms. He lays the unconscious girl on a couch; then, bending over her with a "fierce light kindl[ing] in his piercing, dark eyes," he mutters these vindictive words: "'It is madness to indulge the thought [of adopting her]; I was a fool to dream of it. She would prove heartless, like all of her sex, and repay me with black ingratitude. Let her fight the battle of life unaided.'" (33–34)

Hartwell quickly repents of this resolution, and, as we have seen, takes Beulah home. There he displays a sincere desire to be her guardian, not her ruin. He does so principally by using his penetrating vision in a manner worthy of the Humphreys. The first time he catches her reading alone, for instance, he sneaks up on her "unperceived, and [stands] for some moments at the back of her chair, glancing over her shoulder" (32). It is in this exemplary manner that he continues to deploy his self-proclaimed power to "read the living" (47); like Ellen, Beulah grows up under the super-vision of one who knows and sees all. Even her flirtation with atheism takes place under the doctor's "searching gaze" (41): "[Beulah] scrupulously endeavored to conceal her doubts and questions from her guardian. Poor child! she fancied she concealed them effectually from his knowledge, while he silently noted the march of scepticism in her nature." (181–82)

Plainly, this is no child-seducer. Hovering over Beulah as if she were his own daughter, Hartwell allays whatever suspicions his fierce eyes may initially have aroused. But there is yet something suspect about his looks. Though his intentions are fully fatherly—his formal adoption offer proves it—Hartwell's potent gaze arouses a more than daughterly response in Beulah. From one end of the novel to the other, the heroine is regularly overmastered by the "indescribable charm" of her guardian's "deep-set eyes," now "glittering like polished steel," now "gentle, hazy, yet luminous" (41–42); she grows "dizzy" whenever she gazes into the doctor's "deep eyes" (89), cannot "bear the earnest eyes that look into hers with such misty splendor" (176), quails under "the steady, searching gaze of his luminous eyes" (282), is "dazzled" by his eyes and so must "turn away" (357), and so on. Here is our first solid clue that Beulah's ruling "passion" has to do with sex, specifically with Hartwell's. Further hints dot the opening pages of the book: tantalizing references to the "baffling, fascinating mystery" of the man (41–42); the orphan's inexplicable jealousy of other females with claims on her "father"; most notably, an "inexpressibly thrilling" midnight concert Hartwell performs on his own organ, filling his audience of one with "trembling delight" and transporting her to the "very confines of fabled elysium" (63). Hartwell's may, after all, be the look that ruins Beulah; but, if so, he will not be to blame.

Before we blame Beulah, however, we need to assess her manifest resistance to the doctor. Intrigued though she is by Hartwell's imprisoned radiance, she consistently declines to play Ellen to his John: mesmerized by his Humphreyesque gaze, she yet fends off its complement, the interrogation, habitually quelling Hartwell's queries with variations on the silent "No more!" that stopped him cold at the very start of their relationship. What is more, Beulah's standoffishness is clearly not tactics, but natural aversion: between the "instantly repellent" cast her countenance assumes when Hartwell approaches her at the orphanage (31), and the "feeling" that prevents her from "throw[ing] her arms round his neck" several tumultuous years later (144–45), there stretches a long line of indications to the effect that Hartwell is as repellent as he is irresistible. Indeed, repulsion seems emphatically to gain the upper hand when, at eighteen, Beulah denounces Hartwell's "rod of iron," declines his offer of adoption, and defiantly departs his mansion for the metaphysical mines.

As we have seen, her decision has its proper explanations. Both are inscribed in the pivotal scene in which Beulah definitively wards off her guardian. She "cannot," she cries, crying, be his daughter. The "tyranny" that on a properly feminist reading more than justifies her "cannot" is graphically summed up in Hartwell's cutting response, a "withering smile of scorn and bitterness" that cruelly distorts his "Apollo-like features" (124). But can we be sure that this semidivine expression of displeasure is not a deserved reproof? Provoked by Hartwell's sneer, Beulah "proudly" revises her "cannot" to "will not, then!"; she adds that she "cannot remain any longer the recipient of [his] bounty" (124) because, as she puts it later, she can "have no claim upon him" (160). This is the kind of reasoning that made Milton, in his blindness, suppose he owed God favors. Does the Byronic Beulah want to get away from her would-be father only because pride has similarly clouded her vision?

But does she want to get away from him at all? At a level the critics and Beulah jointly ignore, the heroine's "cannot-will not" tells a different story. Beulah *cannot* be Hartwell's daughter because she *will not* give up the prospect of being his wife. Yet her tears are anything but hypocritical; she wants to be his daughter *too*. Her divided response to the examination obliquely reflects her dilemma. Dwelling on Beulah's transports before Hartwell's penetrating gaze (to say nothing of his organ), the text acknowledges her attraction for her fascinating "father"; playing up her resistance to his probing interrogations, it acknowledges the impediment blocking her patrimatrimonial desire. In the demure language of the novel: Beulah "would like to throw her arms round [Hartwell's] neck . . . but a feeling she could not pause to analyze, prevented her from following the dictates of her heart" (145). Or, in Baym's formulation: Beulah is "anxious to get away from her [guardian] all the more because she loves him." This is not, after all, very different from the orthodox view: Beulah's *passion* is what makes her defy Hartwell. One has only to add—pausing to analyze what neither orthodoxy nor contemporary feminism are inclined to—that Beulah's defiance of Hartwell, her attempt to get away from him, is not unrelated to her passionate desire to get closer to him. The "no more!" with which the orphan wards off her prospective guardian doubles as a hungry cry for *more*.

The proof is the rest of the book. In improper perspective, *Beulah* is about transcending and yet preserving a daughterly relation in a loverly one. The first condition of this transformation is a circumstance orthodoxy and pragmatic feminism must both indignantly deny: for Beulah, Hartwell is also God the Father.[6]

Watch and Ward

A long string of pointed clues identifies the godless doctor with his divine double. There is our early vision of him in purple silk, his almost spiritual rays pouring out of him; a Warneresque passage in which he bears Beulah "out of the house of death" after her sister's early exit (38); his Jehova-like comment thereon ("'now, Beulah, I have saved you, and you belong to me'" [46]); and the covenant he concludes with his "protégée" after the catastrophe ("'I promise you I will guard you, and care for you as tenderly as a father'" [49]). Again, hardly has Beulah settled into her "father's" stately mansion than her Bible happens to fall open to the following "paradox[ical] promise": "'*Whom the Lord loveth he chasteneth*'" (51). The Lord in question is manifestly the One above; but, in the following months and years, it is *Hartwell's* "stern rigidity" Beulah is chastened by. At the very least, this lends color to the idea that the doctor's "rod of iron" also functions as Providence's tool. Other circumstances conspire to suggest that Hartwell is more than a mere instrument of the Omnipotent. For example, a page before Beulah's Bible flaps open to God's paradoxical promise, Hartwell's pious slave Harriet exhorts the orphan to put her "'trust in the Lord.'" When Beulah objects that "'He can never give me back my dead,'" Harriet ripostes: "'But He can raise up other friends for you, and He has. It is a blessed thing to have my master for a friend and a protector. Think of living always in a place like this, with plenty of money, and nothing to wish for. Chile, you don't know how lucky—'" (50).

It would be splitting hairs to ask this faithful servant of her Master's, and her master's, just which "master" she means when. And it is not only slave Harriet who associates Hartwell's doings with the Almighty's. Beulah does too, if less slavishly. Stealing out of Hartwell's house after a spat with his sister (a hateful bundle of malice quite the contrary of John's sister Alice), she lifts her eyes to the "jewelled dome" of a midnight sky, and "seem[s] to hear the words pronounced from the skyey depths: *'Lo, I am with you always, even unto the end'*" (77). Does this set her to thinking about the Lord? Not exactly; it sets her to thinking about Hartwell: "Gradually, the results of the step she had taken obtruded themselves before her: and with a keen pang of pain and grief came the thought, 'What will Dr. Hartwell think of me?' . . . Yet hope whispered, 'He will suspect the truth . . . he will not blame me.'" (77)

Later, Hartwell himself will remind Beulah that he is with her even unto the end. It is Christmas; the "bending sky" is "sunny and beautiful," and Beulah is "looking 'through nature up to nature's God'" (195). Hartwell is nominally absent, having stalked out of Beulah's life after another row. But he is still watching over her, and, to prove it, he sends her a watch. "A folded slip of paper lay on the crimson velvet lining of the box, and recognizing the characters, she hastily read this brief sentence:—"'Wear it constantly, Beulah, to remind you that, in adversity, you still have A GUARDIAN.'" (207) Beulah's reaction shows that she has gotten the Christmas message: "It was very uncertain when she would see him. Yet she felt comforted, for this gift assured her, that however coldly he chose to treat her when they met, he had not thrown her off entirely. With all her independence, she could not bear the thought of his utter alienation; and the consciousness of his remaining interest thrilled her heart with gladness." (207)

It is not, however, always so thrillingly clear that Hartwell has not thrown Beulah off entirely. Sometimes he wrathfully suggests that he has. Each of these terrible outbursts hastens his "progress God-wards" (183) through a kind of surreptitious apotheosis by rhetorical association. Here is what Beulah's would-be savior says when she quashes his plans to adopt her: "'Mark me, Beulah! Your pride will wreck you . . . Leave me.'" (124) "'Would he,'" the rejected rejecter is moved to wonder, "'relinquish all interest in one whom he had so long watched over and directed?'" (130). The tone grows still more Miltonic when Beulah spurns Hartwell's next offer of grace, "passionately" calling him a "tyrant" and declining to return to his stately mansion (180). Hartwell says—"calmly": "'Fierce, proud spirit! Ah! it will take long years of trial and suffering to tame you. Go, Beulah! You have cast yourself off. It was no wish, no work of mine.'" (177) Beulah's refusal to become her savior's bride brings on the Biblical crescendo: "'Poor child, it needs no prophetic vision to predict your ill-starred career. . . . Remember, when your health is broken, and all your hopes withered, remember I warned you, and would have saved you, and you would not.'" (285) Finally, there is the anguished cry Beulah's guardian wrenches from her when, after she has balked at his offer of marriage, he departs for "Baalbec, Maroc, Tartary, India, China," and other places. This is Beulah's Golgotha: "'Oh, I am so desolate . . . My heart dies within me. . . . Oh, my guardian, don't forsake me!'" (286).

Hartwell, in sum, is Beulah's father twice over. The capital consequence is that she can lose and yet keep him: Beulah's guardian may forsake her, but her GUARDIAN cannot. The doctor's surreptitious apotheosis thus provides a kind of incestuous insurance policy, freeing the paternal Hartwell to resign his office for an appointment as Beulah's lover without ceasing to be, in his celestial dimension, her loving Father. This entails an additional, and no less capital, benefit: her "father" bifurcated into her Father and her lover, Beulah, like little Ellen, can satisfy her incestuous longings on the grandest possible scale.

Why, then, does she not simply take patrimatrimonial advantage of her lover-Father? Having stymied her guardian's adoption attempt and so cleared a path for his "even more tempting" offer (Baym), why does she reject that offer too when it comes? The answer is that it comes for the wrong reasons—or, more exactly, from the wrong Hartwell. For the flawed hero's two natures, like the heroine's, are not only different, they are flagrantly at odds: this is part of what it means to say that *Beulah* exemplifies the double plot. To understand how that complicates the family affair, we need to turn our attention to the split in Hartwell's only imperfectly divine soul.

A Case of Displaced Onanism

Hartwell-God's godlessness is the palpable sign of his duplicity. Unlike Jesus Christ, or, perhaps, John, the Faustian (meta)physician is not of one substance with the Father; he is man *plus* God, an unbeliever who diaphysitically figures the divinity. The resulting difference between God-Hartwell and himself drives a wedge between Beulah's "father" and her lover: if her GUARDIAN cannot forsake her, her guardian certainly can. Hartwell's marriage bid pinpoints the danger involved. "'Once I asked you to be my child . . . now, I ask you to be my wife'": the chilling contrast between the "once" and the "now" suggests that Hartwell has simply thrown off the father's role for the lover's, that he wants a regular romance, not a family affair. Rebuffed, he says as much, uttering the words Beulah must dread above all others: "'I am not your guardian, Beulah.'" (286) Well may the heroine's "heart die within" her, for her heart's wish hangs in the balance. Beulah left her "father" so that she could marry him, and now he is refusing to be her father.

"'*You* refused to make *me* such,'" is Hartwell's Parthian shot (286; emphasis added). Of course he is right. But he tells only part of the story. What he fails to see, or, in any case, to say, is that Beulah had no choice but to reject him. To have embraced his adoption offer while her whole nature cried out for "something superadded" would have involved her in the most damnable sort of double dealing. Desiring her "father," she *had* to de-sire him. Yet this strategem cannot deliver Beulah from her dilemma, as we realize by the time she spurns her guardian's more tempting offer. For Beulah, there *is* no getting away from father, for father is the only one she desires. Her second refusal to become a Hartwell therefore poses, in inverted form, the question tacitly framed by the first. She almost sees this herself: "She loved him above all others; loved him as a child adores its father; but how could she, who had so reverenced him, consent to become his wife?"[7] (294)

Yet how could she not? The one prospect more fearful than life with father is the prospect of life without him. Beulah's struggle with the demons of philosophy has taught her at least this: outside the labyrinth of the fatherly gapes the "deepest, blackest gulf," the Tartarean no-woman's-land reserved for women who would shun the land of Beulah. Coupling with the father she desired would have led Beulah straight to the bottomless pit; but coupling with a de-sired Hartwell would lead straight to the same place.

Only if one appreciates this hellish double bind can one make sense of Beulah's reaction to Hartwell's marriage offer, a hysterical, histrionic eruption for which there is no proper explanation. Hardly has Hartwell opened his mouth to propose than Beulah gives vent to a "half-smothered groan," and cries, "shuddering violently": "'Impossible. Do not ask it. I cannot. I cannot.'" A moment later she adds, for emphasis, "'Oh sir, I would rather die!'" Lest one suppose this is just talk, the heroine reinforces her words with some unmistakable body language: "She shrank away from the touch of his lips on her brow, and an expression of hopeless suffering settled upon her face" (283–84). It is a highly overdetermined expression. Beulah shrinks and shudders before the horror of incest: still a slave of the child-womanly passion that once squeezed the purple drops from her lips, she is appalled by her own half-smothered urges. But she also trembles before the specter of an *un*incestuous coupling. Her womanly intuitions tell her that, in freeing Hartwell from the trammels of the incestuous dialectic, she must set loose the unfatherly sex fiend we decided he wasn't when he first took her in. Beulah is therefore doubly right to regard marriage with the depaternalized Hartwell as a fate worse than death, for that alternative to patrimatrimony could only yoke the monsters that prowl just beyond the confines of domestic ideology: the insatiable female animal and her unrestrainedly (self-)abusive mate.

There is, to be sure, no direct evidence that Beulah has transformed the once paternally minded Hartwell into an excessively amative maniac. As for the notion that, driving him into the wastes of Tartary, she also drives him into a waste of shame, the reassuring references to his "iron rod" pointedly advertise its absurdity: nothing is less likely than that her disowned "father's" substance has been sapped by unmanly habits. But her "brother" Eugene Graham's has.

Because Beulah's "father" and her "brother" are more closely related than either suspects, we need to investigate Eugene's case.

Eugene was Beulah's childhood beau. Long ago, he dwelt with her in the orphan asylum, and loved her, despite or perhaps because of the difference in their ages, "as well as if she were his sister" (8). We know how well that is: before Beulah moved in with Hartwell, she and her "brother" had begun "[speaking] of their future as one" (192). But the stream of events carries this prospective John Humphreys off to distant Heidelberg, where he must manage without a devoted American female to monitor him. The results are predictable. When, years later, Eugene returns to the United States, Beulah's "infallible" "womanly intuitions" (160) immediately tell her that "the idol of her girlhood" is not what he was; she feels "contempt" welling up in her for the "weakness" she senses in him, and knows instinctively that she can never again "love him, save as a friend, as a brother" (164). Her intuitions are all too accurate; Eugene is in the clutches of a "fatal habit" (191). Here is what his adoptive sister Cornelia has to say about it: "'Oh, it is like a hideous nightmare! I cannot realize that Eugene, so noble, so pure, so refined, could ever have gone to the excesses he has been guilty of. . . . My parents will not see it; my mother says "all young men are wild at first"; and my father shuts his eye to his altered habits.'" (190–91)

A bit further on, Cornelia notes that Eugene's unmanly habit has become well-nigh universal among young men:

> "[I]t has become so prevalent in this city, that of all the gentlemen whom I meet in so-called fashionable society, there are very few who abstain. . . . I have seen them at parties . . . talking the most disgusting nonsense to girls . . . and oh, Eugene is following in their disgraceful steps! Beulah, if the wives, and mothers, and sisters, did their duty, all this might be remedied. If they carefully and constantly strove to shield their sons and brothers from temptation, they might preserve them from the fatal habit, which, once confirmed, it is almost impossible to eradicate." (191)

We have, to be sure, not cited this passage properly. Though Eugene is indeed guilty of abusing himself by distilling a poison into his frame, the disease that threatens to destroy him is not spermatorrhea, but cirrhosis of the liver. Eugene cannot keep his hands off the *bottle*. Emboldened, however, by Cornelia's description of his malady and the prophylaxis she recommends in closing, we will not hesitate to diagnose a case of displaced onanism. The rest of Eugene's history bears out the diagnosis. He had come home from Germany thinking to marry his metaphorical sister; rebuffed, he is soon ensnared and dragged to the altar by his beautiful but promiscuous cousin by adoption, Antoinette. He is of course incapable of chastening this quasi-Creole "flirt" (298); his nervous substance eaten up by his fatal habit, he must weakly countenance her "downward departures." The moment of his deepest degradation occurs one evening as he sits abusing himself in the company of some equally degenerate friends. Two of his companions do not scruple to conduct the following conversation under his very nose:

> "Where is Fred, anyhow? He is a devilish fine fellow for a frolic. I—"
> "Why, gone to the coast with [Eugene's] pretty wife. He is all devotion. They waltz, and ride, and in fine, he is her admirer *par excellence.*" (296)

Eugene's flaccid reaction shows just how unmanly his habit has made him: "Eugene half rose at this insulting mention of his wife's name, but . . . song was now ringing around him, and sinking back, he too raised his unsteady voice." (296) Antoinette, one hardly need add, will continue to ride to her heart's content.

Eugene, in contrast, cannot ride any more at all, as he convincingly demonstrates in the wake of his carouse. Though he can "barely sit erect" (297), he foolishly engages in a buggy race with one of his besotted companions. In a trice, he is thrown senseless from his carriage—as luck would have it, practically on Beulah's front door. The heroine emerges "fearlessly" from her study to the spot where his "prostrate form" is lying; "bend[ing] over his body," she observes that "one arm [is] crushed beneath him," nearly faints at the grisly sight, but then rallies and goes for help (297). Eugene's turns out to be a fortunate fall. Beulah patiently nurses her former "brother" and his crushed arm back to health; as he convalesces, she comes to "supply" his wife's "place" (300) in weaning him from secret sin. In return, a chastened Eugene symbolically supplies Beulah's father's place; in wistful memory of his big-brotherly days at the asylum, he sires a daughter on his faithless wife and decides to name her Beulah.

So much for Eugene. What does his crushed and regenerated arm have to do with Hartwell's iron rod?

They are, to begin with, linked by the structure of the novel. The long second phase of Beulah's relationship to her guardian—the one that begins when she declines to be Miss Hartwell and extends well past her refusal to become Mrs. Hartwell—has a curious feature: Hartwell is absent during most of it. But Eugene isn't. He reenters Beulah's life just before she compels Hartwell to drop his paternal suit; the story of his moral decline is interwoven with the story of her descent into the metaphysical mines; his fall occurs just after Beulah turns down Hartwell's more tempting offer; and his recovery under Beulah's care parallels her reascension toward Hartwell and Heaven. This counterpoint bears examination. Eugene's adoptive sister Cornelia shows us how to proceed when she reminds us, and Beulah, that "if the wives, and mothers, and sisters, did their duty," "their sons and brothers" might be preserved from their fatal proclivities. Here is Cornelia's brother's other "sister's" precipitate response: "'If a man's innate self-respect will not save him from habitual, disgusting intoxication, all the female influence in the universe would not avail. . . . If Eugene once sinks so low, neither you, nor I, nor his wife—had he one—could reclaim him.'" (193)

This is heresy. Pace Beulah, the *only* force that can reclaim Eugene is female influence. One sees, then, to what noxious conclusions Beulah's alienation from Hartwell and God is leading. But it is ironic that Cornelia should be the one to gesture at them, inasmuch as she too is a notorious renegade from the faith of her fathers. She underscores the irony, as well as her warning, by promptly dying an apostate's death. Watching the reprobate in her death agony, we understand that *her* female influence is powerless to exorcise her brother's deadly defect:

[A] wailing cry broke from [Cornelia's] lips; and extending her arms toward [Eugene], she said sobbingly—

"Shall I see you no more—no more? . . . are we now parted forever—forever?"

He laid her head on his bosom, and endeavored to soothe her; but, clinging to him, she said huskily—

"Eugene, with my last breath I implore you; forsake your intemperate companions. . . . Eugene, promise, promise!—Eugene!" (277)

Cornelia draws her last breath in vain. She is not cold in her grave before Eugene shows up at the revel that nearly costs him his arm. This is what makes her death so sad. But we do not need the evidence of Eugene's fracture to know that Cornelia has botched her exit; we have seen the scene played properly before, and can attest that the present rendition is a cruel mockery of the real thing. Unlike Alice Humphreys, Cornelia does not expire serene and satisfied in her brother's encircling arms; she goes gasping into eternity with "no hopes of a blissful future" (266), and hence no hope of rejoining "the only being she ever loved" (237) in a family reunion beyond the grave. Unlike John Humphreys, Eugene does not tenderly lay his dying sister on her deathbed, and then "go down the mountain together" with his other "sister"; he throws himself into Cornelia's "vacant chair, and sob[s] like a broken-hearted child" (278). "What an exit," groans the narrator (297), doubtless thinking as much of the living as the dead: of Eugene, whose future incapacitation is heralded by his unpromising performance here; still more, perhaps, of his quondam "sister," who, with what emotions one can imagine, witnesses Cornelia's unchristian end. With the emotions, let us say, of an apostate Ellen Montgomery, summoned to watch an infidel alter ego give up the ghost without benefit of Father or "brother." To be sure, Beulah's (ex-)"father" delays his departure for Tartary and so forth long enough to make a fleeting appearance on the somber scene; "put[ting] his hand tenderly on [Beulah's] head," he offers to lead her from Cornelia's deathbed as he once led her from Lilly's (278). This abortive gesture, however, only reminds us the more poignantly that Beulah has not yet secured what Cornelia will never enjoy: a chastely incestuous match with a paternal-fraternal chastener. Tellingly, Beulah passes the night alone on a couch near the corpse, in morbid "self-communion" (278).

On the couch, she doubtless reflects on the doctor's anguishing absence, and the reprobate's admonitory failure. Perhaps she notices, if only subconsciously, that that failure reflects on her own. Cornelia's tragic story turns on its missing hero; but *his* absence is finally that of the godly monitor who should have shielded him from sin. Cornelia could not fill the role, though brother Eugene was "the only being she ever really loved," for Cornelia never loved the Father. Beulah likewise fails Eugene, and for a similar reason: she too, for philosophical reasons, is painfully estranged from Heaven. The parallel should recall a matter much graver than Cornelia's defection: the potential tragedy of Beulah and Hartwell is *also* about its missing heroine. Watching Eugene decline while Beulah sinks ever deeper into the cavernous mines of metaphysics, we cannot forget that Hartwell, largely absent from the moment Beulah first drops him, must also make do without an elevating female influence. In Eugene's case, the upshot is a potency problem and the corresponding failure to establish a properly patrifratrimatrimonial bond. In Hartwell's case, the provisional result is the same, except that Hartwell's problem is not impotence, but the equivalent, hyperamative hardness. Via Cornelia/Beulah, Eugene's crushed arm points, directly if limply, at Hartwell's iron phallus.

It thereby points to the immediate reason for Beulah's shuddering response to Hartwell's proposal: Beulah senses that Hartwell can do to *her* what Eugene does to his *arm*. But we have already made this pragmatic-feminist argument in other, improper-feminist terms. To say that Beulah trembles before Hartwell's steely ardor is the same as to say that she trembles before the thought of taking the lover whose fatherly affections she has alienated. Because Beulah is estranged from the Father, Hartwell is *excessively* amative from the moment he begins to be amative. The female godlessness that drives Beulah's "brother" to nearly terminal self-abuse must drive her de-sired "father" to abuse his ex-daughter and prospective wife. In the end, Eugene's debility is Cornelia's fault. It follows, ideo-logically, that Hartwell's hardness is Beulah's fault. It is perhaps unnecessary to repeat that Beulah's fault is the one that, in Mr. Lindsay's words, "cost man Eden": "the primeval curse of desiring." That prim-Eval curse, and its opposite and twin: the primeval curse of de-siring. Only the chastening rod can lift it.

Infidelity, unfaithfulness, Creola-zation

How, if Hartwell was hard to begin with, can one blame his hardness on Beulah's apostasy?

Hartwell himself has already stated the answer. Bending over the twelve-year-old Beulah with that devilish light burning in his semi-divine eye, he predicted that she, like all her sex, would repay his bounty with black ingratitude. Hardly have we met him, in other words, than Hartwell announces he is hard because of (a) woman and predicts that this woman will soon be Beulah. He recalls his prophecy when Beulah, on the threshold of womanhood, meets his adoption offer with black ingratitude: "'I might have known it; I might have expected it; for fate has always decreed me just such returns'" (124). Should we follow Hartwell in identifying Beulah with the heartless woman who hardened him?

Years later, her philosophico-feminist rebellion in full swing, Beulah suggests that we should. Hartwell's devout admirer Clara has just revealed that the woman who embittered Hartwell was his beautiful first wife, Creola. She goes on to hint why Hartwell left her: "'Her conduct was not irreproachable, it has been whispered.'" Beulah spontaneously identifies with this, as she supposes, blameless victim of Hartwell's hard-heartedness: "'Aye, whispered by slanderous tongues! . . . I wonder the curse of Gomorrah does not descend on this gossiping, libellous community.'" (167) Her sisterly solidarity is, however, misplaced, as Beulah definitively learns once she has gone back to Jesus. Mrs. Asbury, a Christian woman who has retrieved her husband from atheism's embrace, reveals that Creola married Hartwell for his money; afterward, "'recklessly imprudent,'" the coquette "'launched into the wildest excesses which society sanctioned,'" carrying on a "'flirtation with one whom she had known previous to her marriage'" (331). "'Poor Guy,'" concludes Mrs. Asbury, praying that "'a merciful and loving God'" may "'bring him to a knowledge of that religion which alone can comfort a nature like his'" (332). Of course, we know as well as Mrs. Asbury who should be helping God bring Beulah's poor Guy to that comforting knowledge. But Beulah's has been more than a sin of omission. She too has betrayed Hartwell à la Creola, carrying on a recklessly imprudent flirtation with metaphysics that has driven her "father" and lover to leave her. In a word, from the moment she jilted Jesus to "begin read[ing] . . . promiscuously," Beulah has been on the road to Creola-zation; one would be hard pressed to say whether the coquette's *infidelity* or the philosopher's *lack of faith* represented the more damnable feminine deviation. And as the identification between Beulah and her sister in sin impresses itself upon us, so too does Hartwell's deeper meaning: what mandates *his* sex's severity is the natural inconstancy of Beulah's.

But Beulah's inconstancy is the sole alternative to incest. (A Creola, witness the name, could never make one of the family; *her* inconstancy thus has nothing to do with incest, it is just plain inconstancy.) Beulah *must* make her lover (too) hard; that is the price to be paid for putting the necessary distance between herself and her loving (ex-)"father," the price, in other words, of her anti-incestuous apostasy. Yet having thus transformed Hartwell from father into excessively amative lover, she must, to excise the excess, make him her father again. It is the complement of the double bind we noticed earlier: once she has re-sired Hartwell, Beulah will be back where she began.

The only "solution" to this dilemma is eminently familiar: Beulah's incestuous urges must be chastened, *so that she may chastely indulge them*. But *Beulah* realizes the com-mutation of passion into passion(lessness) in a mode peculiar to the double plot. Passion forces Beulah to un-father Hartwell, making the hard man hard; making him hard, it *forges the instrument of its own chastening*. Finally, by compelling a chastened Beulah to kiss the chastening rod she has vainly struggled to do without, incestuous passion—now (un)incestuous passion(lessness)—brings the novel nearly full circle. A legitimate father-daughter match redeems the illicit longings that set the incestuous wheel in motion; confined to its proper patrimatrimonial context, unholy passion may be converted into its Holy Familial equivalent. Mrs. Hartwell can at last go about her Father's business, converting her earthly guardian into a type of the GUARDIAN whose type he already unwittingly is. It follows that neither Beulah's self-directed philosophical investigations nor Mr. Lindsay's exposition of the Word is the chief instrument of the heroine's salvation. Credit must rather go to Hartwell's chastening iron.

The irony involved is palpable. Hartwell is practically an atheist, and Beulah finds herself in Christ; moreover, Hartwell has been absent for years when Beulah definitively accepts Him. How can her godless Guy(de) save her in absentia?

He saves her precisely by absenting himself—not by plying the rod, but by withdrawing it. The essence of his technique, in other words, is to threaten to make absolute her willful separation from the fatherly. Accordingly, the peripeteia in Beulah's religious career comes, not when she turns back to the Bible, but rather when the peripatetic Hartwell casts (her) off for Tartary—when he translates the incest taboo, as it were, into geography. Hartwell can do nothing harder than that. But that is hard enough. Two pages after Beulah grasps that her guardian has truly gone ("he has gone—gone!" [294]), she, unbeknownst to herself, converts. As if to prove it, she *re*verts, symbolically closing the distance Hartwell's departure has just opened: she emerges from her study (where she has not long since tearfully penned the heretical sketch "designed to prove that woman's happiness was not necessarily dependent on marriage") to attend to Eugene's crushed arm, thus requiting the brotherly love Eugene lavished on her in their childhood. With this act of osteopathic fratrimatrimony, she begins to set the proposal scene(s) to rights: taking up the torch the expiring Cornelia has somewhat unworthily passed on, she assumes the true woman's patrimony, a normalizing—which is to say incestuous—relation to the male sex. Proceeding to supply Eugene's wife's (and his dead sister's) place by straightening her "brother" out, she serves notice of her willingness to supply her "father's" wife's place too. Having engendered Hartwell's excessive amativeness by her obligatory and yet hopeless struggle against incest, she will now, the text signals, transform it back into a *regulated* amativeness by surrendering to her inborn desire for the paternal.

The narrative, in consequence, begins to reverse itself; once the father is exiled, he can only be recalled. It takes some six years to recall him, providing Beulah a decent interval in which to make ready for the Sunday of her life, that is, to mull over the lesson she unconsciously and instantaneously learns when her forsaken father forsakes her. This chastening interlude ends with a rewriting/re-righting of the drama that preceded it. Hartwell exited abruptly after the tragic developments that culminated in his premature proposal of marriage; now he sweeps back in, and unceremoniously repeats it. If he has changed, the heroine has no time to find out. But he hasn't changed. His Homeric dog Charon recognizes him at a hundred paces, falling "down at his feet and caress[ing] them" (354). As the faithful animal whimpers with delight, Hartwell crushes Beulah to his "strong frame" with a force that "almost suffocate[s] her," providing a palpable reminder of his obviously still steely rod. In the proposal scene that follows, he evinces the uncompromising style ("quick, child, decide") that once goaded the once Byronic heroine into passionate revolt. Lest one overlook the recursive nature of this family reunion, Hartwell invites Beulah to consider that they are simply replaying a drama rehearsed earlier: "'I once asked you to be my wife, and you told me you would rather die'" (355). Everything, he insists that she notice, is just the same.

But everything is also different. The difference, of course, lies in Beulah's eager acquiescence to her Christian com-mutation, which she now knows to be the only alternative to Creola-zation. Her Charon-like welcome of Hartwell makes this plain. Hardly has the faithful creature set to licking his master's feet than Beulah springs

into the doorway, holding out her arms, with a wild, joyful cry—

"Come at last! Oh, thank God! Come at last!" Her face was radiant, her eyes burned, her glowing lips parted. (354)

Those glowing, parted lips provide the (im)proper answer to the question Hartwell first posed six years ago. Now Beulah would rather die than *not* be Mrs. Hartwell. But the text is not content to leave matters there. It offers a theological reprise as well:

"You have changed in many things, since we parted, nearly six years ago?" [Hartwell asked].
"Yes, I thank God, I am changed. My infidelity was the source of many sorrows; but the clouds have passed from my mind; I have found the truth in holy writ." (356)

Beulah's "infidelity" was a source of many sorrows; the greatest of her sorrows was Hartwell's absence; the cause of Hartwell's absence was Beulah's infidelity. In the same measure as she was unfaithful to her guardian, Beulah was unfaithful to herself, and to her name; she tried, in violation of her nature, to become a Creola, to cut the Holy Familial tie Creolas are not bound by. We hardly need to see a picture of the faithless creature to be reminded of Beulah's perhaps graver breach of faith. It so happens, however, that Hartwell is staring at one as he proposes. The stare, needless to add, is stern.

Sterner, perhaps, than it need be. For Beulah is exactly right when she says that Hartwell has come back "because for weary years [she has] prayed for [his] return" (355). The wish, in this instance, is father to the father: Hartwell has changed back into Beulah's "father," has "come back," because she has submitted her daughterly desire to the Father in chastening prayer for the father. Now, at last, she is willing to be her guardian's daughter, willing to confess—however coyly—that he has all along been both source and object of her desire:

"Beulah, do you cling to me because you love me? . . . Answer me, Beulah."
"Because you are my all."
"How long have I been your all?"
"Oh, longer than I knew myself!" was the evasive reply. (356)

The reply is in fact anything but evasive: Hartwell has in truth been Beulah's all longer than she has known herself. Moreover, as significant as the reply itself is the fact that Beulah no longer avoids replying. She sees, now, that it would be futile: Hartwell has long known her self better than she has. He probably still does; his "splendid, dark eyes" are "unaltered" and penetrate Beulah as easily as when she was a child. "Silently regarding" her at the beginning of the scene (354), and, at the end, "scan[ning her face] earnestly, as if reading all that had passed" (356), Hartwell reestablishes himself as past master of the mastering gaze. With her submissive replies, Beulah, like Ellen, subjectively affirms a submission her "[child-]woman's nature" has long since tendered for her. Consenting to be her guardian's wife, she consents to be his daughter too.

Beulah's chastening permits this impermissible union. But her chastening began with a wrenching separation from God/Hartwell that she "voluntarily" induced; it ends by reuniting her with the fatherly. Shall we say, then, that chastening represents a transitory moment of difference, annulled when the rebellious daughter becomes the dutiful child-wife? Is the female animal's incestuous desire sated under "religion's happy reign?"

Not quite. Like *The Wide, Wide World*, *Beulah* strains to close the incestuous circle; yet this novel too can loop the loop only in a perpetually receding future. In Warner's tale, as in other instances of the simple plot, the irreducible difference between perfect hero and flawed heroine interminably postpones (unim)paired bliss. John's/Jesus' rod is forever both incestuous carrot and anti-incestuous stick; the master can never leave off chastening his charge, by holding her at a permanent if permanently decreasing distance from the object of her always vestigially unchaste desire. Beulah's godless, amative hero has a much shakier claim to superiority over his ward. His chastening superiority, however, is divinely prescribed. *Beulah* offers an elegant solution to this fundamental domestic crux. Simply, Hartwell will continue to better Beulah forever because the daughterly infidelity that enabled their incestuous union has also engendered the gap that calls it permanently into question. Hartwell's residual unfatherly amativeness is the scourge that will continue to subdue his little girl. Having, à la Creola, separated lover, father, and GUARDIAN, Beulah must spend the rest of her days helping God join together what woman has rent asunder. Her life's work and wife's holy mission will be to reform her too amative chastener forever. And that never-ending effort will endlessly chasten *her*.

Hartwell doffs his hat right after reminding Beulah she once said she would rather die than marry him. A gloss accompanies the gesture: "'I am no longer a young man. Look here.'" He threw off his hat, and passing his fingers through his curling hair, she saw, here and there, streaks of silver. He watched her, as she noted it. She saw, too, how haggard he looked." (355)

"He watched her, as she noted it." Has Hartwell recognized Beulah's desire for a father? Beulah now loves her father in her husband; will he, reciprocating her incestuous passion(lessness), apply the rod with paternal grace? In proper terms: will Beulah convert Hartwell, whether to Methodism, pragmatic feminism, or some combination of the two? The question hangs heavy over the novel's unwritten sequel. But the scene that closes the book provides solid grounds for hope. (Assigning the grizzled veteran of four proposals a "willingness to compromise at last," Baym, only a bit overeagerly perhaps, converts this hope into a fact). Once again, Hartwell's unhatted head speaks for him.

It is Beulah's wedding day. Yet the bride has a "troubled heart," and a feeling she has still not paused to analyze: "She loved her guardian above everything else; knew that, separated from him, life would be a dreary blank to her; yet, much as she loved him, she could not divest herself of a species of fear, of dread. The thought of being his wife filled her with vague apprehension." (359)

The text specifies two reasons for Beulah's nonspecific anxiety. Beulah named the first while accepting Hartwell's final proposal, when she mentioned what she had "prayed for not less fervently than for [his] return"—namely, that "God would melt [his] infidel heart" (356). The second reason is inscribed in a "free" association; as a tremulous Beulah goes out to tie the knot, "the image of Creola [rises] before her" (359). By now we know that the two reasons are one. And we also know, better than proper readers perhaps, why it is Beulah's ex-father's graying hair that casteth out her Creolan fears, greatly facilitating the business the man of iron is about to consummate. The consummation occurs, predictably, in Hartwell's "well-remembered house" (360):

She felt that a pair of eyes were riveted on her face, and suddenly the blood surged into her white cheeks. Her hand lay clasped in his, and her head drooped lower, to avoid his searching gaze.

"Oh, Beulah! my wife! why are you afraid of me?"

The low, musical tones caused her heart to thrill strangely; she made a great effort, and lifted her head. She saw the expression of sorrow that clouded his face; saw his white brow wrinkle; and as her eyes fell on the silver threads scattered through his brown hair, there came an instant revulsion of feeling; fear vanished; love reigned supreme. She threw her arms up about his neck, and exclaimed—

"I am not afraid of you now. May God bless my guardian! my husband!" (507)

It is, unmistakably, Hartwell's silver threads that catalyze the instant revulsion of the revulsion the adolescent Beulah left unanalyzed. As well they might: for they pledge that Mrs. Hartwell's husband-guardian will *re-ward his ward*, that his last proposal includes a renewal of his Ur-proposal. Tipped with silver, Hartwell's iron proclaims that Beulah may henceforth serve God and "nature's God" simultaneously; it promises too that, through her "holy work of love," she may look forward to sem-paternally reconciling the de-sired father with his desired double. This side of the Great Divide, the child-woman can come no closer to Beulah.

Writing, Re-righting, Clara-fication

Writing was for Beulah a "source of many sorrows"; from Spinoza to her skeptical essay on marriage, it was the origin and issue of her infidelity. Rewriting provided a vehicle for her return to the faith; in the essays "warning others of the snare in which she had so long been entangled" (327), she sought to repair the damage her literary promiscuity had wrought. The indispensable condition and goal of her reconciliation with the Word was likewise writing, but of a special kind—Scripture, the originary writing wholly faithful to the Father. From deviant writing to rewriting to holy writ: was this odyssey of the signifier salutary? Or should the early Beulah have followed the orthodox advice the later Beulah dispenses, and never have strayed from the "only sure fountain" of truth?

There is a character in *Beulah* who never does: Clara, Beulah's artless and spotless friend. Clara and Beulah have a good deal in common. Clara too has been treated cruelly by fate, and philanthropically by Hartwell. She was quite as destitute an orphan; sat next to Beulah at school; and loves her former deskmate's guardian as ardently as Beulah does. The heroine calls Clara's, and our, attention to the parallels: "'Clara, I believe there is less difference in our positions than you seem to imagine'" (98). There *is*, however, a difference. An ethereal being of "angelic sweetness and purity," Clara, as we have seen, thinks that Beulah should "almost worship" Hart-well. She, for her part, comes close to doing literally that. Not coinci-dentally, she also unswervingly maintains "a perfect faith in the reli-gion of Jesus Christ" (252). Clara is thus permanently in the position Beulah attains only at the end of *Beulah*.

Moreover, Clara helps Beulah attain it. When the apostate's philo-sophical infidelity is at its height (or nadir), Clara points sorrowfully to the "utter revolution of [Beulah's] nature," from Christian faith and joy to skepticism and chronic depression. After reminding Beu-lah that, her prodigious "mental endowments" notwithstanding, she has "a woman's heart" (251), her friend pleads: "'Oh, Beulah . . . come back to Christ, and the Bible'" (252). The plea is gently rein-forced by further remembrance of things past: "'There is another heart, dear Beulah, a heart sad, but noble, that you are causing bit-ter anguish'" (253). That heart is of course Hartwell's. One more dear heart remains to be mentioned; having evoked Beulah's Father and (ex-)"father," Clara brings up the heroine's disowned "brother," whose star-crossed journey to Heidelberg, she quietly recalls, once led Beulah to seek out the Father: "'Do you remember, that about six years ago, a storm . . . tossed the Morning Star [the ship Eugene took to Europe] far from its destined track, and for many days it was unheard of? Do you remember, too, that . . . you bowed your knee in prayer to Almighty God imploring him to calm the tempest . . . ? Ah, Beulah, you distrusted human pilots then.'" (253) This makes Beulah think: "[M]emory had flown back to the hour when she had knelt in prayer for Eugene. . . . He had left her, an earnest believer in religion; he came back scoffing at everything sacred. . . . Was there an intimate connexion between the revolutions in his nature?" (253)

There was, we know. We know too, what Clara is perhaps too sweet to say, that there is an equally intimate connection between the ongoing revolution in Eugene's nature and the upheaval in Beulah's. Finally, we know that only a counterrevolution in Beulah will suc-ceed in bringing about the restoration of Eugene (and, by implica-tion, fend off the disintegration of Hartwell). That redeeming coun-terrevolution must be a process that halts and reverses Beulah's creeping Creola-zation: namely, Clara-fication. To save and be saved, Beulah must become like her childlike friend.

But let us not be too quick to conclude that Beulah should have abided by the only sure fountain, like Clara. For Clara's "Madonna-like serenity" (246) has to be its own reward. It never occurs to Hartwell to make her his daughter and/or his wife. Beulah, who swings from faith to infidelity and back again, is the one who gets her guardian.

Not coincidentally, *Beulah* follows a trajectory parallel to Beulah's. For the unwritten rule of the novel, as Susan Warner has taught us, is that holy writ has to be wholly rewritten. That is, fiction must be unfaithful to God's Truth in order to be faithful to it; fictional Clara-fication of the Word implies its Creola-zation. Wading through the murky waters of metaphysics back toward the limpid fountain that once refreshed her, Beulah merely acts out the dialectic of deviation and return inherent in the clarifying fictionalization of holy writ.

Yet though the Word has to be Clara-fied, it is not the Word that is unclear. What muddies the fountain of truth is the infidelity of the novel: for example, the novel philosophies that lead Beulah astray, but also the novel as a genre that necessarily (dis)figures the eternal verities. Congenitally deformed by this contradictory relation to its source, *Beulah* is cloven by the same hostility to itself that one observes in *The Wide, Wide World*. It erupts in Beulah's hostility to *her*self—for example, to the impious essays she issued, appropriately, "under various fictitious signatures" (327). Disavowing this work, Beulah advertises *Beulah's* aspiration to replace the fictitious with the true, to reduce original and therefore errant scribbling to Scripture. As the wide, wide world "and all the works that are therein" will one day reenter the eternal Word that spawns them, so *Beulah*, like all proper novels, seeks to lose itself in the unchanging truth whose transparent shadow it longs to be. Beulah's self-effacing evolution as a writer images that of the self-destructive writing that helps re-right her.

So does her emotional evolution as a child-woman—or, more precisely, as a child-woman-child. Rejoining the Father and the father, Beulah recovers the "pure faith of her childhood" (320): re-warded by her guardian-husband, she recuperates her true child-womanly nature. With that restoration and return, the novel strains to couple its beginning and its end, and so to exclude its middle: it symbolically erases all the writing that recounts Beulah's perverse involvement with false writing. As it does, it also symbolically eliminates everything that intervenes between Hartwell's proposals of adoption and marriage. Indeed, going even farther than Beulah's (ex-)"father," it strains to eliminate a crucial little bit more. Unlike Hartwell, who finally only wants to efface the loverly refusal at the *end*—not the daughterly refusal at the *beginning*—of Beulah's hysterical phase, the novel aspires to eliminate her "No's" in both places. That is, it aspires to remove the impediment blocking full union with the paternal rod; its textual desire is to collapse inward on an all-embracing, all-consuming primal-and-final scene that would, telescoping adoption and marriage, obliterate the narrative that joins as it separates them. *Beulah*'s passion for truth remains *entirely* faithful to Beulah's passion for Hartwell.

Yet the latter passion, paradoxically, shows why the former must be forever frustrated. To suppose that *Beulah*, like Cousin's God, can be "at once . . . end and middle" (316) is to succumb to the classic fallacy the Hartwellian phallus is there to ward off. *Beulah* cannot exclude its middle because it cannot exclude Beulah's: the pulsation that contaminates woman's—and woman's fiction's—purity is also the textual energy driving fiction toward truth. That is why the novel must contain the womanly desire that motivates its incestuous deference to the Word; but that is also why it must contain it. *Beulah* needs all of Beulah to entice Beulah (back) to Beulah.

Beulah must, in other words, undergo Creola-zation so that her Clara-fication may begin, and never end. Clara, who is always already—and therefore never—Clara-fied, fails to graduate from the school she and Beulah attended; she drops out, and slowly fades from the text. Beulah is forever graduating, thanks to her Creolan "past [that] can never die" (361). The truth of holy writ is forever wedded to woman's unholy passion. That, as Beulah tells us after her own fashion, is why one must read *Beulah*.

5

GO AWAY AND DIE:

The Lamplighter, 'Lena Rivers, Ernest Linwood

His forbearing at present . . . is on purpose to try their love.
—John Bunyan

Go away and die, come back and let me love you.
—Armenian saying

George Sand's remark that *Uncle Tom's Cabin* (1852) is essentially "domestic and of the family" finds its extension in the modern critical commonplace that Stowe puffs household affection and deflates romance. "The sentimental novel," Philip Fisher declares in an essay on *Uncle Tom*, "argues first of all for the reality, strength, and priority of an emotional life not based on sexual passion. It is not the relations between men and women that are its central reality . . . but the relation of a parent to a child." "*Eros*," affirms Stephen Railton, after citing Stowe's "archly smug" aside on the superiority of Rachel Halliday's matronly "cestus" to Venus's venereal one, is "replaced by mother love" in *Uncle Tom*. "Kinship titles of *Mammy, Uncle*, and *Aunt* applied to slaves throughout the novel," says Severn Duvall, "reinforce the familial metaphor. . . . Mrs. Stowe represents the easy domestic intermingling of black and white, and a parental privilege appropriated with equal familiarity in both groups." Amy Schrager Lang observes that Augustine St. Clare's "time and attention are entirely absorbed in the care of his child," who, she pertinently reminds us, is "his mother's namesake." That "motherly little girl" is, of course, little Eva, tutelary spirit of all the family-oriented critics of *Uncle Tom*. If Stowe's novel celebrates domestic love's moral victory over the dark slavery of the passions, as they insist, then the book is essentially a eulogy for America's archetypally passionless mother-daughter.[1]

All this might seem to set the stage for a facile reversal. But we are not about to accuse scribblerdom's most vestal virgin of taking an untoward interest in her "adoring papa"[2]—to say nothing of her doting Uncle. The notion that little Eva is even a little incestuous is the most preposterous sort of tomfoolery. The same, however, can properly be said of the incestuousness of any scribbler heroine. The special virtue of Stowe's perfected version of Beulah or Ellen, Alice or Clara, is simply that little Eva throws the preposterousness of the idea that true womanhood springs from incest into even sharper relief than do her at least provisionally passionate sisters. For if the mid-century reading formation put the forbidden passion into every woman's fiction, scribblerdom's eminently good little girls, with little Eva at their head, quite as systematically consigned it to the limbo of the utterly nonsensical. It is in that (non)sense that incest haunts *Uncle Tom's Cabin*—"as a memory does its loss: by its censorship."[3] But the negative dialectics involved are not negligible because they are nonsensical. Indeed, it could be argued that they are powerful enough to kill little Eva.

Why did God cut the little evangel off when he did? Such ultimate questions are, notoriously, unanswerable. But, whatever His reason, it almost certainly was not to punish any actual immorality. Always draped in white, like her father's departed mother, little Eva lives and dies "without spot or stain";[4] she goes to Heaven before becoming even a little like Eve. As to her unincestuousness, the evidence is positively overwhelming. To be sure, Eva resembles the Father's bride much more closely than does Marie St. Clare, the Queen of Heaven's nominal representative in *Uncle Tom*, and it is quite true that her father unambiguously prefers her to his unlovable wife ("hang the woman!" [184]); but this hardly warrants the suggestion that *Eva* aspires to her mother's place in her father's affections. Again, St. Clare gives his daughter his mother's name in the hope that "she would prove a reproduction of her image"—a "thing" which, coupled with his "absorbing devotion to the child," excites Marie's "petulant jealousy" and "dislike" of her daughter (171–72). But Eva, obviously, had no hand in her christening; and nothing else justifies the suspicion that she harbors the least desire to become her father's mother (a "divine" woman [243] once explicitly associated, in a rather tasteless jest, with "the Virgin Mary herself" [246]). That Eva is "zealous in kind offices" for the Uncle who "almost worship[s] her" (280) has, evidently, nothing to do with incest; Tom is a domestic, but he is manifestly not part of the family. As to her admiring, hot-blooded cousin Henrique, one cannot fail to be struck by the fact that Eva receives his "flushed" compliments "with perfect simplicity, without even a change of feature" (293)—quite as if she took the young gallant's ardor to be purely fraternal. In fine, the non-sense of little Eva's death is that she dies for her incestuous *non-sins*. And the beauty of it is the total absence of positive proof.

Unless the proof positive is precisely this absence, corroborated by prepubescent Eva's (un)timely death itself. One may or may not find with Ann Douglas that the proto-"Teen Angel's" lingering departure is "archetypically satisfying"; but who would deny that (to borrow Stowe's notorious phrase) it somehow "feels right"? Yet why should it? Why doesn't Simon Legree die at the age of twelve? "All [the scribblers] agree," Nina Baym incontrovertibly claims, "that total self-abnegation is suicidal." In innocent Eva's condemned person, Elizabeth Ammons argues, Stowe "resurrects" Eve "from infamy." Mundane chastening (like Ellen's or Beulah's) is Ammons's paradox leavened with Baym's tautology: the average scribbler Eve is "resurrected" from infamy without being totally (ab)negated. Yet the infamous crime she (on an improper view) longs to commit calls for nothing short of total annihilation. Eve/Eva's murderous resurrection squares the celestial accounts: perfectly chaste, Stowe's "feminine Christ" is nevertheless chastened to death. Or is she perfectly chaste because she is so chastened—unincestuous by virtue of the lethal "censuring" of her incestuous cestus? Is the child-woman's congenital fault the reason "the 'carnal' and the 'charnal' are inextricably linked"?[5]

There is no way of telling. That, perhaps, is what makes the "pre-pubescent corpse as heroine" so archetypically satisfying;[6] always al-ready (ab)negated, she eternalizes that death-in-life where "total self-abnegation" is coeval with Christian-feminist "resurrection," where incestuous non-sense survives *as* its obliteration by non-incestuous sense. Preventively executed before she can launch woman's congen-itally motivated insurrection, laid to rest by a rodless Uncle and "womanish" (251) father incapable of instigating it, the prepubescent and therefore pre-incestuous corpse passes "from death unto [eter-nal] life" (319) as a paragon of unimpregnable female innocence. Little Eva rediviva—a dead ringer, in improper perspective, for little Eva, dead—eternally suspends the overwhelming question posed by the substitution of "mother love" for "Eros": the question as to whether the prim-Eval is con-genitally evil, or untarnishably little-Eval.[7] Sacrifice or sanction, liberation or preventive detention, Eve/

Eva's (un)timely transfer to the beyond leaves improper criticism grasping at the merest wisps: not even non-sense, but non-sense's ghost.

How, then, can one test the improper hypothesis that little Eva was prophylactically dispatched for unconscious intent to commit incest? The method here adopted—admittedly oblique—turns on ransacking scribblerdom for other evidence of real or symbolic gyn-ocide. Specifically, it seeks to determine what happens to the scribblers' *post*pubescent corpses—or, rather, "corpses," since they return with astonishing frequency from figurative graves. Do their authors have them tried for imaginary crimes, and packed off into chastening exile? Do they arrange for carbolic acid to be decanted into their adolescent eyes, and celebrate the morally restorative effects thereof? As for those heroines who marry while still unchastened: are they summarily executed for their unseemly haste, and do they come to bless their executioners? And is something like incest evoked at each punishing turn?

It seems highly unlikely. But then so does the nonsensical notion that the moving death of little Eva is an exercise in the mortification of the incestuous female flesh.

God's Griselda

It is time we turned the light of Maria Susanna Cummins's *The Lamplighter* (1854) back on the source. *The Lamplighter*, it will be recalled, affirms, *expressis verbis*, that the secret of true happiness lies in kissing the Father's rod ("a foretaste of heaven").[8] One might reasonably expect the text to reinforce its unbending orthodoxy on this cardinal point by arranging, like the best-sellers we have already examined, for a fatherly martinet to discipline and then marry a congenitally wayward child-woman. But Cummins's novel develops and suppresses its patrimatrimonial implications with a lighter touch. Though it displays the typical features of the double plot—a pious-passionate heroine, a flawed but perfectable father figure, and an impressive array of chastening trials and tribulations—it scrambles them, fragmenting, in particular, the main incestuous relationship. Thus *The Lamplighter*'s version of the Law-Man meets his appointed ward appallingly late in the day; he chastens not her but her bosom friend, and that years before the action of the

novel proper begins; he is debarred by a long absence from super-
vising the heroine's sentimental education. Yet though the hero is
seemingly dispossessed of rod and ward, his division and dismember-
berment obeys quite the same ideo-logic as do more conventional
scribbler procedures. Or, rather, (dis)obeys it. For what the novel
chops up and buries is eventually resurrected; and it turns out to be
another avatar of the improper tale domestic ideology and the domestic novel jointly conspire to ignore.

The fragments come together in *The Lamplighter*'s climactic chapters. They are dominated by a Mysterious Stranger. We will recognize him: "His features were rather sharp, but expressive, and even
handsome; his eyes, dark, keen, and piercing, had a most penetrating look, while his firmly compressed lips spoke of resolution and
strength of will. But the chief peculiarity of his appearance was his
hair, which was deeply tinged with gray . . . strikingly in contrast
with the youthful fire of his eye." (421)

As the narrator gratuitously puts it, this young-old man embodies
"contradictory claims" (421). Before long he is pressing them on the
novel's nubile heroine, Gerty. He uses his eyes, "eyes whose earnest,
magnetic gaze had the power to disconcert and bewilder" (428).
What he proceeds to say—ostensibly on the topic of the surrounding
scene, perhaps not coincidentally that honeymoon haven, Niagara
Falls—has the same thrillingly confounding effect as his gaze: "'You
have never seen anything so beautiful before in your life.' He did
not seem to question her; he spoke as if he knew" (428).

This proves to be the kind of line Gerty falls for. It is not half a
page before she is sitting "entranced with admiration and delight"
(428) as the stranger talks on; the "confusion" engendered by his
piercing-penetrating gaze and no less probing pseudo-question
swiftly modulates into "so much ease and freedom from restraint"
that she soon finds herself conversing "familiarly with a complete
stranger," even leaning familiarly on his arm (429). Is that append-
age, we catch ourselves wondering, paternal or loverly? Gerty's
avuncular friend Dr. Jeremy, who has been voyeuristically eyeing
the scene, prompts us to spy out the lover: "the doctor tried to rally
Gertrude a little about her gray-headed beau, declaring that he was
yet young and handsome, and that she could have his hair dyed any
color she pleased" (429). But this and other hints of budding romance are coupled with intimations of impending paternity, as when
the gray-haired stranger "look[s] at Gertrude in such a benignant,

fatherly way that she hesitate[s] not to take his offered hand"; or,
again, when he decently avoids "bestowing upon her the keen and
scrutinizing gaze which had proved so disconcerting" (429). Receiv-
ing signals so thoroughly mixed, one hesitates to take up a definitive
attitude toward the Mysterious Stranger. The text coyly leaves one
hesitating.

In time, of course, it releases the reader from her embarrassment.
But not, as we began by saying, classically. The stranger does not
adopt Gerty; she does not fall semi-incestuously in love with him; he
does not chasten her unlawful desires; she does not, once chastened,
set to curing him of his heathenish hardness; filial and conjugal passion do not at last lie down together under religion's happy reign.
An unwonted complication blocks this standard resolution of the incest problem. The stranger is not Gerty's "father," but her father.

The romantic promise hovering over their family reunion does
not, for all that, go unfulfilled. Nor is the stranger superfluously
endowed with a chastener's sine qua non, the power "to inspire awe,
and even fear" (431). Gerty marries her father after all, but by
proxy. Though she has been thoroughly chastened long before she
first meets him, he may justly claim credit for the chastening. And
he reaps the usual benefit from this devious patrimatrimony; an embittered Hartwellian agnostic when he spills the secret of his identity,
he develops a Christian appreciation for "the good, the pure, and
the truly great" (457) as a result of his symbolic union with his chastened daughter.

Their marriage at one remove is made possible by a web of relationships involving four characters: Gerty, her loving father, Philip
Amory (emphasis added), her lover, Willie Sullivan, and her main
mentor, Emily Graham. Gerty has a typically troubled prehistory.
Brought as a baby from malarial Rio to a Boston slum, she wastes
her infancy in the house of the hateful Nan Grant, who hates her.
Predictably, the little orphan grows up a casebook passionate child:
"her little, fierce, untamed, impetuous nature had hitherto only expressed itself in angry passion, sullen obstinacy, and even hatred"
(218). The first to help her become better (if we do not count Nan's
catalyzing cruelty [see p. 77]) is the motherly, titular lamplighter
Trueman Flint, who takes her from the nasty Nan's house to his
humble home. But Flint does not live up to the promise of his pa-
tronymic; though he has "as good and honest a heart as ever
throbbed" (217), Trueman is not made of the stern stuff that alone

can tame female passion. He is already wobbly when he unofficially adopts Gerty, and becomes even wobblier later; though he makes her happy, "the fire of her little spirit [is] not quenched" (247) by this Van Bruntish odd old man, who symbolically ends his days as an "old paralytic" (447) under Gerty's motherly-daughterly care. Fortunately, Gerty is befriended by two other characters not long after Trueman takes her in. One is Willie Sullivan, a poor but diligent young man whose doting mother has raised him in the spirit of Jesus. The other is the blind Emily Graham, a woman whose love for doing good and enduring evil borders on the saintly.

Willie is not only "manly and noble," but also possesses "uncommon beauty." Not long after they meet, he and Gerty are tightly attached by ties of mutual devotion. An honorific consanguinity cements their bond; as Willie bubbles to Gerty, "Uncle True's your uncle, and mine too;—so we're cousins" (236). This gives us grounds to speculate that Willie will quench Gerty's fires even as he kindles them, à la John Humphreys; or else that he will, à la Eugene Graham, leave the incestuous promise of their childhood romance tragically unfulfilled, perhaps sinking into the dismal swamp of self-abuse. In the event, he does neither—after seeming to be on the point of doing both.

Initial indications are that Willie is being groomed for the Humphreyesque role. He teaches Gerty about God, protects her from the neighborhood bullies, and soon advances from honorific cousin to quasi-brother. His mother calls attention to his change in status: "I think [Gerty] and Willie could not love each other better, if they were own brother and sister" (291). But circumstances prevent Gerty's "brother" from becoming a full-fledged John. Well before he can begin to educate her in earnest, Willie has to sail to India to seek his fortune. This will put us in mind of Eugene's fateful voyage to Heidelberg, the more so as *The Lamplighter* repeatedly evokes the terrifying possibility of Willie's dissipating while so far away from his pure American mother. Willie does not, however, follow Eugene's example any more than he follows John's. After an absence of several hundred pages and complications we will prudently ignore, he returns to Boston unseduced and unspoiled. There, without lifting a finger to chasten his childhood sweetheart, he marries her; and with that, *The Lamplighter* ends.

The course of this mundane romance would seem at least a bit less anomalous if some other familiar male authority were to chasten

Gerty in her beloved's absence, and then pass on, bequeathing her her Willie. One could, for example, imagine her biological father in the role. It is, however, the conspicuously feminine Emily Graham who cures Gerty "of her dark infirmity" (263) by "teaching her the spirit of her Divine Master" (271). Moreover, Emily cures her as thoroughly as one can cure congenitally infirm woman; Gerty attests her true womanhood in all manner of self-abnegating ways well before Willie and her father reappear on the scene. Still more problematic, one has to strain to link the "dark infirmity" Gerty exposes to Emily with woman's natural inclination to incest. Finally, as Emily is neither Gerty's sister nor her "sister," nothing indicates that Gerty is motivated to kiss the chastening rod by the same incestuous impulses the rod chastens. Indeed, we cannot even legitimately speak of the rod, for the blind Emily, not surprisingly, does not have one; the point is foregrounded in various tableaux like the one in which Gerty's frail teacher, "in her sweet and gentle helplessness, lean[s] . . . trustingly" on her pupil, "bright, erect, and strong" (424). At least until her father Philip Amory's ambiguous entrance late in the novel, then, domesticity's incestuous dialectic would seem to find little enough to latch onto in *The Lamplighter*.

In fact, it would have needed nothing more than the cues already mentioned. For the mid-century reading formation, female "infirmity" automatically evoked incest, all the more so if it was "dark"—just as, when young men journeyed to distant climes, the danger of solitary and/or social fornication automatically sprang up. Thus, even if Gerty's father had never surfaced, *The Lamplighter*'s audience would have sensed the domestic dialectic skulking in the decorous darkness. But such a thesis is convincing only if one already believes that the mid-century reading formation answers to our description of it. Happily—that is, almost tragically—the last part of *The Lamplighter* provides the basis for a narrower argument, retrospectively mandating an improper reading of the first, apparently unincestuous part. Having brought Gerty's tale nearly to its climax, the novel pauses to review Emily's; and Emily's silently exposes the incestuous affinities of the whole.

We hear Emily's story from her own mouth. Examined with due attention to, as John Humphreys might have said, providentially planned trifles, it confirms what the perverse reader will in any case have concluded upon learning that this saintly female is blind: namely, that she has been blinded for incestuous insubordination, and that she is saintly—read: passionless—because she has been blinded. The tragedy (which is, need one say, only apparently a tragedy) occurs when Emily is sixteen. She has been living with her father, her good Christian stepmother, and the latter's son. (Un)expectedly, her stepmother dies, but not before charging her beloved Emily to "'be a guardian-angel to [her] boy!'" (466). Almost everything speaks for entrusting the task to Emily, since the boy—let us provisionally call him Emily's "brother"—has for years been her "sole companion," and the devoted "partner of all [her] youthful pleasures" (465). The one problem is that Emily's father, Mr. Graham, has from the first looked with a jaundiced eye upon "his step-son's familiar intimacy" with Emily. Accordingly, when she reaches "the period of womanhood," he resolves "to put an immediate check upon [their] freedom of intercourse" (467).

Looking back, Emily finds her father's resolution anything but surprising, since, when he announced it, the "'attachment between [her and her "brother"] could no longer be considered a childish one'" (467). Yet, as Emily admits in the next breath, there was "'no reason to believe that the idea of romance . . . entered at all into [her "brother's"] calculations'" (467). There is, one therefore suspects, reason to believe that it entered furtively into hers. If so, one has a way of explaining why she so readily accepts her father's suggestive interpretation of a manifestly innocent childhood attachment. Unobtrusively, to be sure, the prologue to Emily's drama thus alerts us not only to incest, but also to the familiar theme of woman's special predilection for it.

The ensuing scene broadens this trifling hint of specifically feminine guilt. Emily, as she herself only too gladly confesses to Gerty, was a "spoiled child" before her great "trial" (468). The epigraph to the chapter in which she tells her tale has already prepared us to give "spoiled" its full theological weight:

> When, lo! arrayed in robes of light,
> A nymph celestial came;
> She cleared the mists that dimmed my sight—
> Religion was her name.
> She proved the chastisement divine,
> And bade me kiss the rod;
> She taught this rebel heart of mine
> Submission to its God. (465)

The relevant rebel heart is in this case Emily's. On its promptings, the spoiled child "lent [herself] unhesitatingly to a species of petty deception" (468) in order to preserve her "familiar intimacy" with her "brother." Did she thereby prove "faithless to the trust" her step-mother reposed in her, as she herself wonders (466)? Should the would-be guardian angel have guilefully maintained a no longer childish attachment to her familiar intimate—*before* kissing the rod? Was her passionate fidelity to him the worst sort of faithlesssness? The ambiguity of woman's position, as Beulah in particular shows us, precludes a simple answer. The essential point is simply that her position is ambiguous.

The day she loses her eyes, Emily is in this highly ambiguous position—"quite alone," weakened by a recent illness, "half reclining upon the sofa" in her father's library (468). For the past six weeks, she has "enjoyed no society but that of [her] nurse, together with periodical visits from [her] father." Naturally, she feels "no common satisfaction and pleasure when [her] most congenial but now nearly forbidden associate unexpectedly" enters (469). Having entered, the nearly forbidden associate gives nearly full play to "all the fire of a hot and ungoverned temper," fanned as it is by his "woman's depth of feeling." He too derives uncommon satisfaction from this forbidden tryst, as he shows by "expressing again and again his joy" (469). The only other thing he does is to bathe Emily's temples with cologne for several most congenial hours. That, however, is enough.

Indeed, it is much too much. The con-genitally flawed Emily is "spoiled," that is, unchastened, while her "congenial companion's" "woman's depth of feeling" has betrayed him into giving a fillip to the passion he should rather manfully squelch. Something must induce him to take up the chastening rod, and that quickly. Otherwise, he may never take it up, and Emily's pure morality will probably be destroyed forever.

Emily's father Mr. Graham is the godsend. Bursting upon the scene as night draws nigh, he flings a "double accusation" in his step-son's teeth: he charges that the boy means to "win the affections . . . of his only child," and, further, that he has committed "forgery of a large amount . . . upon his benefactor's [Mr. Graham's] name" (469). The first offense, Mr. Graham adds, is "a secondary and pardonable crime" (469); we are left to conclude that the other is primary and unpardonable. The (un)true accusation has consequences only Providence could have foreseen. Emily's "brother" storms in a frenzy toward his accuser, races solicitously back toward the fainting Emily, and accidentally pours "a powerful acid" (470) into her eyes. The epigraph helps one put this Oedipal tragedy in (im)proper perspective. Emily's blinding is "the chastisement divine" (465) for her natural rebelliousness—for, let us say, her excessively familiar intimacy with her "brother."

It is not for naught, then, that Mr. Graham charges his stepson with misappropriating the name of the father. The false accusation comes true when the young man reaches for the acid: (mal)adroitly pronouncing the father's "No," Emily's "brother" slips into the role of the forbidding father whose name he stands accused of usurping. That, perhaps, is why Emily's father's face vanishes in her recollection of her chastisement divine, to be replaced, as she tells Gerty, by her "brother's": "'My father stood with his back to the light, and from the first moment of his entering the room I never saw his face again; but the countenance of the other, the object of his accusation, illumined as it was by the last rays of the golden sunset, stands ever in the foreground of my recollection'" (469). But if Emily's "brother"—the setting son and future father—thus takes the accuser's role, who takes the accused's? We need only recall that this is *Emily's* "trial." The real object of Mr. Graham's and his stepson's fury is the unchastened, ambiguously positioned seducer.

With the benefit of hindsight, it becomes clear as day to Emily that this distribution of roles is meet and right. "'I was then,'" she confesses to Gerty, "'a child of the world, eager for worldly pleasures.'" Her blinding, however, opened her eyes, and "lit the lamp of religion" in her soul. She can now say, with the Evangelist, "'Once I was blind, but now I see!'" (471): she sees that she brought her chastisement upon herself for hating instruction and despising reproof. She should therefore, according to the usual pattern, be allowed to satisfy the forbidden desire for which one is chastened. That is precisely what happens, after a decent interval. Her "brother," whom she erroneously supposed had died "'in a foreign land, alone, unnursed, untended, and uncared for'" (471), comes home long years after involuntarily chastening Emily, and marries the woman he maimed.

What does all this have to do with Gerty?

To begin with, it involves her in incest-by-association. Emily makes the association for us, and Gerty, when she pauses in the middle of her autobiography to remark to her confidante, "'How often, when you have spoken of the assistance Willie was to you in your studies, have I been reminded of the time when I, too, received similar encouragement and aid from my own youthful companion and friend'" (467). Emily's "brother" was to Emily as Willie was to Gerty; the analogy expands to accommodate all the essentials of Gerty's troubled history. In this new frame, details we may have skimmed over before invite a longer look. When Willie left for India, for example, Gerty exclaimed to her mentor: "'Miss Emily, you do not know how I love Willie'"; only now can we appreciate the full import of Emily's truncated reply: "'I, Gertrude! *not know*, my child! I know better than you imagine. . . . I, too, had—'" (296). Just what did Emily and Gerty both have, and why have both been divinely chastised for it? When Willie's dying mother wanted to embrace her son more than she wanted to go to Jesus, why did Gerty compassionately cry, "'It cannot be a sin, that which is so natural'" (349)? Was it because Gerty loved Willie the way his mother did—the way Emily loved her forbidden associate? Did Emily suffer for Gerty's sins as well as her own?

If so, it makes sense that Emily tells Gerty her story just after Willie returns from India. For, to Gerty's dismay, long absence has made Willie an associate nearly as unapproachable as Emily's "brother" ought to have been: "Had they both been children, as in the earlier days of their brother and sister hood, it would have been easy, and but natural, to dart forward, overtake, and claim him. But time, in the changes it had wrought, had built up a huge barrier between them." (451)

In principle, this barrier has already been surmounted, for Gerty has already been chastened by Emily. Because her chastening has been accompanied by only the barest evocation of incest, however, Gerty, and duller readers, may not have grasped what women are chastened *for*. It is harder not to understand after Willie comes back, shielded by that nearly insuperable barrier. The text helps one along by again evoking, after a long silence on the subject, Gerty's "ardent and excitable . . . temperament" (453). With the inaccessible Willie waiting tantalizingly behind his barrier, this newly remembered ardor is subjected to the restraining influence of Emily's chastening story; the immediate context of that instructive tale is provided by several more chastening experiences. They seem, for a time, to have cordoned Willie off for good. Thus the controlling pattern of Emily's biography is belatedly replicated in Gerty's. More precisely, the concluding episodes of Gerty's tale belatedly signal that the whole of it hews to the pattern of Emily's. *The Lamplighter*'s crowning scene is therefore as unsurprising as Emily's long-awaited match with her "brother": as Willie's late loving mother beams down from on high, "the son and daughter of her love" (544) plight their troth on Trueman Flint's grave.

But this is only the small change of an improper reading of Cummins's classic. Eclipsing the analogy between Emily's and Gerty's amours is the *identification* of the two long-suffering ladies. This identification is buttressed by a "singular coincidence" (535). To everyone's astonishment, Gerty is revealed to be the daughter of Emily's "brother," who is none other than Gerty's strange familiar gentleman, Philip Amory. The singular coincidence plus the identification of the two women who coincide in it add up to the real stakes of the novel: Gerty's (re)union with her biological father.

The coincidence caps a process of identification that has been underway throughout the novel. Emily has been assiduously promoting it, much as Alice promoted *her* identification with Ellen. Overseeing an exemplary program of Christian nurture, "the blind girl" "simply and gradually . . . impart[s] her light to the child's dark soul" (266). Soon the two "people of God" (471) are living "in a beautiful world of their own," bound "heart to heart in the closest bonds of sympathy and affection" (327), finding their "happiness . . . almost wholly in each other" (362). Gerty's relation to Emily, indeed, only echos her relation to her self: "to pour out her thoughts to Emily was like whispering to her own heart, and the response to those thoughts was as sure and certain" (426). This mingling of self and self is consummated when Emily tells her story to Gerty, as it were transferring her remembrance of things past to her alter ego. Gerty's receptive response shows how entirely she makes her story her own: "When [Emily] laid her hand upon [Gerty's] head, and prayed that she too might be fitted for a patient endurance of trial, and be made stronger and better thereby, she felt her heart penetrated with that deep love and trust which seldom come to us except in the hour of sorrow, and prove that it is through suffering only we are made perfect." (471)

Of course, the story Gerty thus makes her own is already her own story. This is true in a generic sense, as was noted a moment ago: Emily's is only a variant on the archetypal story of woman's chasten-

ing. It is also true in the specific sense that the two women are enduring parallel deprivations: Emily has (apparently) lost Philip
Amory, Gerty has (apparently) lost Willie. Finally, and most impor-
tantly, Emily's story is also quite literally Gerty's, though neither of
them knows it as the story is being told. The history of Emily's chastening is the prehistory of Gerty's: unintentionally chastening his
"sister," Amory unintentionally forged the true woman who in turn
supervised the chastening of his daughter. Without going into detail,
let us note that Amory has also had a direct hand in Gerty's moral
education: abandoning her as an infant in Rio, he initiated the long
train of trials that made Gerty susceptible to Emily's pious influence.
Mr. Graham thus spoke doubly true in falsely accusing Amory of
forging the name of the father, for by the seminal act of pouring
acid into Emily's eyes, Amory became not only Emily's spiritual father,
but, through her, Gerty's as well. Here is the ultimate source of the
identification between Gerty and Emily: both play the role of chastened heroine in the incestuous drama whose hero is Philip Amory.

But how can we accuse Gerty of taking an incestuous interest in
Amory when she doesn't even know him? The scenes that confront
the heroine and her mysterious-yet-familiar stranger seem designed
to meet precisely that objection; they afford Gerty the opportunity
to fall in love with her father the only time she decently can, that is,
when she doesn't (really) know him. Not coincidentally, the first of
these titillatingly ambivalent encounters takes place only two pages
before Willie reenters Gerty's life. The history of her relation to her
older admirer is thereafter interwoven with that of her relation to
her younger one. Moreover, Emily tells her chastening story somewhere toward the middle of these combined developments. One
might almost conclude that the already pious Gerty was being vicariously rechastened in anticipation of an impending union with her
fatherly friend.

One might conclude, too, that he is being chastened in anticipation of his union with her, in accordance with the demands of the
double plot. He certainly shows himself to be in dire need of chastening. We have already noticed the Hartwellian streaks in Amory's
hair; as with Hartwell, this premature gray is the outward sign of
inner turmoil. Gerty's father has lost his faith, in man and in God.
So much so, in fact, that at one point, his somewhat acidulous "manner," if not "his look," implies a shocking "slight sneer" at the Holy

Sabbath (432). Later he tells Gerty, "with bitterness," that he "trust[s] no one" (457–58). Who bears the responsibility for this falling off? The answer will not amaze us: Amory's apostasy is ultimately Emily's fault.

The proof is that Amory lost his "faith in Heaven" at a precisely identifiable moment, shortly after putting out Emily's eyes, when someone convinced him that his fickle companion no longer loved him. This was the "final blow, beneath which his manhood had fallen"; in that instant "the blight had come" (517). Why was Amory so easily persuaded of Emily's flagging faith? The text tells us as delicately as possible when it informs us, through Emily herself, that she was not one of the "people of God" at the time of the fatal encounter with her familiar intimate. When Amory unstoppered the acid, Emily, by her own admission, probably "uttered words that seemed like a reproach" (470), instead of patiently suffering her Father's will. Amory's account of the episode confirms that Emily's comportment on this trying occasion was less than true-womanly; when he approached her as her eyes were dissolving, "she repelled [him] with her hands" (514). Worse, as a "child of the world," she dwelt in "the darkness of despair" for a long time after her trial (471), unable to accept the chastisement divine. She was in this subjectively unchastened state when Amory came to seek a reconciliation. Is it any wonder that he readily believed she now hated him, that he instantly turned from God, and that he soon contracted a dangerous marriage with a "half-child, half-woman" (518), a (pre-chastened) orphan whom "sorrow made [his] sister" (519)?

As with Hartwell, so with Amory: masculine unbelief must at least *begin* to give way to faith before there can be any question of patri-matrimony and a happy end. The turn does, indeed, occur, shortly after Amory returns to America. But Gerty, not Emily, induces it. Gerty is "the young and ardent worshipper of the beautiful and the true" who begins to teach her father "to love and pity . . . that miserable thing called man" (436); it is Gerty's brightly shining light that sheds the first rays on Amory's road to Heaven. The road to Heaven, as we know, also leads to the hearth. All is thus building toward the climax that does not, of course, come, since it would involve Amory in a "crime" even more "deep, dark, and disgraceful" (511) than the one Mr. Graham "falsely" accused him of committing. If this foul offense is to be avoided, something more than the chastening rod must ultimately be interposed between father and daughter. Emily is.

The sickly Emily, however, is only a pale substitute for Gerty, an ersatz sister/daughter who gets to do, by default, what the real one cannot. This is indicated plainly enough with Amory's first, pre-paternal appearance. His potent gaze speaks for him: it penetrates both Gerty and Emily. Emily comes first. The mysterious stranger's attention is, however, "at once transferred from the lovely and interesting face of Emily to the more youthful, eloquent, and beaming features of Gertrude" (420–21). There follows the (in retrospect) horrifying interlude in which Amory completely wins his daughter's heart while Emily dawdles in the wings. But Emily is, fortunately for all concerned, eventually drawn back into the scene: "Emily, whose nervous system was somewhat disordered, clung tremblingly to Gertrude; and Gertrude found herself, she knew not how, leaning on the arm of [Amory]" (429). We do not need to chart the ensuing climax in detail, for its contours are familiar enough. Somehow, Emily takes Gerty's place on Amory's arm; he and Emily "me[e]t again" "as children" (531), they are married, and Emily undertakes to carry on with Gerty's holy work of love, securing Amory's "hold on eternal life" (552). There are barriers even scribbler heroines cannot cross: Gerty has to satisfy herself with Willie.

More to the point, perhaps, we have to satisfy ourselves with our heroine's only allusively incestuous match. But *The Lamplighter* would not have been the literary beacon it once was if it did not offer some compensation for this mildly disappointing ending. It does so principally in the scene in which Gerty, willy-nilly, plights her troth to her, as she now knows, real father. Here is the novel's other climax. Like many another scribbler dénouement, it needs no comment, if quoted at proper length and read in the (im)proper spirit:

Mr. Amory, with folded arms and a fixed countenance, is watching for her coming . . . she bursts into a torrent of passionate tears, interrupted only by frequent sobs, so deep and so exhausting that her father, with his arms folded tightly around her, and clasping her so closely to his heart that she feels its irregular beating, endeavors to still the tempest of her grief, whispering softly, as to an infant, "Hush! hush, my child! you frighten me!" And, gradually soothed by his gentle caresses, her excitement subsides. . . . Wrapped in the folds of his heavy cloak . . . and still encircled in his strong embrace, Gertrude feels that their union of spirit is not less complete; while the long-banished man . . . glows with a melting tenderness which hardening solitude has not had the power to subdue. . . . Mr. Amory . . . asks . . . "You will love me, then?" "Oh, I do! I do!" exclaims Gertrude, sealing his lips with kisses . . . the strong man weeps. Not long, however. Her self-possession all restored at seeing him thus overcome, Gertrude whispers, "Come!"

"Whither?" exclaims he, looking up in surprise.

"To Emily." (529–30)

Innocence Is No Defense

At a climactic moment in Mary Jane Holmes's 'Lena Rivers (1856), the titular heroine's once and future lover Durward Graham writes her the following lines:

> I would rather see you dead than the guilty thing you are, for then your memory would be to me as a holy blessed influence, leading me on to a better world. . . . But now, alas! . . . I saw you throw your arms around *his* neck—the husband of *my* mother. I saw you lay your head upon his bosom. I heard him as he called you *dearest*, and said you would never be parted again![9]

Durward has not been quick to condemn. Almost a hundred pages earlier, his mother tried to prejudice him against 'Lena by remarking, in characteristically sardonic fashion, "'that it would be extremely pleasant to marry a bride with whom one's father was in love'"; Durward dismissed the insinuation with a properly loyal "'How ridiculous!'" (137). Though Mrs. Graham countered with crushing evidence of the deepening bond between 'Lena and the elder Graham, Durward's faith in his beloved remained firm. He would doubtless have rushed her to the altar if his mother had not, in the nick of time, found a compromising picture of 'Lena in her husband's possession, a picture 'Lena could only feebly protest she had never had taken. Even in the face of this seemingly incontrovertible proof of 'Lena's double-dealing, her lover hesitates to pronounce her guilty, preferring to regard her as a more or less innocent victim of his stepfather's foul and unnatural lusts. Only after Durward actually witnesses 'Lena and his alleged rival embracing passionately in bed does he—more in sorrow than in anger—pen the indictment just cited, reluctantly concluding that "uncertainty [has been] made sure," and bidding his "lost 'Lena" "farewell for ever" (232). 'Lena does not blame him. Indeed, she almost seems to confirm Durward's verdict; as she thinks back over his words, "her own heart sadly echo[s]" the sentence "*'lost for ever'*" (232).

Yet, though Durward's senses did not deceive him, the apparently "lost" 'Lena is as blameless as scribbler heroine ever was. There is a perfectly innocent explanation for what Durward thinks he saw. The man he caught 'Lena in bed with was her father.

Durward, at any rate, considers the explanation perfectly innocent, and so, emphatically, does the narrator. Having turned a more skeptical eye on our heroines' shenanigans, we may be inclined to take 'Lena's exoneration as proof that she is an even guiltier thing than Durward supposed, and to conclude that the scene he witnesses displays—behind the scarcest of veils—the heroine's con-genital fault. But the rest of *'Lena Rivers* makes one feel mildly guilty for so blithely assuming 'Lena's—and, indeed, her sister heroines'—guilt. For one thing, 'Lena demonstrates no excessive interest in her father before discovering that that is who he is; she is neither transfixed by his piercing eyes nor overmastered by his penetrating questions. Mr. Graham, for his part, seems hardly to possess a chastening rod. Indeed, no one deliberately applies the chastening rod to 'Lena; embryonic asides about Durward's ability to "control [her] wild nature" (232) remain just that, making the absence of a fully developed male master-figure all the more palpable. Again, one does not, simply because the chastening Law-Man is largely absent, find the text thickly littered with ominous hints of the heroine's incestuousness, such as might justify one's suspicions of 'Lena, and a perverse reading of the bedroom scene. On the contrary, Holmes eschews that species of cheap sensationalism with true-womanly dignity, matter-of-factly letting the reader in on the secret of Mr. Graham's identity long before her plot requires her to. The threat of inadvertent incest titillatingly if briefly evoked by *The Lamplighter* is thus, in *'Lena Rivers*, dispelled before it can materialize. The novel does not even grant us the subsidiary thrill of supposing, for a while, that 'Lena's beloved Durward has turned out to be her biological brother: we have long since learned that he is Mrs. Graham's son by a former marriage. The single satisfaction we are afforded when Mr. Graham acknowledges he is 'Lena's father is that of snickering knowingly as her loathsome rival ignorantly gloats that Durward's new-found "sister" can't marry him. It seems small compensation for the interdicted pleasures we could have had.

All this might predispose one to read *'Lena Rivers* as an indignant denunciation of Victorian misogyny. Far from being haunted by an abiding sense of woman's lawless passion, the argument would run, the text truculently puts her to bed with her father, defying one to suppose that something wicked might happen there. This is a perfectly proper line of reasoning. In other words, it violates the implacable rule of improper logic which states that to defend a child-woman against a charge of con-genital crime is, ipso facto, to charge her with same. For, in the measure that the defense implies an incriminating understanding of the indictment, one is prevented from concluding that 'Lena's innocence somehow extricates *'Lena Rivers* from the toils of the incestuous dialectic. And in the measure that *'Lena Rivers* is enmeshed in the incestuous dialectic, one is prevented from concluding that 'Lena Rivers is innocent. Or, rather, one must conclude that she is just as innocent as Ellen, Beulah, Gerty, et al.; that is, that she belongs with her sisters in the dock.

We do not need to dwell at undue length on the process through which *'Lena Rivers* associates girlish guilelessness and girlish guilt. It is enough to know that *'Lena Rivers* is the record of 'Lena Rivers' great "trial" (Emily). No matter that the accused is so pure of heart as not even to understand Mrs. Graham's "dark insinuations" about her relationship with Mr. Graham (155); this means only that *'Lena Rivers* makes its dark insinuations by insisting that there are none to be made. By now, the procedure involved can hardly surprise us: in scribblerdom, the hints and guesses that justify chastening trials are rarely much more substantial than Mrs. Graham's baseless allegations. Beulah, and before her Ellen, are tried for incestuous impulses they will never suspect they had; *The Lamplighter*, taking the method a step further, tries Gerty for incest by association with a woman at least as sexless as Ellen; *'Lena Rivers* unblushingly declares its heroine "wholly innocent" (155), and then *tries her anyway*. It is almost as if innocence were only suppressed incest; as if the perfection of scribbler justice would involve purging the innocent, *without trial*, in order to preserve them from wrong; as if what might appear to be cruel mistrials were in fact divinely ordained and redemptive miss-trials. One might go so far as to speculate that the author of the miss on trial could not decide if the defendant, though "as innocent as a little child" (191), was not also guilty as con-genital sin. It could even be argued that that is why she is tried; and that the result of the operation can only be, in Durward's polysemous formulation, that "uncertainty is made sure."

In 'Lena Rivers, the uncertainty is introduced by way of the standard references to the orphaned heroine's "passion." Frances Cogan,
lauding ten-year-old 'Lena as a shining example of "the Real [as opposed to the True] Womanhood ideal," alerts us to the real dangers
ahead. 'Lena, she notes—and we tremble—"defends herself brilliantly against a bullying . . . cousin" by "'hitting him a blow in the
face'" and "'snatch[ing] a cigar from his mouth.'" Cogan further
commends the little hoyden for "mounting her horse" without little
Durward's help—for, as it were, riding alone.[10] We may add that the
unchastened creature "passionately" rails at her grandfather (13),
flies "into a violent passion" when her bullying cousin teases her
(38), "inflict[s] a long scratch upon the forehead" of another cousin
(60), and commits several other such significant miss-demeanors.
Her future lover Durward laconically delivers scribblerdom's usual
verdict on the Real Woman: "too passionate" (61).

Passion does not, however, peak in attraction for a familiar gentleman. Instead, 'Lena is confronted with the groundless accusation
that she has been encouraging her father's sexual advances. Unlike
the characters who credit this foul slander, we know that Mr.
Graham's advances are not sexual at all, but paternal; moreover, we
know that 'Lena, who doesn't know Mr. Graham to be her father,
has in any case not been encouraging his advances. The "libelous"
suggestion (Beulah on Creola) that our heroine might be guilty of
incest is therefore doubly preposterous—at two removes, so to
speak, from the realm of the possible. At that safe distance from the
fiction proper, it flourishes.

It is nourished by an atmosphere delicately laced with intimations
of incest. They emanate mainly from the cattish Mrs. Graham, who
of course does not dream that 'Lena is her husband's daughter. That
that lady should be their source bespeaks an ingeniously perverse
logic. If 'Lena were consorting with her father, she would be his
wife's natural rival; however, if Mrs. Graham were consorting with
her son, 'Lena's ostensible affair with her father would make her
Mrs. Graham's unwitting accomplice in a crime still more (un)natu-
ral than patrimatrimony (namely, that horror of horrors, filial ma-
trimatrimony). But then 'Lena's romance with Durward would represent for Mrs. Graham a threat even more menacing than 'Lena's
alleged romance with Mr. Graham. Mrs. Graham seems to be blessed
with an instinctive grasp of this convoluted logic. "'When I take
'Lena Rivers into my family for my husband and son to make love

to, alternately,'" she declares in response to her husband's proposal to adopt 'Lena, "'I shall be ready for the lunatic asylum'" (93).

A bit later, Mrs. Graham will tell her son over breakfast that her husband breathed 'Lena's name in his sleep the night before. Durward—either "to tease his mother, or to make his father's guilt less heinous in her eyes"—reports that he too dreamed of 'Lena. The narrator notes, with proper irony, that "a double task was now imposed upon [Mrs. Graham]—that of watching both husband and son" (105–6). Eventually, watching the one gives Mrs. Graham hope, for a while at least, of restoring her uncontested dominion over the other: informing Durward that she has found his beloved's picture in "his father's" possession, Mrs. Graham calls a temporary halt to her son's budding romance. She should be sorry, for this unburdens her husband of a rival for 'Lena's affections. However, "so peculiar was her nature," as the narrator puts it, "that she would not have had matters otherwise if she could" (152). If it were not impossible, given Mrs. Graham's ignorance of Mr. Graham's real relation to 'Lena—and unthinkable besides—one might conclude that Mrs. Graham welcomes her husband's involvement with his daughter because it gives her a free hand with her boy.

None of this, however, implies that 'Lena wants to commit incest. Indeed, through Mrs. Graham no less than her husband, 'Lena Rivers seems unambiguously to identify incest as the sin of the mothers and fathers, not the daughters. 'Lena did not, appearances notwithstanding, present her picture to Mr. Graham: it turns out that what Mrs. Graham found in her husband's possession was a daguerreotype of 'Lena's mother, Mr. Graham's first wife, who almost exactly resembled 'Lena. Pursuing his daughter, Mr. Graham would seem to be pursuing his (dead) bride even more obviously than Mrs. Graham would seem to be pursuing a lifelong affair with Durward. What, under such circumstances, could possibly justify speaking of 'Lena's incestuous passion?

Her miss-trial does: 'Lena Rivers concentrates on chastening its heroine, not the Grahams. Moreover, although Mr. Graham is not endowed with a rod anything like John Humphreys's, her author appoints her father 'Lena's chastener; timorously concealing the fact that she is his daughter, he initiates a series of trials as severe as any Ellen's. Eventually everyone, even 'Lena's dear old grandmother, is persuaded of her moral turpitude. To make a long story short, the passionate young lady is thereupon turned out of doors, becomes "a

wanderer in the world" (211), contracts a dangerous fever, and
nearly dies. Chastening the innocent abroad with her cowardly father's connivance, Providence treats her, despite her innocence, as if
she were guilty as sin.

The cardinal merit of *'Lena Rivers* lies in its crass insistence on that
"as if," the condensed expression of the union of proper and improper in domestic fiction. Through it, the text admits the wom-
anological thesis the story rules out of court. 'Lena's terrible trial is
exposed as a mistrial when it is publicly revealed that the "lover"
Durward espied couching with her was actually her father. But her
author's—and her Author's—plot against her nonetheless accom-
plishes the great end of scribbler (in)justice: it affords us, and Durward, the opportunity "to see if there [is] in ['Lena] aught of evil"
(95). The elegance of the plot lies in its showing us that there *is* even
as it shows him that there *isn't*; the evidence that vindicates her incriminates her. And, even more elegantly, the process that vindicates
as it incriminates her also fearfully chastens her: the "uncertainty"
that attaches to women from birth is "made sure" by the same chastening process which establishes that 'Lena was never, in any proper
sense, uncertain. This guilty innocence, finally, justifies the cruel
conspiracy of circumstance that is the sum and substance of *'Lena
Rivers* and its sister novels, and the her-story of the wide, wide
world: it reminds us that only miss-trials can reveal the truth about
female innocence and female guilt. Lying in her father's arms, 'Lena
neatly figures both.

Shooting the Signifier; or, The Importance of Being Ernest

"The literary domestics," says Mary Kelley, "exposed their
own tale." This might be construed as a comment on the self-reflex-
iveness of domestic fiction. But Kelley does not mean to say what she
here seems to. Indeed, she means to say quite the opposite: that the
scribblers' tale is emphatically *not* about their tale. It is rather, as she
reads it, exclusively about "Hymen"—whose "temple," she affirms,
"encloses the secret of [Victorian] woman's life."

The immediate reference is to a passage in Caroline Lee Hentz's
novel *Ernest Linwood* (1856) in which the first-person narrator, Gabriella Linwood (née Lynn), breaks the flow of her story to ruminate
upon her activity as a writer. Or, more precisely, her (non)activity:

Gabriella calls attention to her authorial function only to deny that she has one. "Book!—am I writing a book? No, indeed!" It is somewhat as if the narrator were abruptly to intrude upon her narrative to confess truthfully that she was lying: "this writer of a book who has not written a book, has never written a book, paradoxically no longer dreams of being an author."

But the paradox, so Kelley, is more apparent than real. If our (non)author declares that she is not an author, the reason is that she really isn't. And, indeed, never really was. "True," the narrator does recall that, as a little girl, she fled a "male teacher" who ridiculed her poetry, to seek refuge in a sylvan "'by-path'" she considered hers, and not "the world's." We are also told, Kelley reluctantly concedes, that the little girl later "become[s] a secret writer of poetry," and that her secret path in "'the woods'" is evidently an emblem of "that secret so-called writer." But these are details and by-gones. "If there was a suggestion of hidden desire foreshadowing the secret writer, nevertheless the lasting impression was that the desire, rather than being nurtured, wilted in the woods." The impression is cemented by the fact that, up to the moment when the "little girl writ older" emits a "few detached offbeats" denying she is a writer, "there has not been any reference whatsoever to the fact that Gabriella is either writing or has written the book that she is narrating." Hence the voice we hear here must not be Gabriella's, but Gabriella's echoing Hentz'. The "suspended moment" is just that: the "once-removed author" has momentarily "usurped the place of her narrator, delivered her curious messages out of the context of the novel, and once again relinquished the tale to her fictional persona."

Yet the balance of Kelley's argument suggests that the "once-removed author" does not so much usurp Gabriella's place as that she shares the non-place Gabriella does not occupy. As the ventriloquized "Gabriella's" apparently self-reflexive writing is not really about *her* writing, so what Hentz is apparently writing is not really *writing*. It is "life," "truth," "home," "the heart." "Hentz, viz. Gabriella" does not write about having "entered the 'temple' of culture because she is actually speaking of the temple of domesticity, a temple she has never left." On closer inspection, what one might take to be the novel's "imaginary parts" melt back into their flesh-and-blood counterparts: Hentz's fiction "relates" no more nor less than woman's "life of domesticity," "not a literal transcription of her domestic life," to be sure, "but its inner truth." Having renounced any desire "'to possess the wand of the enchanter,'" says Kelley, taking her cue from her (non)author, Hentz-viz.-Gabriella restricts herself to recreating the dreary round of life on the hearth: "'the measured duty, the chained-down spirit, the girdled heart.'"[11]

"Revelation," Kelley also says with reference to the scribblers, "often came fast on the heels of denial."[12] Her own revealing appropriation of Gabriella's viz. Hentz' viz. all-scribblerdom's self-portrait does more than illustrate the point: it reveals that revelation often comes *as* denial, the improper as the disowned twin of the proper. As we prepare to exit scribblerdom by way of *Ernest Linwood*, it may be useful to examine this complicity in the light of its critical reflection. Let us, then, pause on the threshold of Hentz's "temple of Hymen" to glance back over the road we have come, and guess what, given Kelley's advance report, is likely to lie ahead. Reading Hentz's denials in Kelley's transcription, what can one surmise about *Ernest Linwood*? What does Kelley reveal by denying—or revealing—that the scribblers expose their own tale? What does Gabriella reveal by denying that she is writing a book?

Not, perhaps, that she is not writing one—but that her heart deserves girdling *because she is*. Not, to extrapolate from our anatomy of her sisters, that she lacks "imaginary parts"—but that her imaginary part is precisely what must, yet cannot really, be girdled. From which it would follow that our surrogate scribbler's repudiation of the "wand of the enchanter" should take the form of a process and not a preliminary, prolonged self-denunciation and not simple renunciation; and that the seemingly "detached off-beats" which chirp that hers is a text-which-is-not-one must ride the ground bass—the "*deep, under chord*" (129)—of her (non)book. Like the "chaining down" of Gabriella's-viz.-Hentz's heart, the "chaining down" of her art should emerge as a major concern of her whole text.

Our acquaintance with Warner et al. emboldens us to go a speculative step further. In scribblerdom, we have suggested, the dialectic of the detextualized text chimes with that of the desexualized sex: girdling their heroines' hearts, the scribblers chain down their own tales. It would therefore be puzzling if Hentz did not develop the paradox of the (non)book in terms of the parallel paradox of passion(lessness). The enchanting wand *Ernest Linwood*'s (non)author is not supposed to have should accordingly conjure up an incestuous imaginary part. It should also, transmogrified into a chastening rod, symbolically detextualize Gabriella's-viz.-Hentz's incestuous tale by symbolically desexualizing Gabriella. We may, then, anticipate the recurrence of a deadeningly familiar configuration: as we are likely to discover Gabriella, pace Kelley, writing about her writing (Hypothesis 1), we will almost surely find that she does so by (Hypothesis 2) writing about her righting.

This much follows directly from the ABC's of improper criticism. But *Ernest Linwood* adds a twist that calls for more strenuous speculation. A rarity in bestsellerdom, Gabriella is both heroine and first-person narrator. Hence Hentz, writing about her writing, is also writing about her—Gabriella—writing. What concrete effects can one expect this to have? Our theory generates an unlikely, not to say outlandish, answer (which, admittedly, we will have to temper upon turning to the novel proper). If it is true that the scribbler signifier, like the scribbler heroine, is innocent and incestuous at once, then the scribbler heroine who scribbles the story in which she represents the scribbler signifier will be even more conspicuously (not) guilty of incest than are her sisters. One may consequently (Hypothesis 3) look for her text to preach the fitness of inflicting a particularly dreadful punishment upon her, while profiling her as the hapless victim of a terrible travesty of justice. Indeed, her doom is likely to be augmented in proportion to the intensification of her sinful innocence. It would be surprising if the upshot did not bear a striking resemblance to homicide. Or, rather, womanslaughter.

To be sure, scribbler heroines who are not first-person narrators also innocently commit dreadfully deadly sins. One can, however, plead mitigating circumstances on their behalf: that their con-genital fault is not their fault; that they suffer, in consequence, for the sins of their creator; indeed, that their crimes are strictly imaginary, not only because they have no real equivalent outside scribblerdom, but also because they are not really committed even in that paper realm. But a scribbler who writes about her own righting indicts *herself* as the author of her imaginary crime. No matter that she writes, like Hentz-viz.-Gabriella, from the viewpoint of one already chastened for it; she must imaginatively recommit it in committing her history to paper, and so sin in much the same imaginary manner that earns her her original chastening. Retelling the story of her incestuous passion(lessness), she has no choice but to tell the story of her own incestuous tale. Or, to put it the other way around, the narrative of the heroine's chastening necessarily exposes the unchasteness of the narration of the heroine-become-narrator. In such a heroine turned

scribbler turned heroine and so on, incest insists beyond the possibility of its elimination; insists, indeed, in the measure that it is
"eliminated." In a word, however firmly girdled the chastened nar-
rator-heroine's heart, the imaginary part of her self-referential art
will not be chained down.

There is a patent analogy between this irreducible remainder of
writerly guilt and that residual maidenly passion which survives its
conversion into wifely passion(lessness). But the analogy points back,
as so often in scribblerdom, to the (as it were) incestuous relation
between the terms it relates. For, as was just noted, domestic fiction
engenders the incestuousness whose persistence it attests. If the
scribbler's heart, as Kelley affirms, "directs her pen," the pen itself
conjures up the incestuous "inner truth" of the directing heart.[13]
The natural sin that defiles the temple of Hymen goes forth from
the temple of culture. How then should a scribbler, if she is to tell
her own chastening tale consistently, reflect the irreducibly unchaste
effects of the telling within the action of the tale itself? To ask the
question is to answer it: by directing a scribbling heart to direct a
pen to direct an incestuous scribbler heart into the temple of Hymen—*unchastened*.

Gabriella may consequently be counted on (Hypothesis 4, susceptible of modification) to enter into a marriage involving amorous
trysts with her father and/or brother. For obvious reasons, one may
further anticipate (Hypothesis 5) that she will be meted out a punishment calculated to convert passion into passion(lessness), and,
concomitantly, writing into (non)writing. Finally, it seems clear that
the compound and cumulative nature of the passionate woman-
writer's crime will call down an unprecedentedly fearful chastisement upon her heart and head. For the scribbler signifier become
flesh, a few (un)deserved miss-trials, a sprinkling of acid in the eyes,
or a tender death by tuberculosis (to say nothing of mundane tribulations like humbling in the dust or philosophical fustigation) would
be too little too late. Gabriella-viz.-Hentz could only conclude about
her writing—with scribblerdom's most Draconian critics—that she
ought to be (Hypothesis 3a) summarily shot for it.

Alternatively (to return to our point of departure), the writer of
Enerst Linwood might seek to avoid this ineluctable conclusion by
pleading that her "secret desire" to create has long since "wilted in
the woods." Gabriella can make the argument rather plausibly: insofar as she is relating what really happened to her, she is manifestly

not forging any imaginary parts. But by denying that her fiction is truly fiction, she unwittingly passes the incriminating enchanter's wand back to Hentz.[14] The latter may therefore be expected to develop a supplementary strategy to shuffle off the burden of authorship. For example, she might put Gabriella up to insinuating that one's Author must take sole responsibility for what is nominally one's own perversity. That general theory has, as we learned from Warner in particular, a special aesthetic variant. It posits, be it recalled, that woman's fiction is naturally bound to the divine truth as the child-woman is to her (Heavenly) father. In other words, that the scribbler text, however passionate its attachment to its living Spring, cannot be blamed for its textual impropriety—because it was God in His wisdom Who made the signifier incestuous.

This may explain why Gabriella weds a reflection on aesthetics to one on fornication, while pondering marriage in its relation to "the Father of the fatherless" (52). The passage is particularly poignant because the Gabriella who pens it had herself been passing through a fatherless period at the time she writes of ("I was fatherless" [17]). Not only had she never known anything of her earthly father; her angelic mother had forbidden her, from earliest childhood, so much as to mention his name. So keenly did the little orphan feel her condition that she sometimes caught herself wondering if her sire had not been "like one of those gods of mythology, who, veiling their divinity in clouds, came down and wooed the daughters of men" (17). This is not without relevance to Gabriella's sally into aesthetic theory, if only because the latter prefaces the heroine's reading of a manuscript by her late mother which promises "to reveal the mystery of [Gabriella's] parentage" (164). But the links between the theory, its biographical background, and the reading it prefaces go well beyond the circumstantial—in ways the theory itself help one explain.

"How," Gabriella the narrator wonders, can a writer guarantee the fidelity of her art to truth? "Only follow nature," cries she, generically invoking "the critic," "and you cannot err." But, she knows well, "the great motive principle of nature" is "love"; and love is *un*natural, a source of "pestilence and death," unless it "bathes" in the purifying waters of "heavenly union" with the Father. By this point, however, a scant page after taking up the theory of the (non)novel, Gabriella is thinking more of matrimony than her muse. Her further reflections develop along lines conveniently drawn together in E.D.E.N. Southworth's observation that marriage unites *three* parties: husband, wife, and Heavenly Father.[15] The overall implication is therefore that art attains its proper end only if informed by that fidelity to Heaven whose earthly type—holy patri-matrimony—provides the main matter of Hentz's (and all scribbler-dom's) art. We are all too familiar with the fatal flaw in this circular scheme: the "God-resembling love" that binds father to daughter as it does husband to wife and signifer to transcendental signified has a perverse tendency to breed the very "pestilence and death" it is the sole means of averting. Feminine art, like the feminine heart, is held to what Kelley aptly calls a "familiar course" by an "inner compass"[16] that directs it, so Gabriella, back toward the "living spring" "from which it descends" (163–68).

"Whither am I wandering?" Gabriella therefore wonders, immediately after explaining the principle of nondeviation from the living Spring (164). One may combine this with a pair of questions she asks somewhat later: "Where was I? Who was I?" (184). Synthetically: which "I" is wondering whither it is wandering? Is it Gabriella-the-writer's "I," or is it the innermost Gabriella's, the "I" of the character who is written about? Or is the wandering in question that of the "I" itself? Is Gabriella-the-writer, renegade representative of the temple of culture, meekly meandering after the innermost Gabriella into the temple of Hymen? Is it the innermost Gabriella who is both wondering *and* wandering, with Gabriella-the-writer simply serving as her sounding board? Or is Hymen only the writer's tympanum, and are the quest and the question both hers? And why is *either* Gabriella either wandering *or* wondering, if she knows that, in "follow[ing] nature," one "cannot err"?

But the two "I's" cannot be separated as easily as such questions suggest. The main reason is that the innermost Gabriella is herself a writer. Heir to "an imagination of the high-pressure kind," she very early connects it to the "escape-pipes" of textuality, intermittently pumping out a "gushing stream" of "poesy," and, later, "exuber-an[t]" personal letters (94). Just as early, these effusions encounter high-pressure counterpressures. They are applied, most notably, by Gabriella's "Olympian king-god" of a schoolmaster, a philosopher who, though remarkably "kind and indulgent," dams up her "poetic raptures" with murderous resolve (and so diverts them into the woody "by-path" mentioned by Kelley). He is at it on the first page of *Ernest Linwood*. To Gabriella's pained surprise, the "master" does not laud the ode that his fatherless pupil, a "burning Sappho," has "scribbled" in praise of her beloved mother, and read out in class in anticipation of "a scene of triumph." Quite the contrary: sitting "enthroned" under the "cupola" of his "academy," whose "giant pen dip[s] its glittering nib into the deep blue ether" (the reference is to a weather vane), the philosopher drives his "iron wedge" "with cleaving force" into the twelve-year-old's dithyramb. Gabriella-the-(non)writer repeatedly alludes to this traumatic "incident" of her childhood, which "cut into" her as into "a tender loaf of bread" (pp. 5–11). We are given to understand that, if she did not go on to compose, say, a best-selling novel capable of thrilling "unborn millions" (69), the primary reason was her "kind" and yet "cruel" master's poeticidal conception of "school-girl propriety." To the adolescent poem he "so ruthlessly murdered" (64), Gabriella traces the origins of her literary (non)career.

Is the poeticide therefore to be condemned, to cite his own ironically intended words, as a bloody "Draco," a "tyrant" out to beat down budding talent "with an iron rod" (6)? Let us not rush to judgment. The philosopher is not the only person in Gabriella's entourage to suggest that "wander[ing] idly . . . in the flowery paths of poetry" (27) can make a young lady forget her "measured duty." Gabriella's angelic and moribund mother likewise earnestly entreats her not to "indulge too much in the dreams of imagination" (18). The (non)poetess herself, upon producing a particularly poetic passage of her lyrical (non)novel, defensively asks us and God: "Is this poetry? Is it sacrilege? If so, forgive me, thou great Inspirer of thought,—'my spirit would fain not wander far from thee'" (28). Tellingly, these and other pregnant allusions to the seductive pleasures of scribbler art pair off with reminders of the insidious and pernicious passions of the child-womanly heart—and the treatment they cry out for. Thus our young poetess, displaying a feline fury reminiscent of tigress Beulah's, "jump[s] up with the leap of the panther" (10) to defend her poetic progeny against her teacher's "iron wedge"; an hour later, she ruefully notes that "she had no right to rebel," and should have kissed the rod instead (14). Again, riding alone through a significantly somber night, she reflects on her failure to bow to Divine might, and cries, "Oh! rebel that I was, did I not need the chastening discipline, never exerted but in wisdom and love?" (43). Plainly, the occasion for these and a rash of similar comments is not writing alone. Nevertheless, the steady alternation of references to the pen and the rod indicates that our "burning Sappho's" "sultry heart" (11) glows with a "fire" (9) perceptible principally insofar as it overheats her adolescent lyre. Nor are we left wondering about the links between the sexual and the textual: often enough to make the message unmistakable, the poetic is all but explicitly linked to passions more pelvic. The following warning, issued Gabriella by her "admirable, high-minded, and God-fearing" stepmother (226), shows how:

> "I would save you, if possible, from becoming the victim of a diseased imagination. . . . With your vivid imagination and deep sensibility, there is great danger of your yielding unconsciously to habits the more fatal in their influence, because apparently as innocent as they are insidious and pernicious. A life of active industry and usefulness is the only safeguard from temptation and sin." (67)

All this sheds a troubling light on young Gabriella's poetic bent. Thinking back, one is almost tempted to conclude that the poeticide which introduces *Ernest Linwood* represents the opening salvo in a salutary struggle to regulate a potentially "diseased imagination." Was the master's objective not simply to rule out those "fatal" eventualities Gabriella's benevolent stepmother also warns of? Did he not aim to recall his immoderately poetic pupil to her "measured duty," at a season when one stray verse might have destroyed pure morality forever? Ought one, then, to condemn his "Draconian" rule out of hand? Should one not rather commend his "dark, formidable ferula" (130) for plugging the escape-pipes of Gabriella's high-pressure imagination, and so keeping her "long imprisoned yearnings" (7) bottled up? It is too early to answer these questions. But it is perhaps not out of place to note that Gabriella's young friend and admirer Dick, who defies the feral "king-god" in order to protect the fledgling poetess from his "Olympian" rage, subsequently evolves into her brother, and couches lovingly with her in high grass. As to Regulus himself—for such is the master's name—he exhibits a monstrously irregular attitude toward his pupil's long imprisoned yearnings: having, when Gabriella was twelve, pilloried poesy with the rigor we have seen, he develops a taste for its "mystical beauties" (85) as she approaches eighteen, abjectly begging Gabriella's pardon for the "harshness and injustice" (131) with which he once sought to girdle her swelling muse. This change of heart presages another: "in love with a young girl . . . much his junior," Regulus soon makes himself "ridiculous" (133) with a proposal distinctly patrimatrimonial ("'Gabriella, my child. . . . if you would trust your orphan youth to my keeping . . .'" [131–32]). What does this suggest, if not that the (so to speak) de-Regulation of the signifier can take the lid off irregularities of the most "dread[ful]" and "bewilder[ing]" kind (131–32)? But the "diseased imagination" here de-Regulated is patently not (the innermost) Gabriella's. She quite unambivalently rejects Regulus's proposition; whatever may have been the case earlier, she now takes no romantic interest in her fatherly preceptor—nor, for that matter, in young Dick. Whose incestuous textuality, then, is symbolically liberated here?

If Gabriella were *making up* her story of her old master's proposal, then the incestuous textuality in question might be charged to her account. But there are no "imaginary parts" in Gabriella's real-life confessions. Hence the culprit must be Hentz. The ultimate target of the prophylactic "murder" that once so severely cropped Gabriella's adolescent art would appear to be her *author's* all too springing imagination. If so, then Gabriella-the-narrator, as representative scribbler, incurs the punishment for her author's "diseased imagination"; the innermost Gabriella, in turn, serves as scapegoat for Gabriella-the-representative-scribbler. Yet these innocent victims could not satisfactorily represent the guilty if they did not somehow appropriate their guilt. The distance that, as was just seen, initially separates Gabriella from patrimatrimonial iniquity must therefore be closed. On the other hand, the guilty will naturally prefer to prove their representatives as innocent as so many little Evas, "wrapped in the spotless whiteness of the winding-sheet" (144). The procedure that Gabriella—and, hence, Hentz—follow to establish their prim-Eval innocence is that of *disowning their own tale*. Inconveniently, this also turns out to be the surest way of making their prim-Evally guilty tale theirs.

Of course, one cannot hang a charge of textual impropriety on the sole peg of Regulus' proposal; even a Mary Jane Holmes might hesitate to pronounce that adequate proof of the incestuous complicity of innocence with guilt. Let us, then, rejoin Gabriella wondering whither she is wandering, and see if she is not about to incriminate herself further by innocently and yet culpably straying toward the forbidden passion. When we left her, she had just closed her meditation on "the living spring." She is now sitting, after having spent a frustrating hour in bed "clasping" an unsympathetic pillow "to [her]

bosom," on her recently deceased mother Rosalie's grave, cradling
Rosalie's Ms. in her hands; and, authorized by the "awaken[ing] to . . .
woman's destiny" (143) that her pillow-clutching betokens, is on the
point of breaking the "hermetic seal" on her mother's text. What
does she discover in this tale-within-a-tale?

She discovers the story of her mother's awakening to woman's destiny, and a strategically placed injunction to read it only if she can
"sympathize with [its heroine's] emotions" (178). They are strong
emotions indeed, as strong as the tale of love Rosalie tells; and
"strong indeed must have been the love that triumphed over principle, honor, and truth, that broke the most sacred of human ties, and
dared the vengeance of retributive Heaven" (179–80). A love perhaps as strong as those recounted in the "wild, impassioned romances" which, Gabriella reads, her unregulated mother used to
read; indeed, to devour, for young Rosalie's "imagination was preternaturally developed," and, "unguarded by precept," voluptuously
"yielded . . . [it]self to the wizard spell of genius and passion" (167).
Rosalie's own tale, however, is as innocent as Rosalie herself, as spot-
lessly white as the winding-sheet she is wrapped up in. Hence Hentz'
tale—at least to the extent that it is Rosalie's—is too.

Yet Rosalie's-viz.-Hentz' tale is also two. If the proper one is as
white as a winding-sheet, the other is as black as sin; and, as Gabriella soon discovers to her cost, to be wrapped up in the one is to
be buried in the other. For Rosalie's tale breathes the deadly mia-
smas that Regulus seemed to suspect emanated from every "garland
of poesy"; the Ms. is, as Gabriella says (in what is properly speaking
another context), "a bridge of death," "woven of flowers" (144).[17] We
can guess what is at the root of this deadly duplicity: the "living
spring."

Thus Rosalie's tale turns on her relationship with her "demi-god"
of a father, who relives his love for his late first wife with her
daughterly "representative" just when the latter awakens to
"woman's destiny"; on the wifely daughter's embittered relationship
with her demi-trollop of a stepmother, who, after the "demi-god's"
demise, mistreats his quondam favorite "as a rival of her maturer
charms"; on the immediate object of this unseemly rivalry, a man
named St. James,[18] introduced to Rosalie by, for obvious reasons,
George Washington ("'as your father's friend, and your country's
father, dear child, permit me . . . '"); on Rosalie's triumph at the
altar over her (step)maternal rival ("she never forgave me for win-

ning the love of the man she had herself resolved to charm"); on Rosalie's long-distance chastening at the hands of the (apparently) bigamous St. James, whose (apparently) senior spouse comes rapping at Rosalie's door after St. James has sired Gabriella upon Rosalie and then (apparently) deserted them both; and on several other things (165–84). But we will leave the other things to the silence of the tomb, because we have already disinterred enough to answer the question that concerns us. Whose "love" "dared the vengeance of retributive Heaven"?

There are, of course, two culprits: St. James and Rosalie. Addressing the junior Mrs. St. James, the other one reminds her of the crime she has been innocently committing; "'if you still persist in calling [St. James] your own,'" "the avenger" (195) thunders, "'it will be in defiance of the laws of man and the canons of the living God'" (182). Rosalie does not persist; she confirms the real Mrs. St. James's sentence by swooning at the feet "of her whom [she] had so guiltlessly wronged" (184). But she is wrong to think that she "has guiltlessly wronged" her. Properly speaking, she is wrong to think that she has wronged her: as will appear in due course, Rosalie did not in fact marry the real Mr. St. James. Improperly speaking, she is wrong to think that she is guiltless. Yet if she shares the blame for "bigamy," it is not with St. James (her marriage with whom was not, despite appearances, bigamous), but with George Washington's other friend: her beloved father.[19] As sympathetic readers will long since have gathered, Rosalie's crime is to have "follow[ed] nature" straight back to her "living spring": that is, to have triumphed over her "maturer" "rival" of a (step)mother by reliving with her fatherly "demi-god" "the pure, fond love of his early years" (168). Well might Rosalie retrospectively bless the "bigamous" St. James for chasteningly degrading her, and so reconciling her with the wrathful Father. Only the long life of "holy sorrow" (142) he imposed on his wife by leaving her could have atoned for her "idolatrous"—that is, incestuous—passion for the Father's lower-case equivalent (197).

Admittedly, the case against Rosalie could no more stand up in court than she can stand up before the true Mrs. St. James's false accusation that she is not truly her false husband's wife (indeed, she is not; she is truly her father's). It is a good thing for improper criticism, then, that her Heavenly Judge grants the mor(t)ally guilty and yet perfectly innocent Rosalie an eternal stay of execution. For He thereby makes possible the incestuous continuation of her trial—

namely, as Gabriella's; and it is in the course of the latter that the author(s) of *Ernest Linwood* are conclusively proven (not) guilty of fomenting incest. How, we must therefore now ask, does Gabriella's tale dovetail with Rosalie's?

They are joined, to begin with, by the "sympathy" one female heart, awakening to "woman's destiny," must feel for another; this was, we remember, the condition for Gabriella's reading her mother's Ms. at all. But the sympathy Rosalie's story elicits from Gabriella runs deeper than ordinary sisterly solidarity. The reason is not simply that Rosalie is her reader's mother. Thus, coming upon a passage in which the writer interrupts her narrative to commend her fatherless daughter to (in Gabriella's paraphrase) the Father's "all-embracing arms" (168), Gabriella throws down her story to speculate, "trembling" (170), about its dénouement. Of course, the fatherless daughter in question is Gabriella, and the dénouement is *Ernest Linwood*. We have, then, caught the innermost Gabriella in the act of *reading her own tale*; the sympathy it awakens in her is auto-affection. But not only is this reader in the text in the text she is reading; the text she is reading becomes a part (and, as we will see, a determining part) of the text she is destined to write: *Ernest Linwood*. The implication seems to be that the (non)writer of this (non)novel is best represented by the sympathetic but passive witness of woman's/her mother's/her own unfolding destiny. Kelley accurately restates the implicit message, though her reference is to real and not fictional biography: "Hentz may not have written her novel 'at random,' but in a sense she recorded it without choice."[20]

One can go farther. Not only does the tale-within-Gabriella's-tale suggest that "the secret so-called writer" of *Ernest Linwood* is nothing more than God's secretary; it creates a kind of vanishing perspective that makes the observing and recording "I" disappear in what the "I" observes. Gabriella-the-(non)writer (to say nothing of Hentz) adopts the viewpoint of the former self she is contemplating, who in turn finds herself absorbed in the contemplation of an even earlier self: the Gabriella who already knows how her tale will come out regresses toward the one who anxiously observes its unfolding, who regresses toward the Gabriella who does not observe at all, but is only observed. Gabriella infans, finally, might be said to vanish altogether in her mother's tale, taking Gabriella the reader, and hence the writer, with her. As if to underscore the point, Gabriella-the-reader throws her Ms. down for the second time at the mortifying moment when her mother shrieks and falls down as if dead before the "real" Mrs. St. James. The mortified Gabriella thereupon shrieks and falls down "dead to the present," more or less atop her dead mother, her "head rest[ing]" on her tomb, "the inexorable past" "grinding [her] with iron heel into the dust of the grave." It is in this dramatic context that Gabriella—the writer and/or the innermost Gabriella—asks, "Where was I? Who was I?" (184–85). The answer would seem to be that she is on her way into her mother's grave, or even that she *is* her nonexistent mother; perhaps, more radically, that she is nowhere and nothing. The poetological implications of this portrait of the (non)writer as young corpse are not far to seek. The scribbler who *is not* does not scribble at all: she *is scribbled*, and hence erased. The nominal author of *Ernest Linwood* thus has every reason to "doubt of [her] own identity" (191). Ground into a past that continues to write her out of existence, she can only watch as a "giant pen"—(mother) nature's, or the Father's—writes the lethal "Mene Tekel of [her] clouded destiny on the palace walls of Heaven" (188).

Is it, however, only in this purely negative sense that Gabriella-the-writer is weighed in the scales and found wanting? The "giant pen" suggests otherwise. Referring us back to the "glittering nib," and thence to the poeticidal Regulus, it links the "iron heel" that grinds the "awakening" woman into Rosalie's grave with the "iron wedge" that "murdered" Gabriella's pubescent poem. In that context, the celestial "Mene Tekel" appears as a backhanded warning that Gabriella is about to be punished for doing something she ought not to; her indirect plea that she writes "without choice" begins therefore to look suspiciously like an oblique admission that she is guilty of writing the story she claims she is only recording/reading. The "hidden desire" of the "little girl writ older" may not have wilted after all, and Regulus's work may be still to do. If so, the swoon precipitated by Gabriella's reading of her own tale might well be an earnest of the destiny "retributive Heaven" reserves for unreconstructed woman writers.

Gabriella seems to suspect something of the sort. "Raised . . . from the ground" by Ernest Linwood (we will be properly introduced to him in a moment), she tells him she is in despair. "Despair," replies he, "belongs to guilt" (184–85). Ernest means, to cite Regulus, that it is not possible for "a feeling to find entrance into [Gabriella's] heart, that angels might not cherish" (134). Perhaps; and yet, as Regulus once knew, unangelic feelings may find their way into the most "guileless" (134) angel's *art*, and thence, by retroaction, into her heart after all. What if the young poetess so severely Regulated for having "scribbled" a poem about her mother were (like) the (non)writer who scribbled her mother's tale? In that case—and assuming that Rosalie's tale is as incestuous as an improper reading indicates—one could imagine (1) this passionate (non)author (not)authoring an impassioned tale about (2) a passionate (non)author (not)authoring an impassioned tale in which (3) her passionate (non)author of a mother has (not)authored an impassioned tale in which (4) she reads "a wild, impassioned tale" that, finally, (5) some "wizard . . . of genius and passion" has positively, if anonymously, authored. But then this wizard of passion would (not) bear a strong resemblance to (1), and hence would be (not) guilty of committing imaginary incest. Ignoring, for a moment, the "nots" in this long chain, one can see why Hentz might prefer, to cite Kelley, to "relinquish her tale to her fictional persona," and why the latter would be inclined to pass the compliment along: namely, in hopes of shifting to another's shoulders the burden of guilt that writing entails. The problem is that the bequest incriminates both legator and legatee: the one because she receives it, the other because she has it to give. The proliferation of writers in/of *Ernest Linwood* only multiplies the number of "wizards of passion" guilty of conjuring up incest with the enchanter's wand.

But we are getting ahead of ourselves. If the insinuations just proffered are not to seem like the rantings of a diseased imagination, Gabriella's tale must be shown to be as incestuous as her mother's. Who, then, is Ernest Linwood, the man who raises Gabriella from her mother's grave?

He is the son of Mrs. Linwood, the wealthy, benevolent widow who unofficially adopts Gabriella after her mother dies, and gives her, together with other good counsel, the lecture on the dangers of the imagination that we have already noted. He is the brother of the "dazzling" but invalid Edith, who, "did the sons of God come down to earth . . . to woo the daughters of men" (79), would most certainly have been assiduously wooed. Because Ernest is off studying in Germany when Gabriella takes up residence at the Linwood mansion, Gabriella's earliest introduction to him comes by way of the rapturous accolades of his mother and sister. They are rapturous indeed. The gentle Edith, who, though "not passionless," does not "attract . . . the admiration of the other sex" (79), does not seem to mind: she is content to adore and be adored by her brother, and loves to sing his praises to her new "sister" (95). His doting mother's attitude is nicely summed up in the confession that Ernest, as precious to her "as [her] heart's best blood," is "the one idol that comes between [her] and [her] God" (224). What Gabriella hears about this idolized son and brother ("'he shall be your brother too, Gabriella'" [95]) intrigues her, the more so, perhaps, as the period of Ernest's absence is one in which neither her fatherly teacher Regulus nor her brotherly companion Dick is having much success in plucking her "masterchord" (89). When Ernest comes home, he promptly plucks it.

His technique reminds one, superficially at least, of John Humphreys's. Introduced by Mrs. Linwood to the "child of [her] adoption," Ernest instantly "claim[s] the privilege of an adopted brother," warmly extending his hand to Gabriella before turning lovingly to sister Edith (106). The gesture is Humphreyesque, if the hand that makes it isn't: "delicately moulded," "as if it might have belonged to a woman," it is a hand apparently not "formed to wield the weapon of authority" (106). Yet Ernest is no namby-pamby either, as Gabriella's rapt description of his reunion with Edith makes plain:

> Edith occupied a low ottoman at [Ernest's] feet. One arm was thrown across his lap, and her eyes were lifted to his face with an expression of the most idolizing affection. And all the while he was talking, his hand passed caressingly over her fair flaxen hair, or lingered amidst its glistening ringlets. It was a beautiful picture of sisterly and fraternal love. . . . I remembered [that]. . . . the Saviour of mankind called himself our brother,—stamping with the seal of divinity the dear relationship. . . . If [Ernest] paused . . . Edith would draw a long breath, as if she had just been inhaling some exhilarating gas. (106–7)

It is, of course, not gas, but Ernest's unmanning gaze that exhilarates Edith. Gabriella too comes powerfully under its influence. Her newly adopted "brother" has, she notes, "a power about him which overmastered" (125); he is richly endowed with "that searching eye, which, next to the glance of Omnipotence, I would shun in guilt and shame" (143). She does not, however, shun it. This troubles the invalid Edith, who seems to wish that Ernest would pluck her masterchord rather than Gabriella's:

"I believe it would kill me, Gabriella," [said Edith], "to know that [Ernest] loved another better than myself."

For the first time I thought Edith selfish, and that she carried the romance of sisterly affection too far.

"You wish him, then, to be an old bachelor!" said I, smiling.

"Oh! don't apply to him such a horrid name. I did not think of that." (111)

Such remarks give Gabriella pause. She would not willingly displace the angelic Edith, nor displease her stepmotherly benefactress, who also appears less than enthusiastic about her poor, fatherless protégée's budding interest in Ernest. Yet, despite a self-sacrificing resolution not to "intermeddle with [her "mother's" and "sister's"] joy" (99), Gabriella cannot help dangling before Ernest "the counter charm that can rival [theirs]" (122). Ernest takes it. A scene that unites him, Edith, the temporarily indisposed Gabriella, and the physically absent Mrs. Linwood on a sofa graphically illustrates the (un)natural dynamics involved:

Sitting by me, [Ernest] said, as I was an invalid, I should be peculiarly favored.

"Methinks she is not the only favored one," said the sweet voice of Edith, as she floated near.

"There is room for you, dear Edith," said I, moving closer to the arm of the sofa, and leaving a space for her between us.

"Room on the sofa, Edith," added he, moving towards me, and making a space for her on his right. . . . "Thus would I ever bind to my heart the two loveliest, dearest, best."

Edith bent her head, and kissed the hand which held hers. As she looked up I saw that her eyes were glistening.

"What would mamma say?" she asked, trying to conceal her emotion. "Surely there can be none dearer and better than she is." (215–16)

Gabriella thinks she has the right answer to this one: "'I am not a very good metaphysician,' I answered, 'but I should think the heart very narrow, that could accommodate only those whom Nature placed in it'" (217). Ernest pronounces her metaphysics good; clasping both Edith's and Gabriella's hands in "one of his own," he intones, "earnestly": "'A triune band . . . that must never be broken. . . . Love each other now, love each other forever, even as I love ye both'" (217).

This is exactly "as it should be" (Ernest, p. 216), for reasons Susan

Warner has taught us: Gabriella is to *supplement*, not supplant, Edith
("'a sister can never be supplanted'" [Ernest, p. 189])—and, by implication, "mamma" as well. But the rest is exactly as it should *not* be.
If Gabriella once loved her mother with a "passionate earnestness"
(30) that attested a "need" for "chastening discipline" (43), she loves
Ernest with a passion that positively cries out for the rod. *Ernest Linwood*, however, rushes its sisterly supplement to the altar as is. Or,
rather, Ernest Linwood does. Though blessed with the Master's
prowess, even with His voice ("'love each other forever, even as I
love ye both'"), Ernest is fatally disinclined "to wield the weapon of
authority" which alone can transform a brother/lover into a type of
the "Saviour of [wo]mankind." His one wish is to sweep his adoptive
sister into that "'inner temple [Edith] cannot enter'" (Ernest, p. 227),
while Gabriella is still, as he says, "'in the bloom of her innocence'"
(230). Gabriella is nothing loath. "'O that I too had a brother!'" her
"craving heart" earlier led her to cry (103); granted a brother-surro-
gate who bids fair to satisfy this craving and more, she is only too
willing to be hastened, unchastened, into the "dream of heaven"
(236) represented by his encircling arms. Her heart ungirdled, her
girlish bloom all uncropped, Gabriella enters the temple of Hymen
as no scribbler heroine should—and as no scribbler should permit
her heroine to.

That the heroine, if not the scribbler, must pay a high price for
this folly is made clear even before she ties the knot. Thus it is quite
unambiguously announced, as Gabriella is offering Ernest the charm
that can rival his mother's and sister's, that an "invisible sword
[hangs] trembling" over the impending match (202). Ernest, Mrs.
Linwood warns her prospective supplement, has inherited "dark
passions" from his paternal ancestors; "jealousy, like a serpent, lies
coiled in his heart" (202). Hardly have Gabriella and Ernest rushed
to the altar than the sword-serpent strikes. The new bride feels herself "observed by an eye that watched [her] every movement" (244),
an eye quick to construe 'Lena-like innocence as the blackest guilt.
The Linwoods' marriage quickly degenerates into an endless succes-
sion of crises: repeatedly, Ernest confronts Gabriella with wild accu-
sations of infidelity, retracts them in paroxysms of remorse, and
then levels new and more disgraceful charges. Gabriella endures it
all for one reason only: she feels she is "loved, even to the madness
of idolatry" (298).

According to our general theory, she should endure it for a quite different reason: because her premature marriage allows her to couple with her father and/or brother. This, in turn, should provoke feckless Ernest into administering a murderous postnuptial chastening. But no theory is perfect. What actually happens is that Ernest *thinks* he catches Gabriella conniving to go to bed with someone she *claims* is her father. In fact, the man turns out to be her father's *twin brother*, and Gabriella does not, despite appearances, connive to go to bed with him. (At the risk of being charged with clutching at straws in an attempt to bend *Ernest Linwood* to our preconceptions, we will note that the resemblance between the twins "was so perfect that even their own mother was not able to distinguish the one from the other" [436]). Somewhat later Ernest comes upon his bride lying in the grass with Dick, the intimate companion and still, despite appearances, unrequited "lover of [her] youth" (385). At this point, she, Dick, and the reader erroneously believe him to be her brother. Ernest does not believe Dick to be her brother, or unrequited, and so shoots him and Gabriella. Here too our theory fails to measure up to the fictional reality: no avenging "iron heel" fulfills the Mene Tekel of Gabriella's incestuous destiny by grinding her into her incestuous mother's grave. The text offers only "a cloud . . . heavy as iron," which comes "lowering and crushing" the heroine into (temporary) "darkness,—silence,—oblivion" (386). Finally, even Dick lets us down. He is not Gabriella's brother, but her father's twin's son— and thus only her first cousin.

In short, Gabriella is quite as innocent as 'Lena, and Ernest quite as deranged as his insanely suspicious model, the borderline paranoiac Nicholas M. Hentz.[21] Yet, whatever the case with Nicholas, there is a certain method to Ernest's madness. Without endorsing his criminal folly, one can go so far as to say that he does not draw his chastening rod without probable cause. We will examine the sequence of events that triggers his response in greater detail later. Here let us note only that, at the highly charged moment when he is finally roused to action, "brother and sister" are "entwined . . . in all the abandonment of nature's holiest feelings" (386). It is then that Gabriella hears the sound of a "gliding snake" in the grass, and looks up to see Ernest fire.

Manifestly, the gliding snake evokes Ernest's diabolical jealousy; Ernest himself says as much in his saner moments. But it also evokes, in line with Biblical precedents, the female animal who evilly couches with her "brother" in the grass. To be sure, this is a line of reasoning that even the mad Ernest would not enter upon. Indeed, if he too had thought that Dick was Gabriella's brother, he would not have shot him, just as Durward, if he had known that Mr. Graham was 'Lena's father, would have embraced the two of them in the very bed in which they lay. Yet as the truth in *'Lena Rivers* matters less than the consequences of the untruth, so, in *Ernest Linwood*, what Ernest would think if he knew the truth matters less than what he does on the basis of his insane insights. "'Do you imply that [Gabriella] needs a restraining influence to keep her from excess?'" he once asks an impertinent acquaintance, with heavy irony. His wife is prompted to remark that Ernest "never spoke without meaning something" (303). One has only to add that he doesn't always grasp what he means. In the shooting scene, he hits upon the meaning he has missed: firing at his wife and her "brother"/"lover," he restrains an excess he doesn't suspect is there. Ernest as gliding snake stiffens into Ernest as chastening rod.

He does not, however, strike solely on the spur of the moment: a long string of insinuations augurs Gabriella's trial by fire. By no means all emanate from Ernest. Most of them bear on our "perfect child of nature's" relation with her supposed father. This is her decidedly unangelic namesake Gabriel St. James, the "polluted," "poisoned," "accursed," "lost," "abandoned," "vile," "ignominious," "degraded," "reckless and dissolute" "libertine" who, on Gabriella's succint appraisal, is "sin and crime . . . in the person of a father" (259–442, *passim*). Gabriel enters Gabriella's life after she marries Ernest, and entices her to several clandestine assignations. "Fierce and deadly passions gleam from his eye" as he draws his "daughter" into "exciting conversations"; his "probing gaze" of "unrepressed admiration" "burn[s her] with its intensity." "'Only let me see your face for the few moments we are together,'" he begs, "'that face so like your mother's'"; "'for one dear embrace, my child,'" he declares huskily not long after, "'I would willingly meet the tortures of the prison-house'" (267–93, *passim*). In time, he meets them, having been condemned to the Tombs to suffer "tortures" destined to continue, as he believes, for "'as long as Almighty vengeance could inflict and immortality endure'" (415). His crime is a fearful one. He is guilty of having "robbed [Gabriella's] husband in the vilest, most insidious manner" by pretending to be Ernest—more precisely, by "committing a forgery in his name" (314).

It should not be supposed that Gabriella helps this self-styled "incarnate fiend" (420) provoke the "retribution of heaven" (316). To the contrary, she feels "polluted, degraded, by contact" with him (276). True, she gives him "the radiant pledge of wedded faith and love" that Ernest had bestowed upon her with "a bridegroom's kiss" (279); she further conceals her degrading commerce with her "father" from her lawfully wedded spouse, betraying "overwhelming confusion" when he finds her out (291). But there are perfectly proper reasons for her conduct (which we will not go into). It is therefore entirely unjust of Ernest to charge Gabriella with letting St. James "desecrate" and "pollute" the "bridal casket" his mother bequeathed her in sacred trust (313); it is terribly wrongheaded of him to accuse her of exchanging "glances" of "mysterious meaning" with the "veteran *roué*" (264). For Gabriella can say with utter truthfulness that "no instinctive attraction drew [her] to this mysterious man" (271).

An instinctive attraction does, however, draw her to her "father's" twin, her father. She first glimpses *this* St. James amidst a wild natural scene of "overpowering magnificence," perhaps not coincidentally that honeymoon haven, Niagara Falls (342). When he doffs his hat, revealing his "originally black" hair, "mingled with snowy locks," Gabriella instantly feels "irresistible desires" and "strange fascinations"; they reap her a "dark-flashing glance" from the ever suspicious Ernest, which, however, cannot prevent her from plunging into "one of those reveries which [she] used to indulge in childhood" (355). At her next meeting with St. James, her father again lifts his hat, and Gabriella again notices "that the dark waves of his hair were mingled with snow" (426). No wonder, then, that on his third encounter with Gabriella, St. James instantly and effortlessly succeeds in doing what her "father" seemed to want to: he draws her "towards him, with a movement [she] had no power to resist, and look[s] in [her] face with eyes in which every passion of the soul seemed concentrated" (429). Gabriella's further relations with this paternal "loadstone" (427) realize the promise tendered here. As *Ernest Linwood* approaches a climax, St. James is fulfilling "all the wants of [his daughter's] yearning filial nature" (433).

All this is, doubtless, perfectly innocent. Yet Gabriella's story is punctuated by a few detached offbeats that, assembled and attached, suggest otherwise to a diseased imagination. Thus Ernest, in one of his fits of pathological jealousy, makes certain innuendoes about Gabriella's early relationship with Regulus. "'Did you ever,'" he angrily asks Gabriella, "'tell me your teacher was your lover? . . . You suffered me to believe that he was to you in the relation almost of a father.'" "'If I have been so unfortunate as to win what your lovely sister might more justly claim,'" responds Gabriella—referring, of course, to Regulus's admiration—"'it has been by the exercise of no base allurement'" (332). This remark resonates all the more powerfully in that the temporarily alienated Ernest has, four pages earlier, decided to "seek consolation from another" than Gabriella—namely, his "lovely sister"; so honored, Edith feels "the joy of being to him all that she had been" (328). "There was something unnatural in [Edith's] exclusive, jealous love of her brother," Gabriella remarks later, after Edith has finally got a lover (348); the man in question, in whose "favor" Gabriella is "extremely prepossessed," inspires in her "the wild idea that he might be [her] unknown brother" (348). She has been thinking a great deal, since meeting her "father," about this mysterious brother, the son St. James is reputed to have; this prompts Ernest's mother to advise her not to "attempt to lift the veil which covers the past" (335). Remarks about veils come thick and fast in the following pages: they are inspired in particular by the journey to Niagara Falls during which Gabriella first espies her real father. "It as if," she says of the Falls, "the veil of the temple of nature were rent" (344). Ernest, who has accompanied his wife to Niagara, is inspired to recite Schiller by her rapturous comment that "nothing but [a] veil of mist" now separates her from heaven; reciting Schiller back to him, Gabriella declaims, "May the horror below never more find a voice . . . / Never more, never more may he lift from the sight / The veil which is woven of terror and night" (345–46). Whatever Schiller may have had in mind, the reader of *Ernest Linwood* cannot help associating "the horror below" with "the remembrance of [Gabriella's] father's crimes." Gabriella herself, two paragraphs later, is remembering that "a passion so wild and strong as that which darkened [her] domestic happiness" can only be curbed by God's "ministers" or His "retributive justice" (336–37). The apocalyptic passion she refers to is, of course, Ernest's mad jealousy. Doubtless, she is thinking of the same wild passion when, fifty pages later, and two pages before passionately embracing her newfound brother Dick, she delivers herself of this reflection: "Reality goes beyond the wildest imaginings of romance. . . . Eye hath not seen . . . the wild extent to which the passions of man may go. The empire of passion is veiled." (382)

Ernest shows us what else Gabriella might mean a bit before he shoots her. He makes the demonstration at a crucial juncture of *Ernest Linwood*. It occurs after some hundred pages of crazed insinuation to the effect that Gabriella is guilty of maintaining improper relations with her "father." Moreover, it comes immediately in the wake of the Linwoods' trip to Niagara, where Gabriella first glimpses her real father, and where Edith has finally learned that "there is a love stronger, deeper than a sister's affection" (352). All this seems to sour Ernest on the Falls. Having "hastened [his womenfolk's] departure" thence (351), he turns, driven by his unaccountable jealousy, to impugning his wife's relations with old friend Dick (who once looked forward to being her "friend, brother, guardian, lover, all in one" [88]).

The immediate occasion for this madness is provided by Dick's return from years of study in Göttingen. Accompanied by an old and dear friend of Ernest's mother, one Dr. Harlowe, he comes to pay the Linwoods a visit. Gabriella is thrilled to see this "companion of her childhood" (356) again. As for Mrs. Linwood, to whom "a young friend on the threshold of manhood" is always "deeply interesting" (90), she feels she is "welcom[ing] back another beloved son" (357). Ernest does not share the two Mrs. Linwoods' enthusiasm. As Dick tells how, in Germany, he frequently "'remembered Edith's heavenly music, and Gabriella's - - - -,'" failing to complete his sentence because he has "become so excited by the recollection he was clothing in words that he [loses] the command of his voice" (357), Ernest, insanely enough, grows more and more agitated. Dick never does clothe in words the "- - - -" of Gabriella's that so excites him; but when Dr. Harlowe jocularly wonders why the "little puss" did not take Dick as her lover, Ernest's dementia gets the better of him. He does not rebuke Harlowe directly, out of respect for his "superior age" (the man is old enough to be his father); but no sooner has the doctor left the room than Ernest turns viciously on his mother. With unwonted roughness, he lays a "withering ban" on her "threshold": her gentleman friend is never to cross it again. "He never comes here," shouts the madman (266), "that he does not utter insulting words." This is, needless to say, the sheerest folly; the last time Dr. Harlowe was at the Linwoods, he did nothing more objectionable than to urge Gabriella to go out riding alone (338). But Ernest will not hear reason. When his mother protests, he gets hysterical: "'Let me die at once; then take this young man [Dick] to your bosom, where he has already supplanted me. Make him your son in a twofold sense, for, by the heaven that hears me, I believe you would bless the hour that gave him the right to Gabriella's love.'" (359)

Quite as spellbinding as this dramatic scene is its abysmal aftermath. Hardly has Mrs. Linwood warned her son of the "terrible abyss" toward which his "unhallowed passion" is driving him, and then shepherded Edith and Gabriella to the safety of her bedroom (360), than a remorseful Ernest reappears on the "threshold" of her "chamber." Ignoring Gabriella, whose impulse is to "steal from the room, leaving [mother and son] to the unwitnessed indulgence of their sacred emotions," the "returning prodigal" begs and receives his mother's pardon (362). Family peace is apparently restored. But then, against Mrs. Linwood's frantic remonstrances, Ernest imposes a terrible penance on himself. As his "Saviour fasted forty days and forty nights in the wilderness," so Ernest vows to "abjure love, joy, domestic endearments, and social pleasures" for just as long (363); he decides, that is, to begin sleeping in his library. We are left in no doubt as to the focus of this, as Gabriella moans, "unnatural and horrible constraint" (365). From the moment Ernest takes his "painful and unnatural vow," Gabriella suffers the "tortures" of "a neglected and avoided wife" (365).

She goes on to tell us, and quite understandably, that "reason condemn[s]" (378) Ernest's strange resolution to shun his wife after briefly laying a ban on his mother's threshold. Yet there is an excellent reason for his course of action, though Ernest may not be privy to it: both Gabriella's mother and her "woman's destiny" have destined our heroine for the "Father's all-embracing arms." Ernest, however, is primarily the son. "Devoted" (156) to his doting mother, whose "kindness penetrated, but . . . also compelled" (114), he has not succeeded in becoming her metaphorical father. The text offers myriad minor proofs of his underdevelopment: he "has the most fastidious taste in the world" (97), loves music (107), plays the harp better than his sister (109), takes advantage of his wealth to "luxuriate in the lap of indolence" (248), and possesses "a smile beautiful as a woman's" (122). He even seems to adore flowers. One notes, too, that, unlike Philip Amory, he is not (not) guilty of committing a forgery in his (step)father's name; his (supposed) father-in-law is guilty of committing a forgery in *Ernest's*. But the clearest sign of the hero's insufficient fatherliness is his indulgence of the insufficiently chastened Gabriella. Ominously, Ernest does not, while courting her, "look upon [her] as a child" (102); as to Ernest the husband (when not insane), "he watch[es Gabriella] as the fond *mother* does the child, whom she has perhaps too severely chided" (272; emphasis added). However overmastering in his own way, such a suitor is not at all likely to "wield the weapon of authority" as a man and Christian should. When Gabriella is humbled in the dust by the Mene Tekel of her destiny, does Ernest not, all "tender and passionate" (185), raise her from her mother's grave? Assure her of her maidenly *innocence*? Answer her "heart's secret prayer" "to be wildly, passionately loved" (190) by hurrying her along to church? One can imagine what a Humphreys or a Hartwell would have to tell a prospective groom who, as Ernest does, urges his love to "come with [him] into the garden" "to hear the language of nature" (152). In brief, Ernest has yet to learn the lesson his jealousy knows: man's God-given duty is to keep female nature chained down.

He begins to learn it in the wake of Dick's return: laying the ban on the elder Mrs. Linwood's threshold, he takes a giant step toward manhood. Indulging his sacred emotions in her chamber, on the other hand, he makes one wonder once again whether he is to be or not to be the fatherly monitor his wife so desperately needs. But then, manfully setting Gabriella "free as before she breathed her marriage vows" (363), he definitively clears the way for a redemptive rewriting of *Ernest Linwood*, one in which he can play his properly heroic role. Therein lies the good sense of Ernest's "frantic vow" to renounce (heterosexual) sex, and with it the "unhallowed passion" that is Gabriella's "heart's secret prayer." Yet, though "the holiness of his purpose" is unmistakable (378), Ernest's renunciation involves a grave danger as well. For a hero can play his proper role only if he also plays his improper one. Passion(lessness), not passionlessness, sustains the female animal's "Divine Love of mankind" (198). The unhallowed must therefore be interdictively hallowed, and not simply shunned. Instead of fleeing, and so freeing, the passionate sister-mother-wife, Ernest must *legitimize* his females' forbidden passion— by, of course, chastening it. The alternatives are the excessive ama-tiveness of the sort that stampedes him into marrying his undis-ciplined wife or the masturbatory isolation suggested by his retreat to his library.

Gabriella's appointed role, accordingly, is to entice her husband's nose out of his books by employing precisely those seductive blandishments which, unchastened, are a call to arms against the law, but which, chastened into passion(lessness), bind man's helpmeet to her lawful Lord and master. The younger Mrs. Linwood therefore goes to Ernest in the library. When she comes upon him, his hand lies "embedded in his dark wavy hair"; he is, momentarily, quite indifferent to her charms. But then, "like one suddenly awakened from a deep sleep," he turns and sees his wife; in an instant, she is "clasped to his bosom with the most passionate emotion" (378). It is the first step back down the road to mental health. Ernest's amativeness has got the better of his manifestly holy, but also "most wretched and deluded" (368) celibacy.

The woman who draws him out of his temporary exile is, however, unchastened, the slave of a forbidden passion that threatens to reenslave her husband as well. One understands, then, why Ernest's initial, apparently healthy reaction modulates into a second, apparently sicker one: "'Temptress, sorceress!' he suddenly exclaimed, pushing me from him with frenzied gesture,—'you have come to destroy my soul. . . . Peace was flowing over me like a river, but now all the waves and billows of passion are gone over me. I sink,—I perish, and you, you—Gabriella, it is you who plunge me in the black abyss of perjury and guilt.'" (379)

This frenzied rejection of the "temptress" is as misguided as his earlier failure to discipline her (im)properly. It seems, for a long moment, as if Ernest were trapped in a vicious circle. But he fights his way out of it in the very next chapter. Taking up the "weapon of authority" at last, he marches out of the library, surprises his "sorceress" of a wife with Dick, and carries out his armed chastening of her. Gabriella was right after all to tempt him from his retreat. Instead of plunging into the "black abyss," he saves himself, thanks to her natural passion, by definitively com-muting the womanly urge that has so long been threatening to "destroy his soul." Saving himself, he saves Gabriella too; shot, the woman he recklessly married "in the bloom of her innocence" is transformed from wizard to true woman. Thanks to Ernest's mad act, incestuous passion may now come forth as incestuous passion(lessness): Gabriella's "long imprisoned yearnings" may at last be legitimately fulfilled.

They are being *illegitimately* fulfilled the moment before Ernest opens fire. For it so happens that an excited Dick, the moment before that moment, imparts "the most astonishing" news to a delighted Gabriella. "Horror and gratitude" "struggling for [the] mas-

tery" of him, our junior Oedipus cries: "'O! Gabriella! you whom I
have loved so long with such fervor, such passion, such idolatry,—
you (O righteous God forgive me!) are the daughter of my father!'"
As "he deplore[s] his sinful passion," Dick rather inconsistently
"clasp[s his sister] to his bosom, and kisse[s her] again and again."
Gabriella responds in kind. Earlier, she had believed she loved Dick
as a brother, until Edith taught her better by demonstrating "how
strong and fervent a sister's love can be" (122); now Gabriella demonstrates what she has learned from Edith. "My soul's desire," she
tells us, "was satisfied. How I had yearned for a brother! and to find
him,—and such a brother! Oh! joy unspeakable. Oh! how strange . . .
how almost passing credulity!" Then, after noting that Dick's "dis-
covery" came "like the music of gushing waters" to one parched by
Ernest's "voluntary estrangement," she briefly reviews the reasoning
that prompted her to "entwine" herself with her supposed brother
"in all the abandonment of nature's holiest feelings": "Ernest could
not be jealous of a brother's love. He would own with pride the fraternal bond, and forget the father's [St. James'] crimes in the son's
virtues." (385–86) This is when Ernest pulls the trigger.

He shoots Gabriella, she declares later, for doing what is only natural, and divine besides: "had I shrunk from a brother's embrace, I
should have been either more or less than woman. I had yielded to a
divine impulse, and could appeal to nature and Heaven for justification" (396). The same divinely natural impulse, it seems to follow,
would justify "embracing" a father no less than a brother: if Gabriella *had* let St. James "desecrate" and "pollute" her "bridal casket,"
as the mad Ernest charged, she would no more have been at fault
than if she had continued to abandon herself to "nature's holiest
feelings" with Dick. Why, then, did she shrink from that "one embrace" St. James would gladly have met "the tortures" for? But Gabriel St. James is not Gabriella's father. As to the St. James who *is*—
the one who awakened her "irresistible desires" at the Falls, forty
pages before her great trial—he is, forty pages after it, satisfying all
the yearnings of her filial nature. It is almost as if Gabriel had
brought the glad tidings of Gabriella's coming union with her father.
Her father, in turn, retroactively transforms her "incest" with her
"brother" into something quite unobjectionable. As Gabriella confesses to St. James that she "'could not love [Dick] better were he
indeed [her] brother,'" a "crimson hue [steals] over [her] face at the
remembrance of a love more passionate than a brother's" (433).

Thanks to St. James, this is now no more than a becoming blush. Gabriella's father has, not two minutes before, revealed that Dick is not Gabriella's brother after all. He is the other, degenerate St. James's son, and thus only her kissing cousin. This affords tremendous relief to all concerned. Gabriella puts it well: "The transition from a lover to a brother was too painful. . . . But a cousin! The tenderness of natural affection and the memories of love, might unite in a bond so near and dear, and hallow each other" (435). Dick echoes her sentiments: "'May you never know or imagine my wretchedness when I believed you to be my sister, knowing that though innocent, I had been guilty, and that I could not love you merely with a brother's love. Thank heaven! you are my cousin.'" (455)

All this might seem to suggest that *Ernest Linwood* complaisantly condones incest and concomitantly condemns Ernest Linwood for intermeddling with Gabriella's family joy. But there is another side to the story. The same Gabriella who protests that Ernest shoots her for doing what comes naturally also blesses his "rash deed" (396) as a kind of *coup de* divine *grâce*. "Shorn of the glory of womanhood" (432) by his avenging rod (the immediate reference is to the convalescent heroine's hair, shaved off for reasons that are not immediately apparent, since Ernest shoots her in the arm), Gabriella unhesitatingly seconds the verdict of the matronly personage who slowly nurses her back to life: "the terrible shock you have sustained will be a death blow to the passion that has caused you so much misery" (409). If the passion in question is fervor for the father, then, as we have just seen, the matronly personage is engaging in some mildly wishful thinking: the "death blow" Ernest almost deals his wife is the prelude to her reunion with St. James, who very ably performs the office her husband, turned fugitive, resigns until *Ernest Linwood* is nearly at an end. We will return to this point in a moment. For now let us stress that Gabriella both insists that "nature and Heaven" can vouch for her innocence, and admits that she is dreadfully guilty: "I had sinned. I had broken the canons of the living God, and deserved a fearful chastisement" (396). In brief, Gabriella knows she deserves a death blow for a crime that is not her fault. Whose fault is *this* perverse state of affairs?

It may be her mother's, or her incestuous tale's; if it is not her Author's, it may be her author's. Noting that the scribblers regarded themselves as "mothers of prose," and their works as their "bantlings," Kelley reminds us that certain of these suspects might be confused with certain others.[22] Hentz makes much the same point by arranging for the "canons of the living God" to thunder twice in *Ernest Linwood*. It will have escaped no one's notice that Gabriella's fearful self-accusation ("I had broken the canons of the living God . . . ") echoes another, equally heavy charge: "'if you . . . persist in calling [St. James] your own,'" we heard the "real" Mrs. St. James roar at Rosalie, "'it will be in defiance of the laws of man and the canons of the living God.'" Her-story repeats itself, in the most literal sense. But *whose* story repeats itself? Whose ordinance, ordonnance, or ordnance does Gabriella (dis)obey?

She herself chooses to see "the divine arrangement of Providence in the apparently accidental circumstances of [her] life" (412). The same arrangement can be discerned in the apparently accidental circumstances of her mother's. As Gabriella's apparent liaison with the criminal St. James brought on her fearful chastisement, so Rosalie's apparently criminal liaison with St. James brought on hers. But Rosalie, we said, only seemed to "dare the vengeance of retributive Heaven" by "guiltlessly wrong[ing]" the "real" Mrs. St. James; her true transgression consisted in stealing that other demi-god, her father, from her (step)maternal rival. Like mother, like daughter: Gabriella "rob[s]" her stepmother and stepsister "of a son and a brother . . . inexpressibly dear" (232). This miss-demeanor, however, is merely a step toward the grand larceny of *Ernest Linwood*'s climax, in which her-story repeats itself far more egregiously. At the tail end of Hentz's novel, Gabriella, like her mother Rosalie before her, becomes a second Rosalie to her father (as Rosalie, whose mother's name was also Rosalie, became a second Rosalie to hers).

Providential arrangements contribute mightily to the advent of this patrimatrimonial "joy so holy" (430). "'You are so like my Rosalie,'" ejaculates St. James, moments after clasping his "lost darling" to his bosom (429–32). He says so because he remembers the wife he long ago abandoned (by mistake) as she was "in the bloom . . . of youth." Since then, of course, Rosalie has been subject to a "mournful process of fading and decay" culminating in her present state of decomposition, one that compares most unfavorably with Gabriella's rosy "freshness." St. James, on the other hand, "breathe[s] an atmosphere pure as the world's first spring"; he has drunk deeply of *"la fontaine de jouvence,"* with the result that he is still *"young,* though past the meridian of life" (451). Is it any wonder that, after their initial embrace, Gabriella is so "overpowered by reverence, love, gratitude, and joy" that she "slid[es] from [St. James'] arms, and, on bended knees and with clasped hands, look[s] up in his face and repeat[s] again and again the sacred name of 'Father'" (430)? Only under the influence of these Beulan "feelings . . . [she] could not analyze" (445) does Gabriella definitively kiss the chastening rod Ernest unconsciously plied on the Father's behalf. "'Forgive me, father,'" she begs St. James; "'I have, father,'" she confesses, "'I have kissed in love and faith the Almighty hand that laid me low.'" She proceeds to kiss his hand. He forgives her (453).

What, precisely, does he forgive her *for*? Gabriella tells us a thousand times. Her sin is the excessive passion she long bore the "hand" who laid her low—namely, Ernest, the Father's vicar, the Ernest who "becomes" the father by laying her low, and then laying low. (As it happens, he scurries off to India, where he may, for all one knows, have befriended Willie.) Or should we rather say that her sin is the excessive passion insanity could suspect her of sating with her "father," now the "sacred ruin" (425) of the Tombs? Certain is that, while this latter-day Oedipus at Colonus is slowly being transfigured (thanks mainly to his mother's Bible) into "a sword in the sunbeams of heaven" (447), his twin is regularly "clasping [Gabriella] to his bosom" (445) much as her new-found "brother" "clasped [her] to his bosom" (385), in a gesture reminiscent of the imperfectly abstinent Ernest's, when he "clasped [her] to his bosom with the most passionate emotion" (378). Gabriella responds with a profession of faith as fervent as the one Gerty proffered Amory: "'I will never leave you again, dear father . . . not even for a husband's unclouded confidence, would I forsake a father's sacred, new-found love'" (445). For his part, brother Dick ("for brother [Gabriella] still called Richard" [452]) seems earnestly to want to finalize this latest arrangement of Providence: "'and if it should be that the ties severed by misfortune and distance are never renewed,'" he declares to Gabriella, "'you will remain with your father, and I will make my home with you, and it will be the business of both our lives to make you happy'" (455). Gabriella, her father, and her "degenerate" (287) "father's" Richard—is this a new, and, perhaps, improved version of the "triune band" that once joined Gabriella, Edith, and Ernest? Can Gabriella at last indulge the "triune passion" that has long "warmed [her] soul" (122)? Perhaps not; in her father's arms, the "poor girl" remembers "Ernest's idolatrous love," and feels "there would always be an aching void which even a father's and brother's tenderness . . . could not fill" (452). On this delicate point, it seems best simply to cite Gabriella. St. James, she exults, makes "the dream of [her] childhood" come true, the one in which she "imagined him one of the sons of God, such as once came down to earth" (433–34). She omits, this time, to specify their reason for making the descent. We will draw our conclusion nonetheless: St. James forgives Gabriella for doing with him what her mother did. And, via Ernest, the "son of God" shoots her for it.

The Father's duplicity, then, and motherly nature, render Gabriella innocent and guilty at once. The "fatal resemblance" which "cause[s] all" woman's "woe" (431) is that between the fatherly "divinity" who chastens her con-genital passion, and his twin, the "fiend" who would pollute her bridal casket; it is likewise that between the mother who couples with her father, and the daughter fated to become her mother. Commending Gabriella to the Father's all-embracing arms, Rosalie anticipated this murderously dialectical arrangement of Providence: woman's destiny, she knew, is patrimatrimony, and therefore also gyn-ocide. We can now interpret the great Mene Tekel momentarily inscribed on the palace walls of Gabriella's Heaven. Because she was her mother's daughter, Rosalie's "perfect child of nature" had to be sinfully united with her father and blasted by the living God before finally being resurrected as the Father's chastened bride. Her-story repeats itself because mother nature does, daring the "vengeance of retributive Heaven" (Rosalie), forcing the Almighty "to reveal Himself in flaming fire as the god of retributive justice" (Gabriella). The aesthetic corollary is the one Gabriella mimed on her mother's grave. Her-story is not the work of any human pen; it is the (non)work of the avenging angel's eternal erase-her, and its ideal type is the spotless whiteness of the winding-sheet.

Yet Ernest charges straight out of a library to reveal himself in flaming fire. Might this signify that he comes straight out of a book—"some wild, impassioned romance" on the order of *Ernest Linwood*? That the tale Gabriella inherits from her mother is not necessarily mother nature's, but her mother the writer's? The natural duplicity of the James brothers notwithstanding, could it be that Gabriella owes her mock execution to the (wo)man-made duplicity of the signifier?

Literally speaking, she certainly does. Ernest does not, be it recalled, shoot Gabriella only for entwining herself with her father's twin's Richard; his jealousy is gradually brought to the flash point by her apparently dubious association with her dubious "parent." This tragedy, in turn, has its antecedents in a fateful misprision, an improper interpretation of a proper name. The fiendish St. James is named Gabriel Henry, the "angel of light" (426) Henry Gabriel; Rosalie was, needless to say, the "earthly divinity's" (414) wife, the "real" Mrs. St. James the demon's; "it is not strange," then, that Rosalie should finally have been persuaded of her husband's "bigamy" by a marriage certificate whose "Gabriel Henry" she misread as "Henry Gabriel" (440). The fatal resemblance that causes all Gabriella's woe is, one sees, double; nature's duplicity has its twin in that of the word.

Ernest Linwood offers further hints about the ambiguous relationship between its real and imaginary parts. Thus, soon after Ernest remarks to Gabriella that she bears a "striking resemblance" to a portrait of an Italian flower girl, Rosalie's daughter finds herself planted before it, "imitating" the flower girl's "attitude." Ernest, who catches her at it, explains why he came to look at the portrait as follows: "'I came on purpose to gaze on that charming representation of youth and innocence, without dreaming that its original was by it.'" Gabriella replies that she does not think she can be taken for the original (123–24). Somewhat later, Ernest seems obliquely to suggest that our heroine's original is to be sought in print: glancing at his library, and then at Gabriella, he evokes that magical moment when a reader, "'glowing with enthusiasm, turns from the page before him to a living page, printed by the hand of God in fair, divine characters'" (128). Has he, one involuntarily wonders, been reading *Ernest Linwood*? Should we take him to mean that Gabriella is (like) a character in a book? Or would Ernest remind us that art's imaginary parts reflect their natural originals, and that Gabriella's original is to be sought in mother nature/her mother's nature? Her mother, however, is a character in *Ernest Linwood*. . . .

More: she is a "mother of prose," amateur author of the story about woman's destiny destined to rewrite itself as Gabriella's. Her daughter is thus doubly descended of her: "art" and "nature," in Gabriella's words, "both seemed my birthright" (62). As we have seen, nature is also her death warrant. But it is such, *Ernest Linwood* suggests, only insofar as it is redoubled in art, just as the James brothers' natural duplicity becomes a "fatal resemblance" only when redoubled by the duplicitous signifier. Natural her-story takes the tragic turn it does with the return of Rosalie's *story*; the self-effacing prophecy which is the Mene Tekel of Gabriella's destiny is born of her mother's Ms. Who can say how Rosalie's tale would have come out if, two years and three paragraphs before becoming "the representative of [her father's] once beloved Rosalie" (167), the passionate reader had not yielded herself to the wizard spell of romances as impassioned as her own (in which romances, perhaps, still other newly awakened Rosalies read impassioned romances by their mothers in which their newly awakened mothers yielded themselves to the wizard spell of impassioned romances, and so on)? Who can say how *Ernest Linwood* would have come out if Gabriella had not read Rosalie?

Yet it would be inaccurate to claim that Gabriella's novel comes out incestuously because she reads her. For, in *Ernest Linwood* as in the rest of scribblerdom, incest does not come out at all. Like Gabriella on her mother's grave, it is thrust prophylactically back into "darkness,—silence,—oblivion." Her-story does not therefore fail to repeat itself; however, to the extent that it is about incest, it repeats itself by repeatedly failing to repeat itself. Like her mother before her, Gabriella is as innocently *un*incestuous as Ernest is mad, "as pure and fresh as the world's first morning, redolent with the fragrance of Eden's first blossoms" (Ernest, p. 127). Incest emerges only in her tale, stirred to life by the duplicitous signifier that tells the story of its nonemergence.

Does the female animal, then, occur neither in nature nor in art? Let us say rather that she owes her (un)natural existence to her (non)emergence in scribblerdom. One can see why Gabriella is "tempted to throw down the pen" (381) just before penning the story of her (un)incestuous escapade with Dick: she would abjure the enchanter's wand before it can conjure the improper out of the perfectly proper, would chain down the incestuous spirit haunting the signifier that chains incest down. In a word, she would write a (non)book, shorn of its imaginary parts, hermetically sealed like the (un)incestuous tale she inherited from her mother. But this is impossible. *Ernest Linwood* therefore takes a different tack: it symbolically transforms its innocently guilty author into a (non)writer.

More specifically, Ernest does, when he opens fire. Who does he fire on? Gabriella indirectly asked the same question earlier, wondering whither she was wandering just before taking up her mother's story, wondering who she was after being laid low for finishing it. Which

Gabriella, we wondered in our turn, was wondering and wandering? The wanderer proceeded to disappear in her mother's tale. But in which sense? Did she become the mother who bore her? Or did she rejoin the "mother of prose"? What sort of gyn-ocide does Ernest commit?

There is good reason for treating it as a case of poeticide. The scene of the crime is rich in poetic associations. It is "the grassy slope," as Gabriella specifies just before being fearfully chastised, next "the welling spring by whose gushing waters [she] had often sat, indulging the wild poetry of [her] imagination" (384). We are not far from that grassy "by-path" in the woods where little Gabriella freely indulged her "own wondrous imaginings" (11). We remember why she was indulging them there: the "gushing stream" of her fantasy had been diverted into that sylvan sanctuary by Regulus's "murder" of her maiden poem. Gabriella's poem was devoted—like whose Ms.?—to her mother and other self. Does Ernest's avenging iron carry on the chastening work begun by the fatherly Regulus's iron wedge? It is perhaps worth recalling that Dick provoked Ernest's assault with revelations that came "like the music of gushing waters" (366) to Gabriella's thirsty ears. One of these revelations, be it noted in passing, was that Dick's mother's surname was La Fontaine; one might also mention, as Gabriella does shortly before Ernest fires, that the spot upon which she often indulged the wild poetry of her imagination was one on which she and the young La Fontaine had often embraced as children. Shortly after Ernest shoots her as she once again embraces "brother" Dick beside the welling spring, she is united with her living spring, the godly father who, steeped in "the wellspring of the heart," the "*fontaine de jouvence*," "breathe[s] an atmosphere pure as the world's first spring" (451). These references might well be supposed to spring from a common source. We need no divining rod to locate it: Gabriella's aesthetic theory long ago located it for us.

It is the loving, living Spring. Art, Gabriella declared, was to "follow nature" back to that ageless fountain. The alpha and omega of every moral tale was to be the "eternal source of love divine" (164): in other words, the Word, or the Holy Father. Has Gabriella-the-writer honored this first principle of scribbler art?

But the writer and her imagination, we were told, wilted in the woods where she once indulged her own wondrous imaginings. Among the imaginings she indulged, one presumes, were the things

she imagined her father doing. If one did not know she had explicitly abandoned the temple of culture for that of Hymen,[23] one might
be inclined to imagine that she was still imagining these things: witness Rosalie's-viz.-Gabriella's wild, impassioned tale about her own
living spring, and the way it dovetails with Gabriella's-viz.-Gabriella's
tale about *hers*. One might further suppose that our (non)writer continued to translate her aesthetic theory into the most natural of
terms even after meeting the fiery fury of Ernest's wilting rod: witness the tail end of her tale, and her living spring's prominent part
in it. Pursuing paradox to the hilt, one could go so far as to say that
Providence arranges to have Gabriella-the-writer shot, much as it
had arranged the murder of Gabriella's pubescent poem, precisely
so that she can spin out the other Gabriella's impious her-story with,
impunity. But then one would have to conclude, in all earnestness,
that Gabriella-viz.-Hentz exposes her own tale—and that Ernest-viz.-
God saves it by shooting it.

Provisional Conclusions

     No better way to conclude a survey of scribblerdom than
with Gabriella's provisional conclusion. Surviving her own execution,
she sums up the great end of scribbler art: to reconcile the final
solution of the woman question with woman's continued survival,
and the scribblers' own self-effacement with the persistence of scribbling. The method to Ernest's madness, in other words, is one we
have been studying since plunging into *The Wide, Wide World*. Shooting his wife, and so saving her, the madman realizes the apocalyptic
promise of the gunpowder in John's soul; his hand-gun is only a
more forceful version of Dr. Hartwell's iron rod; his near-fatal dis-
charge is prefigured in the acid Philip Amory lets flow over his
sweetheart's eyes. The striking resemblance between the gyn-ocidal
maniac and his eminently sane brethren is the index of another: the
one that conflates a 'Lena Rivers's innocence with her guilt, that requires every scribbler heroine to be chastened for a crime she cannot
possibly commit. Whence comes this cruel twinning of sin and sinlessness? Here too Gabriella, in her eagerness to secure the title of
(non)writer, reminds us of answers suggested by her sister scribblers:
it comes, she whispers, from the impropriety of the novel, from the
treacherous duplicity of the signifier. And she prescribes a remedy

we have also seen before: the only sure-fire protection against the corruption of the improper is the spotless whiteness of the (winding) sheet.

But the white sheet shrouds the guilty as well as the spotless. Ernest's aim, after all, was to wrap Gabriella up in one, like her mother before her. Would it have betokened mother and daughter's common martyrdom, or their common crime? God subjects little Eva to similar treatment: can one be sure He did not mean to cure her of the con-genital ailment she inherited from Eve? In its very inconclusiveness, Gabriella's provisional conclusion provides a fitting reprise of this point too: it reminds us that the total self-abnegation which alone preserves scribbler woman from sexual/textual sin eerily resembles the annihilation the living God's canons reserve for the incestuous. White as the winding sheet or black as sin, preternaturally stainless or mortally stained, the only True Woman, in scribblerdom, is a dead woman on leave.

As *The Wide, Wide World* approaches its (un)incestuous climax, Ellen has to promise to do three things for John. The first is to keep up a "full correspondence" with her "brother"; the second, to "read no novels" (563–64). John decorously declines to name his third wish, judging Ellen as yet too unripe to hear it. Her girlish reaction is as predictable as it is winsome: she "puzzled herself a little to think what could be the third thing John wanted of her; but whatever it was, she was very sure she would do it!" (569).

It is only natural that she should be so sure, since it is, after all, her beloved "brother" who wants that third thing; if Ellen did not instinctively want to give it to him, the foundations of the wide world would totter. Yet it is because one is so "very sure" that Ellen and her sisters will "do it" for their respective familiar gentlemen that the foundations of the wide world are forever tottering. To square that domestic(ating) circle, Gabriella submits to symbolic execution by Ernest's chastening rod—and survives to tell the tale that mandates her death by fire. She dies, and rises again, on behalf of all her innocently sinning sisters.

NOTES

Preface

1. The reviews of *Pierre* from which I have culled the words and phrases cited in the text are reprinted in Brian Higgins and Hershel Parker, eds., *Critical Essays on Herman Melville's Pierre; or, The Ambiguities* (Boston, 1983), pp. 46, 60, 22, 43, 35, 55, 48, 63, 64, 58, 69, 42.

2. David Reynolds, *Beyond the American Renaissance: The Subversive Imagination in the Age of Emerson and Melville* (New York, 1988), provides a delightful taxonomy of the sexual perversions that bloomed in the more sensational popular literature of the day; but even Reynolds fails to make good his insight that "the Conventional itself carried the seeds of the Subversive" (p. 159) when he comes to discuss the high-toned and, as he sees it, sanitized domestic novels that were America's best-sellers in the 1850s.

1. The Fictional Subject

1. Susan Geary, "The Domestic Novel as Commercial Commodity: Making a Best Seller in the 1850s," *Papers of the Bibliographical Society of America* 70 (1976): 380; Grace Overmyer, "Susan Bogert and Anna Bartlett Warner," in *Notable American Women*, ed. Edward James et al. (Cambridge, Mass.: 1971), 3:543; Edward H. Foster, *Susan and Anna Warner* (Boston, 1978), Twayne's United States Author Series 312, p. 33; Dorothy Sanderson, *They Wrote for a Living: A Bibliography of the Works of Susan Bogert Warner and Anna Bartlett Warner* (West Point, N.Y., 1976), p. 18; Richard Altick, *The English Common Reader: A Social History of the Mass-Reading Public, 1800–1900* (London, 1957), p. 388.

2. Not just in the United States and England. Bernhard Tauchnitz, a Leipzig-based publisher of English-language books, welcomed *The Wide, Wide World* into his prestigious "Library of British and American Authors" as early as 1854. A German newspaper ran a serialized translation at about the same time; this was probably the text subsequently given a place of honor in Kretzschmar's "*Bibliothek Illustrirter Erzählungen für christliche Familien.*" France had its translation by 1853; it went through four editions by 1856. Polish and Swedish versions followed. "American Literature in Germany," *Norton's Literary Gazette,* n.s., 1 (1855): 3; *Catalogue général des livres imprimés de la Bibliothèque nationale, Auteurs* (Paris, 1959), 218: 502.

3. George Haven Putnam, *George Palmer Putnam: A Memoir* (New York, 1912), p. 438. Frank Luther Mott, *Golden Multitudes: The Story of Best Sellers in the United States* (New York, 1947), p. 124. According to S. Austin Allibone, *A Critical Dictionary of English Literature and British and American Authors* (London, 1871), 3:2585–86, "it was asserted" [by Putnam?] that half a million copies of *The Wide, Wide World* had been sold *by 1860.* Overmyer, "Susan Bogert and Anna Bartlett Warner," p. 543, says that, "according to contemporary records," the book sold one million copies—presumably in the 1850s and 1860s.

4. E. Douglas Branch, *The Sentimental Years, 1830–1860* (New York, 1934), pp. 128–29; Leslie Fiedler, Introduction, *The Monks of Monk Hall, or The Quaker City,* by George Lippard (New York, 1970), p. vii; and David Reynolds, *Beyond the American Renaissance: The Subversive Imagination in the Age of Emerson and Melville* (New York, 1988), p. 207, all put initial sales of *The Quaker City* (1844) in the tens of thousands, but none provides reliable documentation of the claim. Michael Denning, *Mechanic Accents: Dime Novels and Working-Class Culture in America* (London, 1987), p. 88, discusses the novel's extensive sales in separately published installments.

5. "Publishers," *American Publishers' Circular and Literary Gazette* 2 (1855): 165.

6. The three super-sellers of the 1850s were Harriet Beecher Stowe's *Uncle Tom's Cabin,* Susanna Maria Cummins's *The Lamplighter,* and *The Wide, Wide World.* Estimates of the sales of these and other mid-century favorites vary wildly; the general tendency is inflationary.

7. Mott, *Golden Multitudes,* pp. 306–8, pp. 318–20; James Hart, *The Popular Book: A History of America's Literary Taste* (New York, 1950), pp. 305–7. Hawthorne's endlessly cited fulmination may be found in *The Letters of Hawthorne to William D. Ticknor* (Newark, 1910), 1:75. For evidence that the scribblers knew they were scribblers, see Ann Douglas, "'The Scribbling Women' and Fanny Fern: Why Women Wrote," *American Quarterly* 23 (1971): 7–8, and Mary Kelley, *Private Woman, Public Stage: Literary Domesticity in Nineteenth-Century America* (Oxford, 1984), pp. 181–84.

8. Gerty's favorite book was the 1854 hit *The Lamplighter,* parodied in the "Nausicaa episode" of *Ulysses.* Its heroine is also named Gerty. Among the other 1850s best-sellers Joyce's Gerty may have treasured were those by

Mary Jane Holmes, Mrs. E.D.E.N. Southworth, Augusta Jane Evans, and (possibly) Sylvanus Cobb; the collected works of these luminaries were continuously in print until the end of the nineteenth century. Esther Carrier's investigation of library records indicates that Holmes, Southworth, and Cobb also numbered among the writers most often checked out of public libraries late in the 1800s. See her *Fiction in Public Libraries, 1876–1900* (New York, 1965), pp. 75, 79–80, 175.

9. Thus the publishers Street and Smith, who brought out a resplendent 100–volume edition of Mrs. Southworth shortly before the war, were by 1937 happy to reduce the remainder at twenty-four titles for a piddling $1.75. See Regis Boyle, "Mrs. E.D.E.N. Southworth, Novelist" (Washington, D.C., 1939), p. 162.

10. Some continue to be charmed. For example, Jane Tompkins, in her afterword to the Feminist Press reprint of *The Wide, Wide World* (New York, 1987), p. 584, judges the novel "compulsively readable, absorbing, and provoking." De gustibus . . .

11. The term "cultural work" is borrowed from Jane Tompkins, *Sensational Designs: The Cultural Work of American Fiction, 1790–1860* (Oxford, 1985). Cathy Davidson documents pre-Jacksonian America's tendency to leave its cultural workers unhonored and unsung in *Revolution and the Word: The Rise of the Novel in America* (New York, 1986), pp. 30–31. Reynolds's *Beyond the American Renaissance* represents a truly Herculean effort to (among other things) do these faceless pioneers posthumous justice.

On the ongoing internationalization of the American best-seller, see John Sutherland, *Bestsellers: Popular Fiction of the 1970s* (London, 1981), pp. 14, 21, 29–30.

12. Fredric Jameson, citing Jean Baudrillard on capitalist mass art, in "Reification and Utopia in Mass Culture," *Social Text* 1 (1979): 135.

13. Hawthorne, *Letters*, 1:75.

14. Koch, Introduction, *Tempest and Sunshine by Mary Jane Holmes and The Lamplighter by Maria Susanna Cummins* (New York, 1968), p. viii.

15. Johanna Brenner and Maria Ramas, "Rethinking Women's Oppression," *New Left Review* 144 (March–April 1984): 61.

16. "Image" and "imitation," as Jacques Derrida notes in what is presumably a glancing allusion to Jacques Lacan, have the same root. See *Dissemination*, trans. Barbara Johnson (Chicago, 1987), p. 188.

17. John Cawelti, *Adventure, Mystery, Romance* (Chicago, 1976), p. 10.

18. Henry Nash Smith, *Democracy and the Novel: Popular Resistance to Classic American Writers* (New York, 1978), pp. 12, 14–15.

19. This happy formulation is borrowed from Elizabeth Stuart Phelps, *The Sunny Side; or, The Country Minister's Wife* (Boston, 1851), a better-seller that climaxes in an emotional account of the minister's wife's redeeming love for her son.

20. Caroline Kirkland is thus quite right when she observes that, in *The Wide, Wide World*, Warner "has not taken pains to hide her foundations."

Kirkland identifies those foundations as religious; but, inadvertently or not, she points to incest as well (see chap. 4, n. 7). Review of *The Wide, Wide World, Queechy*, and *Dollars and Cents, North American Review* 76 (1853): 115.

21. Leslie Fiedler, *Love and Death in the American Novel*, 2d. ed. (New York, 1966), pp. 415–420, and Sally McNall, *Who Is in the House? A Psychological Study of Two Centuries of Women's Fiction in America, 1795 to the Present* (New York, 1981), pp. 33–63, both register the incestuous implications of the 1850s best-seller, but neither develops them in detail. Tompkins, *Sensational Designs*, pp. 172–84, faces up to scribbler sadomasochism, but scotomizes incest. Mary Hiatt, "Susan Warner's Subtext: The Other Side of Piety," *Journal of Evolutionary Psychology* 8 (1987): 250–61, develops, with respect to *The Wide, Wide World*, Alexander Cowie's point that in later domestic fiction "an erotic element (for which the author acknowledged no responsibility) became apparent between the lines." Cowie, "The Vogue of the Domestic Novel, 1850–1870," *The South Atlantic Quarterly* 41 (1942): 417.

22. Cowie, "Vogue," p. 417.

23. *The Rise of the American Novel* (New York, 1951), pp. 443, 441. Cowie's spoof of scribblerdom is hilarious; no one will regret taking the time to look it up. Drier formulations of the idea that the scribblers preached compliance are to be found in Fred Pattee, *The Feminine Fifties* (New York, 1940); H. Ross Brown, *The Sentimental Novel in America, 1789–1860* (Durham, N.C., 1940); Mott, *Golden Multitudes*; Hart, *The Popular Book*, pp. 85–105; Leslie Smith, "Through Rose-Colored Glasses: Some Victorian Sentimental Novels," in *New Dimensions in Popular Culture*, ed. Russel Nye (Bowling Green, Ohio, 1972), pp. 90–106; Henry Nash Smith, "The Scribbling Women and the Cosmic Success Story," *Critical Inquiry* 1 (1974): 47–70; John Frederick, "Hawthorne's Scribbling Women," *New England Quarterly* 48 (1975): 231–40; Ann Douglas, *The Feminization of American Culture* (New York, 1977); and (more or less) D. G. Myers, "The Canonization of Susan Warner," *The New Criterion* 4 (December 1988): 73–78.

24. A recent marxist history of U.S. literature provides a textbook example of the casual dismissal of this fiction: "dozens of second-rate and third-rate women writers [published] a flood of sentimental novels in the 1850s and 1860s. . . . These domestic tales often sank to the level of cheap Sunday-school tracts. . . . Conservative in their overwhelming majority, the women writers maintained a stubborn silence on intolerable economic conditions, and avoided making the slightest challenge to the *status quo*" (my translation). Karl-Heinz Schönfelder and Karl-Heinz Wirzberger, *Literatur der USA im Überblick: Von den Anfängen bis zur Gegenwart* (Leipzig, 1977), pp. 159–60.

25. Helen Papashvily, *All the Happy Endings: A Study of the Domestic Novel in America* (New York, 1956), p. xvi.

26. Nina Baym, *Woman's Fiction: A Guide to Novels by and about Women in America, 1820–1870* (Ithaca, N.Y., 1978). Besides Papashvily, Baym's forerunners include Beatrice Hofstadter, "Popular Culture and the Romantic

Heroine," *American Scholar* 30 (1960–61): 98–116, and Dee Garrison, "Immoral Fiction in the Late Victorian Library," *American Quarterly* 28 (1976): 71–89. An article and a book by Frances Cogan reflect Baym's influence: "Weak Fathers and Other Beasts: An Examination of the American Male in Domestic Novels, 1850–1870," *American Studies* (Kansas) 2 (Fall 1984): 5–20, and *All-American Girl: The Ideal of Real Womanhood in Mid-Nineteenth-Century America* (Athens, Ga., 1989). Tompkins's *Sensational Designs* develops a considerably more sophisticated version of the protofeminist thesis.

27. Baym, *Woman's Fiction*, pp. 311, 18, 22, 115, 43, 38.

28. Cogan, "Weak Fathers," pp. 8–9. "Dumbbells" would perhaps have served better than "barbells."

29. "The Sentimentalists: Promise and Betrayal in the Home," *Signs* 4 (1979): 437; also in *Fiction by American Women: Recent Views*, ed. Winifred F. Bevilacqua (Port Washington, N.Y., 1983). Kelley develops the thesis in "The Literary Domestics: Private Woman on a Public Stage," in *Ideas in America's Cultures: From Republic to Mass Society*, ed. Hamilton Cravens (Ames, Iowa, 1982), pp. 27–44, and at length in *Private Woman*. She is anticipated by Mary Ryan, "American Society and the Cult of Domesticity, 1830–1860" (Ph.D. Diss., University of California, Santa Barbara, 1971). Anne Jones, *Tomorrow Is Another Day: The Woman Writer in the South* (Baton Rouge, 1981), pp. 51–91; Beverly Voloshin, "The Limits of Domesticity: The Female *Bildungsroman* in America, 1820–1870," *Women's Studies* 10 (1984): 283–302, reprinted in Voloshin, ed., *American Literature, Culture, and Ideology: Essays in Memory of Henry Nash Smith* (New York, 1990), pp. 95–114; Joanne Dobson, "The Hidden Hand: Subversion of Cultural Ideology in Three Mid-Nineteenth Century American Women's Novels," *American Quarterly* 38 (1986): 223–42; and Hiatt, "Susan Warner's Subtext," are in the same line of descent.

30. Kelley, *Private Woman*, pp. 251, 104.

31. Augusta Jane Evans [Wilson], *Beulah* (1859; London, n.d. [1861]).

32. Voloshin, "Limits of Domesticity," pp. 293–300.

33. Kelley, *Private Woman*, pp. viii, 251.

34. Jones, *Tomorrow*, p. 91; Kelley, *Private Woman*, p. 102.

35. Kelley, *Private Woman*, pp. 215, viii. That some of the (war) reports Kelley considers are literary and others not, changes nothing from the present point of view; we are therefore disregarding her disclaimer to the effect that hers "is a historical study, not, as the term is commonly understood, a literary one" (p. xii).

36. Kelley, *Private Woman*, pp. viii, xii, 258, 56, 251, 145, 279, 329.

37. Elaine Showalter, "Feminist Criticism in the Wilderness," *Critical Inquiry* 8 (Winter 1981): 187, cited (approvingly) in Kelley, *Private Woman*, p. 346.

38. The remainder of this chapter could be called speculative; it explores

the idea that a text's contradictory relation to itself/its readerships might be conceived in terms of an individual's contradictory relation to ideology. Readers who do not go in for that sort of thing are urged to treat the rest of the chapter as a note, and this note as the rest of the chapter—and then to *skip the note.*

39. Louis Althusser, *Lenin and Philosophy and Other Essays*, trans. Ben Brewster (London, 1971), pp. 162–80. For a helpful discussion of the links between Althusser's subject and the rather different subject defined by psychoanalysis, see Warren Montag, "Marxism and Psychoanalysis: The Impossible Encounter," *Minnesota Review*, n.s., 23 (1984): 70–85.

40. "Hailed" is the somewhat inadequate translation of "*interpellé*," which usually has the connotation of being summoned by someone in authority. "Interpol-lation" may give something of the flavor of the corresponding French noun.

41. The Subject involved is "obviously" History because the writing involved is popular fiction. In the case of high art, the Subject is usually just as "obviously" the transhistorical Universal Mind, the ideal reader's Other.

42. R. W. B. Lewis, *The American Adam: Innocence, Tragedy, and Tradition in the Nineteenth Century* (Chicago, 1955), p. 2. I would like to acknowledge my personal and scholarly debt to Professor Lewis, my master in more than one sense of the term.

43. Ibid.

44. Ibid., p. 3.

45. Ibid., pp. 3–4. By "narrative," Lewis here means "fictional narrative."

46. Ibid., p. 67.

47. Lewis's scheme can be overturned, so that *Historie* becomes the commanding person of the historical Trinity *Geschichte*-story-*Historie*; one then has the "modernist" conception according to which historians (or storytellers) forge the "supreme fiction" that retrospectively *makes* the cacophony of cultural conversation *into* an orderly debate. But this palace revolt preserves the essential structure that divides history into distinct moments, posits the primacy of one of them, and then sublates the original distinction by treating all the other moments as reflections of whichever one has been privileged.

48. Lewis, *American Adam*, p. 3.

49. Michel Pêcheux, *Language, Semantics, and Ideology*, trans. Harbans Nagpal (New York, 1982), pp. 118–20.

50. Emile Benveniste, *Problèmes de linguistique générale* (Paris: Gallimard, 1966), 1:247, cited in Jonathan Culler, *Structuralist Poetics* (Ithaca, N.Y., 1975), p. 198.

51. Lewis, *American Adam*, p. 3.

52. For the "bad subject" (it works better in French, since *mauvais sujet* also means something like "bad apple"), see Althusser, *Lenin*, p. 181.

53. Thus Myra Jehlen, "Archimedes and the Paradox of Feminist Criticism," *Signs* 6 (1981): 593, 587, argues that as the "prophets of compliance"

"forswore any claim on the primary vision of art," one "might do better to simply let [them] alone."

54. For example Baym, *Woman's Fiction*, pp. 18–19, concedes that the authors of "woman's fiction" "failed to see that many aspects of their situation might be functions of time and place rather than the will of God," but finds that their books were nonetheless "pragmatic feminis[t]" accounts of the "psychology of women." Her remark that Mrs. Southworth puts an "intensity" into her "platitudes" that "pushes them beyond formula into felt experience" (p. 113) speaks volumes about the ongoing attempt to save the scribblers from oblivion while safeguarding the great tradition.

55. No one has gone all the way down this road yet, but an article on revising the syllabus suggests that someone eventually will: "Another evocative grouping is the quartet of stunning texts published in the watershed years of 1850–1852: *The Scarlet Letter, The Wide, Wide World, Moby Dick,* and *Uncle Tom's Cabin.* . . . To the metaphysical, philosophical, and social concerns of the more familiar texts, *The Wide, Wide World* adds a passionate and minutely detailed account of a young girl's initiation into the . . . realities that severely delimit her identity and enforce her submission to the demands of the authority figures who surround her." Joanne Dobson and Judith Fetterly, "Nineteenth-Century American Novel: A Revised Syllabus," *Legacy* 1 (Spring 1984): 6.

56. On the difference between text and textual mirror, see James Kavanaugh, "'Marks of Weakness': Ideology, Science and Textual Criticism," *Praxis* (Los Angeles) 5 (1981): 27–28.

57. "Binding" is Stephen Heath's term for the process by which enunciation is, as he writes, "held on" enounced in the movies. See *Questions of Cinema* (Bloomington, Ind., 1981), p. 14.

58. Etienne Balibar and Pierre Macherey, "Literature as an Ideological Form: Some Marxist Propositions," trans. James Kavanagh, *Praxis* 5 (1981): 50.

59. Pierre Macherey, *A Theory of Literary Production*, trans. Geoffrey Wall (London, 1978), pp. 227–29, 233–40.

60. *The Illustrated London News*, 12 September 1891, p. 342, reported that Warner's classic was one of the four works most commonly found in "well-to-do English labourers' cottages." (The others were *The Pilgrim's Progress, Uncle Tom's Cabin,* and *Foxe's Book of Martyrs. Clarissa* and *Pamela* also turned up occasionally). See Clarence Gohdes, *American Literature in Nineteenth-Century England* (New York, 1944), p. 32.

61. Edward Salmon, *Juvenile Literature as It Is* (London, 1888), p. 22. Like D. G. Myers, writing almost exactly one hundred years later (see chap. 3, n. 6), Salmon was mystified by Warner's success: "It is not easy to explain the cause of the popularity of 'The Wide, Wide World' . . . [it is] of the severe evangelical order—high in tone, admirably written, well informed in some ways, but dull" (p. 126).

62. Tony Bennett, "Texts, Readers, Reading Formations," *Bulletin of the Midwest Modern Language Association* 16 (1983): 5.

2. The Facts of Life in the 1850s

1. This description of the best-sellers' early readership is suggested by information on people's disposable incomes and leisure time at mid-century, as well as the sales figures of books and magazines.

2. Charles Meigs, *Females and Their Diseases: A Series of Letters to his Class* (Philadelphia, 1848), p. 38. Less reputable popular fiction was more forthcoming about the influence of the female organs and functions on woman's soul. See David Reynolds, *Beyond the American Renaissance: The Subversive Imagination in the Age of Emerson and Melville* (New York, 1988), pp. 212–22.

3. Jonathan Edwards, *Works* (New York, 1881), 3:340, cited in Bernard Wishy, *The Child and the Republic: The Dawn of Modern American Child Nurture* (Philadelphia, 1968), p. 11. Cotton Mather, *A Family Well-Ordered* (Boston, 1699), p. 10, cited in Barbara Epstein, *The Politics of Domesticity: Women, Evangelism, and Temperance in Nineteenth-Century America* (Middletown, Conn., 1981), p. 82. The anonymous minister is cited in Carl Degler, *At Odds: Women and the Family in America from the Revolution to the Present* (Oxford, 1980), p. 86. Here, as throughout this chapter, I have been guided in my travels through America's advice books, medical annals, and religious ruminations by the many scholars who have preceded me; subsequent notes will give some idea of the extent of my debt.

4. Epstein, *Politics*, p. 33.

5. Michel Foucault, *The History of Sexuality*, vol. 1: *An Introduction*, trans. Robert Hurley (New York, 1978), p. 136.

6. For a somewhat different view, see Douglas, *The Feminization of American Culture* (New York, 1977), p. 87.

7. Edward Park, ed., *Memoir of Nathaniel Emmons* (Boston, 1861), 1:434, cited in Douglas, *Feminization*, p. 156.

8. Homer Bostwick, *A Treatise on the Nature and Treatment of Seminal Diseases, Impotency, and Other Kindred Affections* (New York, 1848), p. 184. Heman Humphrey, *Domestic Education* (Amherst, Mass., 1840), p. 77.

In an excellent essay that came to my attention after the present book was completed, Richard Brodhead studies the establishment of the new disciplinary regime in mid-nineteenth-century America and then briefly examines its impact on best-selling novels of the period, including Susan Warner's *The Wide, Wide World*. See "Sparing the Rod: Discipline and Fiction in Antebellum America," *Representations* 21 (Winter 1988): 67–96.

9. J. B. Newman, *Philosophy of Generation: Its Abuses and Their Causes* (New York, 1856), p. 48, cited in Carroll Smith-Rosenberg, "Sex as Symbol in Victorian Purity: An Ethnohistorical Analysis of Jacksonian America," *American Journal of Sociology* 84, Supplement (1978): 232–33.

10. Humphrey, *Domestic Education*, p. 48.

11. Humphrey, *Domestic Education*, p. 47. Bronson Alcott, *Observations on the Principles and Methods of Infant Instruction* (Boston, 1830), p. 22, cited in

Anne Kuhn, *The Mother's Role in Childhood Education: New England Concepts, 1830–1860*, Yale Studies in Religious Education, vol. 19 (New Haven, 1947), pp. 166–67.

12. Foucault, *History of Sexuality*, vol. 1, pp. 141–44. Foucault prefers to speak of the articulation of the disciplinary regime with the politicization of the biological, rather than of the derivation of the one from the other.

13. According to Herbert Gutman, *Work, Culture, and Society in Industrializing America* (New York, 1976), pp. 33–50, large-scale transformation of the labor process and working-class culture began in the 1840s; by then the "normalization" of middle-class culture had been underway for a generation.

14. Catharine Sedgwick, *Home* (Boston, 1841), p. 26, cited in Steven Mintz, *A Prisoner of Expectations: The Family in Victorian Culture* (New York, 1983), p. 37. (Not coincidentally, Sedgwick was an outspoken anti-Calvinist.) William Ellery Channing, quoted in Elizabeth Peabody, *Reminiscences of Rev. William Ellery Channing* (Boston, 1880), p. 30, cited in David Reynolds, "The Feminization Controversy: Sexual Stereotypes and the Paradoxes of Piety in Nineteenth-Century America," *The New England Quarterly* 53 (1980): 99. Max Weber, trans. Talcott Parsons, *The Protestant Ethic and the Spirit of Capitalism* (New York, 1958), pp. 155–83.

15. Catharine Beecher, *A Treatise on Domestic Economy for the Use of Young Ladies at Home and at School* (Boston, 1841), p. 16.

16. For a superb account of the way this contradiction worked out in murderous practice, see Ronald Takaki, *Iron Cages: Race and Culture in Nineteenth-Century America* (Seattle, 1979), especially pp. 67–144.

17. "A Sketch from Life," *Ladies' Magazine* 6 (June 1833): 258, cited in Kuhn, *Mother's Role*, p. 18.

18. Humphrey, *Domestic Education*, pp. 49, 25, 78. Humphrey's style of flexibility recalls that of the New England Theologians inspired by Timothy Dwight: they upheld (at least initially) the doctrine of original sin, while maintaining that many aspects of human nature were essentially innocent, and that children tended naturally to seek God. The liberal minister William G. Eliot takes a different tack, mentioning original sin almost under his breath while stressing a distinction between those he concedes *may* have been born in corruption and those bearing the "burden of actual sin and personal transgression." (*Early Religious Education Considered as the Divinely Appointed Way to the Regenerate Life* [Boston, 1855], p. 100.) Dr. William Acton, the English sexologist, is quite certain that the child's "heart is wicked," but nevertheless deems his mind a "fair book, on whom he who will may write some lasting record" (*Prostitution Considered in its Moral, Social, and Sanitary Aspects* [London, 1857], p. 162). The variations are multifarious, the basic theme the same.

19. Eliot, *Early Religious Education*, pp. 15–16.

20. Though the correlation between class and theological position was not strict, the sects that continued to stress innate depravity and the catastrophic

conversion—notably Methodism and Baptism—included many more working people than did Bushnell's Congregationalists or the explicitly anti-Calvinist Unitarians.

21. Horace Bushnell, "The Kingdom of God as a Grain of Mustard Seed," *New Englander* 2 (1844): 610, in *Horace Bushnell*, ed. H. Shelton Smith (New York, 1965), p. 375. The Bushnell of the 1840s explains himself best in *Views of Christian Nurture and of Subjects Adjacent Thereto* (Hartford, 1847). The principle essay in this collection may be found in *Bushnell*, pp. 378–91.

22. According to Peter Gregg Slater, *Children in the New England Mind: In Death and in Life* (Hamden, Conn., 1977), p. 90, "by the time of the Civil War the debate about [infant depravity] could seem as remote as a medieval disputation."

23. Henry James, Sr., quoted in Douglas, *Feminization*, p. 17.

24. Just how deep the Jacksonian bourgeoisie's humanism ran is another question. Takaki, *Iron Cages*, pp. 11–15, 80–144, richly documents its habit of assigning different groups of people different degrees of humanity.

25. See Henry Nash Smith, *Virgin Land: The American West as Symbol and Myth* (1950; Cambridge, Mass., 1980), pp. 121–32.

26. Henry Wright, *Marriage and Parentage; or, The Reproductive Element in Man, as a Means to his Elevation and Happiness* (Boston, 1854), p. 53. Wright was one of the more exuberant devotees of natural religion.

27. For dithyrambic examples, too long to reproduce here, see Sylvester Graham, *A Lecture to Young Men on Chastity* (1834; Boston, 1837), pp. 34–50; Wright, *Marriage*, pp. 9–14.

28. Foucault, *History of Sexuality*, vol. 1, pp. 121, 123.

29. But see below, pp. 69–73.

30. Steven Nissenbaum, *Sex, Diet, and Debility in Jacksonian America: Sylvester Graham and Health Reform* (Westport, Conn., 1980), p. 28. Nissenbaum reports that only two works condemning male incontinence were published in America in the eighteenth century. Yet as early as 1812, Benjamin Rush was lambasting onanism in what would, by the 1840s, be the standard American terms.

31. George Calhoun, *Report of the Consulting Surgeon on Spermatorrhea or Seminal Weakness* (Philadelphia, 1858), p. 8, cited in Smith-Rosenberg, "Sex as Symbol," p. 235. Frederick Hollick, *A Popular Treatise on Venereal Diseases in All Their Forms* (New York, 1852), p. 69, cited in John S. Haller, Jr. and Robin M. Haller, *The Physician and Sexuality in Victorian America* (Chicago, 1974), pp. 196–97. William Alcott, *The Physiology of Marriage* (Boston, 1856), p. 68. Bostwick, *Treatise*, p. 47. For a sampling of antimasturbation diatribes, see Ronald Walters's invaluable anthology, *Primers for Purity: Sexual Advice to Victorian America* (Englewood Cliffs, N.J., 1974), pp. 21–53, 86–89.

32. Beecher, *Treatise*, p. 233.

33. Bostwick, *Treatise*, p. 183.

34. Orson Fowler, *Amativeness; or, Evils and Remedies of Excessive and Perverted Sexuality* (ca. 1846; London, n.d.), p. 4, laments the "thousands" of

female deaths due to "solitary sexual crime," but concedes that girls are probably "less infected" by the evil than boys. William Sanger, *The History of Prostitution: Its Extent, Causes, and Effects throughout the World* (New York, 1859), p. 320, reports that onanism "is practiced among young women to a great extent, though in a far less degree than among young men." Bostwick, *Treatise*, p. 183, remarks that some female deaths might also be attributed to onanism. The gynecologist Augustus Gardner helps one gauge the force of this "also" in his *Conjugal Sins against the Laws of Life and Health* (1870; New York, 1875), p. 70: "Far less common, indeed, is it among females than among the male youth of this country; perhaps, too, less disastrous in its results."

Fowler, *Amativeness*, p. 2, estimates that 90 percent of boys over eleven polluted themselves. The proportion rose with age until the young men married.

35. John Todd, *The Daughter at School* (Boston, 1858), p. 220; William Eliot, *Lectures to Young Women*, 3d ed. (Boston, 1854), p. 189. A list of mid-century works in which the quoted phrase appears would be long; the idea is ubiquitous.

36. Eliot, *Lectures*, pp. 47–48. Maria McIntosh, *Woman in America: Her Work and Her Reward* (New York, 1850), p. 23. "Editor's Table," *Godey's Lady's Book* 23 (August 1841): 93–94, cited in Kathryn Kish Sklar, *Catharine Beecher: A Study in American Domesticity* (1973; New York, 1976), p. 309. Sarah Hale, *Woman's Record* (New York, 1853), p. xxv, cited in Phillida Bunkle, "Sentimental Womanhood and Domestic Education, 1830–1870," *History of Education Quarterly* 14 (1974): 23. George Weaver, *The Christian Household* (New York, 1854), p. 93.

37. *Godey's Lady's Book*, cited in Meade Minnigerode, *The Fabulous Forties, 1840–1850: A Presentation of Private Life* (New York, 1924), p. 75.

38. G. J. Barker-Benfield, *The Horrors of the Half-Known Life: Male Attitudes toward Women and Sexuality in Nineteenth-Century America* (New York, 1976), pp. 189–226.

39. John Todd, *Woman's Rights* (Boston, 1867), p. 12.

40. Margaret Fuller, *Woman in the Nineteenth Century* (reprint of the 1855 ed.; New York, 1971), p. 96. McIntosh, *Woman*, p. 25. The Seneca Falls Declaration is cited in Elaine Kraditor, *Up from the Pedestal: Selected Writings in the History of American Feminism* (Chicago, 1968), p. 187.

41. Eliot, *Lectures*, p. 74. George Weaver, *Aims and Aids for Girls and Young Women on the Various Duties of Life* (New York, 1855), p. 137. Harriet Beecher Stowe and Catharine Beecher, *American Woman's Home; or, Principles of Domestic Science* (New York, 1869), p. 19. (On Stowe's inclination to make Jesus a mother, see Elizabeth Ammons, "Heroines in Uncle Tom's Cabin," in Ammons, ed., *Critical Essays on Harriet Beecher Stowe*, Critical Essays on American Literature [Boston, 1980], p. 157, and Douglas, *Feminization*, pp. 130–31.) William Alcott, *Letters to a Sister; or, Woman's Mission* (Buffalo, N.Y., 1850), p. 27.

Let us note in passing that, on 8 December 1854, as George Weaver was working on *Aims and Aids*, Pope Pius IX put an end to centuries of controversy by officializing the doctrine of the Immaculate Conception (according to which the Virgin Mother was conceived naturally, yet free of original sin).

42. Isabella Beecher Hooker, Letter of 9 August 1869 to John Stuart Mill, in Jeanne Boydston, Mary Kelley, and Anne Margolis, *The Limits of Sisterhood: The Beecher Sisters on Women's Rights and Woman's Sphere* (Chapel Hill, N.C., 1988), p. 195.

43. Henry Wright, *The Empire of the Mother over the Character and Destiny of the Race* (Boston, 1863), p. 4. Eliot, *Lectures*, p. 179. Sarah Hale, *Woman's Record* (New York, 1853), pp. 151–52, cited in Bunkle, "Sentimental Womanhood," p. 22. Weaver, *Christian Household*, p. 50. Meigs, *Females*, p. 44.

44. Acton, *Prostitution*, p. 20. In his authoritative *The Functions and Disorders of the Reproductive Organs in Youth* (1857; London, 1862), pp. 102–3, Acton confirmed that "in general, women do not feel any great sexual tendencies." Cited in Peter Cominos, "Late Victorian Sexual Respectability and the Social System," *International Review of Social History* 8 (1963): 231–32. The American authority William Sanger corroborated Acton's judgment: "the full force of sexual desire is seldom known to a virtuous woman." Thus Sanger knew straightaway that 513 once virtuous prostitutes were lying when they indicated that they had taken up their trade out of "inclination," which Sanger, logically, took to mean an inclination "to satisfy the sexual passions." Sanger, *Prostitution*, pp. 488–89.

45. On the origins of passionlessness, see Nancy Cott, "Passionlessness: An Interpretation of Victorian Sexual Ideology, 1790–1850," *Signs* 4 (1978): 219–36 (also in *Women and Health in America: Historical Readings*, ed. Judith W. Leavitt [Madison, Wis., 1984]). Carroll Smith-Rosenberg dates the shift in medical opinion later than does Cott. See her *Disorderly Conduct: Visions of Gender in Victorian America* (Oxford, 1985), p. 23, p. 302. See also Peter Gay, *The Bourgeois Experience*, vol. 1, *Education of the Senses* (Oxford, 1984), pp. 154–55; Degler, *At Odds*, pp. 251–54; and [Floyd] Bryan Strong, "Sex, Character, and Reform in America, 1830–1920" (Ph.D. Diss., Stanford University, 1972), p. 17. I have drawn heavily on Strong's insightful and unjustly neglected work on incest in the nineteenth-century American family.

46. *Love and Parentage* (ca. 1844; London, n.d.), p. 35.

47. Graham, *Lecture*, pp. 20, 55. Weaver, *Christian Household*, p. 51.

48. Cominos, "Late Victorian Sexual Respectability," p. 223.

49. Eliot, *Lectures*, pp. 77–79.

50. Orson Fowler, *Perfect Men, Women, and Children in Happy Families* (Boston, 1878), pp. 160, 170, cited in Floyd Bryan Strong, "Towards a History of the Experiential Family: Sex and Incest in the Nineteenth-Century American Family," *Journal of Marriage and the Family* 35 (1973): 462. Compare Sigmund Freud, *Standard Edition*, vol. 7 (London, 1953): 223–24.

51. Bostwick, *Treatise*, p. 185. Todd, *Daughter*, p. 222.

52. Weaver, *Aims and Aids*, p. 182.

53. Foucault, *History of Sexuality*, vol. 1, p. 60.

54. The phrase is Barker-Benfield's.

55. *Love and Parentage*, p. 18. In *Familiar Lessons on Phrenology, Designed for the Use of Schools and Families* (London, n.d.), p. 5, the faculty of amativeness is charmingly defined as "love and kindness between the sexes: a desire to marry, and preference for the society of the opposite sex."

56. Wright, *Marriage*, p. 177. Alcott, *Physiology of Marriage*, p. 46.

57. Acton, *Functions and Disorders* (1857), p. 23. Graham, *Lecture*, p. 73. Alcott, *Physiology of Marriage*, p. 118. John Cowan, *The Science of a New Life* (1869; New York, 1880), p. 103, cited in Walters, *Primers*, p. 89. Edward Dixon, *A Treatise on the Diseases of the Sexual System, Adapted to Popular and Professional Reading* (New York, 1847), p. 220.

58. Alcott, *Physiology of Marriage*, p. 116.

59. Wright, *Marriage*, p. 182.

60. Fowler, *Amativeness*, p. 21.

61. Ibid., p. 16. Wright, *Marriage*, p. 202. The theoretical equivalence between onanism and excessive amativeness notwithstanding, the experts concurred in identifying "solitary fornication" as much the greater danger. See Gay, *Education*, p. 311.

62. Bostwick, *Treatise*, pp. 153–54.

63. Jeremy Taylor, *Holy Living*, cited in Graham, *Lecture*, p. 167. See also Wright, *Marriage*, p. 185: "THE CONDITIONS OF THE WIFE ARE EVER TO CONTROL THE PASSIONAL RELATION." Fowler, *Love and Parentage*, p. 20, states it memorably: "woman is our umpire."

64. Harriet Beecher Stowe, letter of 1845 to her husband, Calvin; Calvin Stowe, letter of 17 July 1845 to his father-in-law, Lyman. Cited in Edmund Wilson, *Patriotic Gore: Studies in the Literature of the American Civil War* (New York, 1962), pp. 22–23.

65. Fowler, *Amativeness*, p. 20.

66. Alcott, *Physiology of Marriage*, p. 13.

67. Fowler, *Perfect Men*, p. 170, cited in Strong, "Towards a History," p. 463.

68. Fiedler, *Love and Death in the American Novel*, 2d ed. (New York, 1966), p. 80.

69. Ibid., pp. 337–90.

70. Fowler, *Amativeness*, p. 19. Weaver, *Christian Household*, p. 51. Meigs, *Females*, p. 40. Harriet Beecher Stowe, *Household Papers and Stories* (1864; New York, 1967), p. 306, cited in Gayle Kimball, *The Religious Ideas of Harriet Beecher Stowe: Her Gospel of Womanhood*, Studies in Women and Religion, vol. 8 (New York, 1982), p. 153. "Grace Greenwood" [Sara Jane Lippincott], *Greenwood Leaves: A Collection of Sketches and Letters*, 3d ed. (Boston, 1851), p. 310. Mrs. John Sanford, *Woman, In Her Social and Domestic Character* (Boston, 1842), pp. 41–42, cited in Barber Welter, *Dimity Convictions: The American Woman in the Nineteenth Century* (Athens, Ohio, 1976), p. 22. McIntosh, *Woman*, pp. 30, 22, 23.

71. Horace Bushnell, *Woman's Suffrage: The Reform Against Nature* (New York, 1869), p. 59. Meigs, *Females*, p. 53.

72. Douglas, *Feminization*, p. 12.

73. For examples, see ibid., pp. 53, 66, 139, 189.

74. William Eliot, *Lectures to Young Men* (St. Louis, 1852), p. 79, cited in Walters, *Primers*, p. 69. Mary Poovey, *The Proper Lady and the Woman Writer: Ideology as Style in the Works of Mary Wollstonecraft, Mary Shelly, and Jane Austen* (Chicago, 1984), p. 19, shows that the dialectic that made the best the worst (or vice versa) had been operating on the other side of the Atlantic from the mid-eighteenth century on. See also her *Uneven Developments: The Ideological Work of Gender in Mid-Victorian England* (London, 1988), especially chap. 2, for a far-reaching discussion of nineteenth-century domestic ideology.

75. Meigs, *Females*, pp. 37–38.

76. Carroll Smith-Rosenberg and Charles Rosenberg, "The Female Animal: Medical and Biological Views of Woman and her Role in Nineteenth-Century America," *Journal of American History* 60 (1973): 668. The essay is reprinted in Leavitt, ed., *Women and Health*.

77. Meigs, *Females*, p. 40. Hugh Smith, *Letters to Married Ladies* (New York and Boston, 1832), p. 174, cited in Welter, *Dimity Convictions*, p. 59. Meigs, *Females*, p. 457.

Carroll Smith-Rosenberg and Charles Rosenberg detail the connections between mental disease and malfunctions of the female reproductive organs in "The Hysterical Woman: Sex Roles and Roles Conflict in Nineteenth-Century America," *Social Research* 39 (1972): 652–78. The essay is reprinted in *Disorderly Conduct*.

78. Gardner, *Conjugal Sins*, p. 22. John King, *Woman: Her Diseases and Their Treatment* (Cincinnati, 1858), p. 10, and Walter Johnson, *An Essay on the Diseases of Young Women* (London, 1849), p. 55, both cited in Welter, *Dimity Convictions*, p. 61. Sanger, *History of Prostitution*, pp. 488–89, p. 320. John C. Peters, *A Treatise on the Diseases of Married Females* (New York, 1854), p. 17, cited in Welter, *Dimity Convictions*, p. 61. Alcott, *Physiology of Marriage*, p. 50. Sanger, *History of Prostitution*, p. 503. Alcott, *Physiology of Marriage*, p. 52.

On clitoridectomy and "female castration," see Mary Daly, *Gyn/Ecology* (London, 1979), pp. 241–45; Strong, "Sex, Character, and Reform," pp. 120–22; and Gay, *Education of the Senses*, p. 304. For an excellent discussion of the psychic and somatic weak points of the nineteenth-century female anatomy, see Carroll Smith-Rosenberg, "Puberty to Menopause: The Cycle of Femininity in Nineteenth-Century America," in *Clio's Consciousness Raised*, eds. Mary Hartman and Lois Banner (New York, 1974), pp. 25–26.

79. Michel Pêcheux, *Language, Semantics, and Ideology*, trans. Harbans Nagpal (New York, 1982), pp. 110–17.

80. Lydia Sigourney, *Letters to Mothers* (Hartford, 1838), p. 10, cited in Douglas, *Feminization*, p. 88.

81. William Acton, *Functions and Disorders* (1865), p. 134, cited in Degler, *At Odds*, p. 254. Washington Irving, "The Love of a Mother," in *Prose Writers*

of America, ed. Rufus Griswold, 2d ed. (Philadelphia, 1847), p. 218. Cf. Freud, *Standard Edition,* vol. 15 (1963), p. 206; vol. 22 (1964), p. 133.

82. Harriet Beecher Stowe, *Lady Byron Vindicated* (Boston, 1870), p. 75. Harriet's cherished brother Henry detailed what happened when the best became the worst in *Twelve Lectures to Young Men, On Various Important Subjects,* rev. ed. (New York, 1875), cited in Walters, *Primers,* pp. 69–71.

83. Dixon, *Treatise,* pp. 224–27. Susan Winnett, "Coming Unstrung: Women, Men, Narrative, and Principles of Pleasure," *PMLA* 105 (1990): 509–11, proposes a theory of reading based in part on the principle of pleasure Dixon blasts here.

84. Graham, *Lecture,* pp. 158–59, describes one relatively mild case, cured by his favorite prescription of a simple vegetable diet.

85. Dixon, *Treatise,* pp. 229–30.

86. Dixon, *Treatise,* pp. 237, 240. Bostwick, *Treatise,* pp. 7, 61, 233–34. Graham, *Lecture,* p. 32. Wright, *Marriage,* p. 11. Sanger, *History of Prostitution,* p. 320. Anticipating Claude Lévi-Strauss (after a fashion), Graham appends the following footnote to his remarks on nature and culture: "By 'a pure state of nature,' be it remembered, I never mean the savage state of man, for that is not his natural state. But I mean that state in which man lives in accordance with all the physiological laws of his nature."

87. Augustus Gardner, *Our Children* (n.p., 1872), pp. 106–7, cited in Barker-Benfield, *Horrors,* p. 233.

88. Fowler, *Amativeness,* p. 26.

89. Eliot, *Lectures to Young Women,* p. 62. I do not know if Eliot ever stumbled across Dixon. Orson Fowler certainly did.

90. Literalists will perhaps object that, according to most experts on onanism, the unmanly habit mushrooms precisely when mother is *not* around (for instance, at boarding school). The objection misses the salient point: mother is *always* around, perhaps most so when she isn't.

91. The metaphor of the rod and the sexist tradition in English literature intersect early on. Here, for example, is Shakespeare on the child-woman:

> . . . maids, in modesty, say "No" to that
> Which they would have the profferer construe "Ay!"
> Fie, fie, how wayward is this foolish love,
> That, like a testy babe, will scratch the nurse,
> And presently, all humbled, kiss the rod!
> *The Two Gentlemen of Verona* (I, ii, 55–59).

92. Fowler, *Love and Parentage,* p. 19.

93. On the class origins of the doctrine of true womanhood, see Gerda Lerner, "The Lady and the Mill Girl: Changes in the Status of Women in the Age of Jackson," *Midcontinent American Studies Journal* 10 (1969): 7–12, and Terry Lovell, *Consuming Fiction* (London, 1987), pp. 84–85, p. 105.

94. Beecher, *Treatise,* p. 2.

95. Humphrey, *Domestic Education*, p. 22.

96. Beecher, *Treatise*, p. 3.

97. Ibid., p. 1.

98. Humphrey, *Domestic Education*, p. 23.

99. Beecher, *Treatise*, pp. 6, 16–17.

100. Humphrey, *Domestic Education*, p. 23.

101. Catharine Beecher, let us note, chose to remain single after her fiancé drowned. But she was all for marriage.

102. Beecher, *Treatise*, pp. 16, 2; Weaver, *Christian Household*, p. 76.

103. Weaver, *Christian Household*, p. 76.

104. Foucault, *History of Sexuality*, vol. 1, p. 113.

105. Nancy Armstrong, *Desire and Domestic Fiction: A Political History of the Novel* (London, 1987), brilliantly discusses the political repercussions of "the power of domestic surveillance" (p. 19) in Britain, emphasizing domestic ideology's disciplinary function. What still needs to be studied is the complementary fantasy of social harmony engendered by the "disciplinary regime."

3. His Sister's Keeper: Susan Warner's *The Wide, Wide World*

1. Susanna Maria Cummins, *The Lamplighter*, in Donald Koch, ed., *The Lamplighter by Maria Susanna Cummins and Tempest and Sunshine by Mary Jane Holmes* (New York, 1968), p. 239.

2. Ibid., p. 297.

3. Baym, *Woman's Fiction: A Guide to Novels by and about Women in America, 1820–1870* (Ithaca, N.Y., 1978), p. 313.

4. Ibid., p. 44; Jane Tompkins, *Sensational Designs: The Cultural Work of American Fiction, 1790–1860* (New York, 1985), p. 163.

5. Taking *The Wide, Wide World* as his/her text, someone shows us what happens when one does: "The fact is that Warner cannot *imagine* what it would mean for such a little girl as Ellen Montgomery to be totally depraved." Myers, "The Canonization of Susan Warner," *The New Criterion* (December 1988): 76. As we will see, this is absolutely correct. Venturing even further than D. G. Myers, we will hazard the assertion that *Ellen herself* couldn't imagine what it would be like for Ellen to be totally depraved. But there is more in *The Wide, Wide World* than is contained in Warner's, Ellen's, or Miss Emily's philosophy. There might even be more there than is contained in D. G. Myers's.

6. Susan Warner, *The Wide, Wide World* (1892; New York, 1987), p. 569. Further references, included in the text, are to the 1987 edition, though the slightly different punctuation of the first edition has been retained. The 1987 publication includes a thitherto wisely suppressed final chapter on Ellen's wedded life, here ignored.

7. The tension between girlish perfection and girlish passion leaves its mark even on *The Wide, Wide World*'s lexicon; "perfect" and "passionate,"

William Veeder reports, are Warner's favorite intensifiers. See *Henry James: The Lessons of the Master: Popular Fiction and Personal Style in the Nineteenth Century* (Chicago, 1975), p. 240.

8. See Elizabeth Wetherell [the pseudonym under which Warner published *The Wide, Wide World*], "Little Ellen and the Shopman," in *The Female Prose Writers of America* (Philadelphia, 1852), pp. 388–95.

9. Cf. Heman Humphrey, *Domestic Education* (Amherst, Mass., 1840), p. 59: "Never use the rod when you are in a passion."

10. Two hundred forty-five times before *The Wide, Wide World* ends, according to one F.S.D., "Tears, Idle Tears," *The Critic* (New York), 29 October 1892, pp. 236–37. F.S.D. lists alphabetically every passage in which Ellen breaks down.

11. Tompkins, *Sensational Designs*, p. 163. As the quoted phrases suggest, Tompkins makes a radically different argument, but we can roundly endorse her conclusion: "It is no accident that [Montgomery] uses her own mother's ring to make the purchase."

12. Unsurprisingly, Ellen's beloved *maternal* aunt has recently died.

13. In fact, as we learn 264 pages later, he is Ellen's maternal uncle. The Ellen in question, however, is not *our* Ellen, but a younger admirer of Ellen's a lot *like* Ellen. Ellen seems to have something of an identity problem; she once asks Ellen, "'We have both got the same name . . . how shall we know which is which?'" (284).

14. In this connection Tompkins, *Sensational Designs*, p. 182, draws a suggestive parallel between *The Wide, Wide World* and *The Story of O*.

15. Tompkins, *Sensational Designs*, p. 170.

16. Mary Hiatt, "Susan Warner's Subtext: The Other Side of Piety," *Journal of Evolutionary Psychology* 8 (1987): 257; Tompkins, "Afterword," *Sensational Designs*, p. 600. Joanne Dobson, "The Hidden Hand: Subversion of Cultural Ideology in Three Mid-Nineteenth-Century American Women's Novels," *American Quarterly* 38 (1986): 232, seizes on the fact that Ellen questions John for manhandling his mount, but omits to mention that it is this very beast, now splendidly disciplined, that carries him to Alice's deathbed as well as to Ellen's rescue. "'Sometimes,'" Alice comments on John's apparent cruelty to animals, it "'is necessary to do such things'" (377). For more on the link between horsewhipping and female education, see the last section of the present chapter.

17. Tompkins, *Sensational Designs*, p. 167.

18. For a sympathetic discussion of Nancy's naughtiness, see Hiatt, "Susan Warner's Subtext," pp. 254–55.

19. The unmistakable allusion to Poe's "The Man That Was Used Up" shows well enough how Nancy has been squandering the time she should have been devoting to her Bible.

20. Ellen is not the only scribbler heroine to cast a "sickened" look at a fractured member, and then take energetic measures to save it. For another instance, see p. 142 below.

21. Kelley, *Private Woman*, p. 293.

22. For an extended treatment of mid-century women writers' guilt-ridden attitudes toward writing, see Kelley, *Private Woman*, pp. 180–214. For a different evaluation of female horsemanship (and, therefore, sexuality) in the domestic novel, see Frances Cogan, *All-American Girl: The Ideal of Real Womanhood in Mid-Nineteenth-Century American* (Athens, Ga., 1989), pp. 50–51.

23. Erich Auerbach, *Mimesis: The Representation of Reality in Western Literature*, trans. Willard Trask (Princeton, 1953), p. 73.

24. A. C. Charity, *Events and Their Afterlife* (Cambridge, Eng., 1966), p. 245.

25. Robert Hollander, *Allegory in Dante's Commedia* (Princeton, 1969), p. 62, cited in Sacvan Bercovitch, ed., *Typology and Early American Literature* (Boston, 1972), p. 60.

26. John Hart, ed., *The Female Prose Writers of America* (Philadelphia, 1852), p. 387.

27. Quoted in Edward Halsey Foster, *Susan and Anna Warner* (Boston, 1978), Twayne's United States Author Series, vol. 312, p. 119.

28. Caroline Kirkland, Review of *Queechy* by Susan Warner and *Dollars and Cents* by Anna and Susan Warner, *North American Review* 76 (1853): 109.

29. No lesser an authority than Humphrey, writing in 1840, concluded—reluctantly, to be sure—that even religious novels worked more harm than good. "What confirms me still more in the opinion," he declared on p. 102 of *Domestic Education*, "is, that even many fathers and mothers in our Israel, who were brought up on the substantial aliment of the old Puritans, are now regaling themselves with the condiments of the nursery, instead of adhering to the meat."

30. Olivia Stokes, *Letters and Memories of Susan and Anna Bartlett Warner* (New York, 1925), p. 14, cited in Foster, *Susan and Anna Warner*, p. 33.

31. Ursula Brumm, *American Thought and Religious Typology*, trans. John Hooglund (New Brunswick, N.J., 1970), p. 60.

32. Augusta Jane Evans [Wilson], *Beulah* (1859; London, n.d. [c. 1861]), p. 271. Beulah, it will be recalled, is the heroine of the best-seller *Beulah*, and an author in her own right. For details, see Chapter 4.

33. By mid-century, a male scribbler and professor of theology at Williams could embolden a heroine of his to exclaim: "Fiction! what else are the parables of the New and Old Testament, and probably the whole book of Job?" Joseph Alden, *Elizabeth Benton; or, Religion in Connection with Fashionable Life* (New York, 1846), p. 145, cited in David Reynolds, *Faith in Fiction: The Emergence of Religious Literature in America* (Cambridge, Mass., 1981), p. 93.

34. Revelations, 1:1–2; Revelations 6:13–15; 2 Peter 3:10; Psalms 102:26; etc. John Humphreys is also, in a sense, citing *his* father, who, like John, is a preacher of the Word—and, incidentally, adores and is adored by his "little girl" (448) Ellen.

35. Caroline Lee Hentz, *Ernest Linwood* (1856; Boston, 1857), p. 69.

36. For a discussion of the English variant, see Sandra Gilbert and Susan Gubar, *The Madwoman in the Attic: The Woman Writer and the Nineteenth-Century Literary Imagination* (New Haven, 1979).

37. Has Ellen been reading Orson Fowler on the sly? He glosses this ambiguous verse as follows: "But, there *is* a 'friend that sticketh closer than a brother.' There is a tie stronger than life. It is that oneness of soul 'which binds two willing hearts' indissolubly together, and makes 'of them twain, one flesh.' Connubial love! . . . Oh, God, we thank thee for emotions thus holy; for bliss thus divine!" *Love and Parentage* (c. 1844; London, n.d.), p. 2.

38. For more on Ellen's relation with Lindsay and her other natural relations in the United Kingdom, see Hiatt, "Susan Warner's Subtext," pp. 257–59.

39. Horace Bushnell, "Our Gospel a Gift to the Imagination," in *Horace Bushnell: Sermons* (New York, 1985), ed. Conrad Cherry, p. 114.

40. *The Phenomenology of Spirit*, trans. James Baillie (Evanston, Ill., 1967), p. 475. For a fuller statement of Hegel's thoughts on this subject in its relation to sister-and-brotherhood, consult the epigraph to this chapter.

41. It is perhaps unnecessary to point out that we have here the supreme guarantee that the child is father to the woman, hence of the identity between man-child and Law-Man, and so between maternal and daughterly incest.

42. Hegel, *Phenomenology*, p. 477. On the multiple links between the Immaculate Conception, the Virgin Birth, Hegel, and sisterhood, see Jacques Derrida, *Glas*, trans. John P. Leavey, Jr. and Richard Rand (Lincoln, Nebr., 1986), pp. 177–84, 222–23.

43. William G. Eliot, *Lectures to Young Women*, 3d ed. (Boston, 1854), p. 85.

4. Life with Father: Augusta Jane Evans's *Beulah*

1. Thus we are referred both to Coleridge and Wordsworth and to J. D. Morell ("one of the most profound philosophical writers of the age"). Augusta Jane Evans [Wilson], *Beulah* (1859; London, n.d. [c. 1861]), pp. 227, 308. Further page references, included in the text, are to this edition. Beulah's reading, be it here noted, is as wide as it is deleterious; the "chaff" a "dire chance throws into her hands," enticing her into a "Cretan maze of investigation" whose "dim devious paths" the "wretched" heroine, in a "perpetual brain-fever," goes "stumbling along" "without chart or compass," in hopeless pursuit of the "awful mysteries of the shadowy spirit realm" in which the "hydra of speculation rears its horrid head" at every turn, consists chiefly, but by no means exclusively, in the pernicious productions of the following deviants: Byron, Carlyle, Comte, Cousin, Cowper, De Quincey, Emerson ("grim"), Feuerbach, Fourier, Goethe, Hegel, Hume, Jean-Paul,

Kingsley, Lamb, Locke, More, Parker ("disgusting"), Plato, Poe, Pope, Reid, Sappho, Schelling, Shelley, Sophocles, Southey, and Spinoza.

2. "Beulah" means "married." See Isaiah 62:4, where the husband in question is Jehovah. Readers who need to brush up on their Old Testament (Evans didn't) may find the following of some help: "[Beulah] was no longer to be a wife deserted by God, but married (1) to God, (2) by a strange application of the figure, to her own sons. In Hos. 1:2 the figure in its first application is reversed. There it is used to point out the faithlessness of Israel to her spouse." James Hastings et al., *A Dictionary of the Bible*, 2 vols. (Edinburgh, 1898), 1:284. That the figure should seem strange is due less to a longstanding corruption of the Hebrew text than to the fact that Hastings et al. missed the multiple connections between the Law-Man, the man-child, and mother—or did not care to know anything about them.

3. Isaiah 4:1.

4. Nina Baym, *Woman's Fiction: A Guide to Novels by and about Women in America, 1820–1870* (Ithaca, N.Y., 1978), p. 279.

5. Ibid., pp. 283–86.

6. The orthodox denial proceeds from Beulah's own mouth; when her friend Clara squeals that Beulah should "almost worship" her guardian, the heroine quite properly rejoins that she is "'not addicted to worshipping anything but God'" (135). We are already familiar with pragmatic feminism's somewhat different strategy for disjoining God and man: "As the women examined the concepts of husband and father most critically in their fiction, they accepted God uncritically by referring to him by such neutral terms as parent and friend. His nature transcended gender" (Baym, *Woman's Fiction*, p. 44). By now it should be apparent why one must most critically examine references to God as a parent. Baym herself points the way: "suitors in these novels are less important than fathers, guardians, and brothers" (p. 40). It would be hard to say it better.

7. Kirkland, Review, p. 116, draws attention to a similar sticking point in *The Wide, Wide World*: "it is hard to imagine Ellen slipping into the quality of wifehood, from the childish reverence which she is represented as feeling, to the last moment, [for John]." Cf. chap. 3, n. 6.

5. Go Away and Die

1. George Sand, review of *Uncle Tom's Cabin*, in *La Presse* (Paris), cited in Kenneth Lynn, Introduction, *Uncle Tom's Cabin, or, Life Among the Lowly* (Cambridge, Mass., 1962), p. x. (For an aperçu of George Sand's understanding of the domestic, see her *François le Champi* [Paris, 1848].) Philip Fisher, "Partings and Ruins: Radical Sentimentality in *Uncle Tom's Cabin*," *Amerikastudien* 28 (1983): 285. Steven Railton, "Mothers, Husbands, and Uncle Tom," *The Georgia Review* 38 (1984): 132. Severn Duvall, *"Uncle Tom's Cabin*: The Sinister Side of the Patriarchy," *The New England Quarterly*

(March 1963): 8. Amy Schrager Lang, "Slavery and Sentimentalism: The Strange Career of Augustine St. Clare," *Women's Studies* 12 (1986): 43. Elizabeth Ammons, "Heroines in *Uncle Tom's Cabin,*" *American Literature* 49 (1977): 170.

2. Ann Douglas, *The Feminization of American Culture* (New York, 1977), p. 1.

3. Louis Althusser, *Montesquieu, Rousseau, Marx,* trans. Ben Brewster (London, 1972), p. 104.

4. Harriet Beecher Stowe, *Uncle Tom's Cabin, or, Life Among the Lowly* (New York, 1966), pp. 162, 244. Further references, included in the text, are to this edition.

5. Douglas, *Feminization,* pp. 1, 3. Nina Baym, *Woman's Fiction: A Guide to Novels by and about Women in America* (Ithaca, New York, 1978), p. 36. Ammons, "Heroines," pp. 169, 164. Frances Cogan, *All-American Girl: The Ideal of Real Womanhood in Mid-Nineteenth Century America* (Athens, Ga., 1989), p. 126.

6. Leslie Fiedler, *Love and Death in the American Novel,* 2d ed. (New York, 1966), p. 267.

7. For an original treatment of the original treatment of this question, see Harold Bloom and David Rosenberg, "The Book of J" [extract from a book of the same name], *American Poetry Review,* Nov./Dec. 1990, p. 30.

8. Maria Susanna Cummins, *The Lamplighter,* in *Tempest and Sunshine by Mary Jane Holmes and The Lamplighter by Maria Susanna Cummins,* ed. Donald Koch (New York, 1968), p. 297. Further references, included in the text, are to this edition, based on that of the 1854 first edition.

9. Mary Jane Holmes, *'Lena Rivers* ([1856]; London, n.d.), p. 231. Further references, included in the text, are to this edition.

10. Cogan, *All-American Girl,* p. 50. The citation from *'Lena Rivers* is to be found on p. 28. Of course, sometimes a cigar is just a cigar.

11. Mary Kelley, *Private Woman, Public Stage: Literary Domesticity in Nineteenth-Century America* (New York, 1984), pp. 217–24. Caroline Lee Hentz, *Ernest Linwood; [or, The Inner Life of the Author]* ([1856]; Boston, 1857), p. 69. Further references to *Ernest Linwood,* included in the text, are to this edition. The subtitle was added by the publisher after Hentz's death.

12. Kelley, *Private Woman,* p. 220.

13. Ibid. Kelley is citing Mary Virginia Terhune, author of several bettersellers, among them *The Hidden Path* and *Eve's Daughters.*

14. As we have seen, Kelley disagrees, both on the grounds that Hentz really isn't a writer at all, and because, for biographical reasons, she thinks that Hentz is only writing about what really happened to *her.* It is in this context that she reduces *Ernest Linwood's* "imaginary" to its "real" parts. See *Private Woman,* pp. 224–32.

15. E.D.E.N. Southworth, Letter of 2 June 1895 to Rose Lawrence, E.D.E.N. Southworth Papers, Library of Congress, cited in Kelley, *Private Woman,* p. 238.

16. Kelley, *Private Woman*, p. 221.

17. The name "Rosalie," according to *Webster's New World Dictionary*, is probably derived from the Latin "*Rosalia*," the annual ceremony of hanging roses on tombs.

18. It will be remembered that St. James, the brother of the Lord, was (say the liberal-minded) one of the ex-Virgin Mary's *other* sons, those *not* of one substance with her Fatherly spouse. To call him a "demi-god" would doubtless be blasphemy; one probably can, however, safely call him Jesus Christ's "demi-brother." In much Catholic commentary, it should be pointed out, this "brother" of the Lord is demoted to cousin, on the basis of rather strained philological arguments.

19. Thrillingly, the father of his country and friend of her father receives Rosalie "with the most endearing familiarity" ("I almost thought he was going to kiss me" [172]) before presenting her to St. James.

20. Kelley, *Private Woman*, p. 230.

21. Ibid., pp. 224–32.

22. See ibid., p. 249. The prose mother who called one of her books a "bantling" was Mary Virginia Hawes Terhune, the author of *Eve's Daughters*.

23. This is perhaps the moment to recall that Hymen, according to most people, was Apollo's son.

INDEX

Library of Congress Cataloging-in-Publication Data

Goshgarian, G. M.
    To kiss the chastening rod : domestic fiction and sexual ideology
in the American Renaissance / G.M. Goshgarian.
      p. cm.
    Includes bibliographical references and index.
    ISBN 0-8014-2559-X (cloth : alkaline paper).
    1. Domestic fiction, American—History and criticism. 2. Women
and literature—United States—History—19th century. 3. American
fiction—Women authors—History and criticism. 4. American
fiction—19th century—History and criticism. 5. Incest in
literature. 6. Family in literature. 7. Sex in literature.
I. Title.
PS374.D57G67   1992
813'309355—dc20   91-55560